NONTRADITIONAL WARFARE

Twenty-First-Century Threats and Responses

EDITED BY *William R. Schilling*

Foreword by Norman R. Augustine

BRASSEY'S, INC.

WASHINGTON, D.C.

Cataloging-in-Publication Data on file with the Library of Congress

ISBN 1-57488-504-9   hardcover
ISBN 1-57488-505-7   paperback

Printed in the United States of America on acid-free paper that meets the
American National Standards Institute Z39-48 Standard.

Brassey's Inc.
22841 Quicksilver Drive
Dulles, Virginia 20166

First Edition

10 9 8 7 6 5 4 3 2 1

CONTENTS

SECTION IV
Models and Tools for Addressing Nontraditional Warfare

SECTION V
Institutional Responses to Nontraditional Warfare

SECTION VI
Applying New and Emerging Technologies to Nontraditional Warfare

FOREWORD

It took just 10 years for the world to go from the euphoria associated with the end of the Cold War to the tragedy of the World Trade Center and the Pentagon. It had been said that the end of the Cold War would make the world safe—but the thing for which it seems to have made the world safe is large numbers of smaller conflicts. As the deterrence effect of the superpower balance evaporated, a new and even more difficult challenge emerged: "How do you deter individuals hidden in society and seeking martyrdom?" One thing is clear: it is not accomplished through Cold War strategies such as mutual assured destruction; such strategies under the markedly changed circumstances of the new world disorder simply assure destruction.

This is a book about these and other related issues, and it does not make good bedtime reading. But it does make very important reading, particularly as we enter the twenty-first century and confront the troubles that as surely lie before us as did those that are behind us. Virtually everyone in civilized society was adversely affected directly or indirectly by the events of September 11, 2001. For some there were tragic losses of family and friends; for others there was the loss of personal freedoms—even such previously unquestioned luxuries as opening one's mail without fearing for the presence of biological agents. In my own case, an office I occupied in the Pentagon many years ago is now gone.

It would seem that in many respects our world has been turned upside down during this past decade and this has occurred in a fashion that would have been unimaginable even a few years ago. The Soviet Union no longer exists—and not a shot was fired on the occasion of its demise. We have experienced the first war in Europe in a half century, a war in which Russia and the United States were at least tacit allies. Hungary, Poland, and the Czech Republic are members of NATO. It is not the Soviet Union that has substantial forces engaged in Afghanistan; it is the United States. Our nation actually breathed a collective sigh of relief when it learned that an airliner crash in New York was "only" due to mechanical problems. And the United States Air Force is flying continuous 24 × 7 combat air patrols over several of the nation's major cities—with the presumed mission to shoot down *our own* airliners should the "appropriate" circumstances arise. And, there is a certain irony that we spent nearly a half century unknowingly preparing to fight exactly the type of war with which Saddam Hussein obliged us in the Persian Gulf.

The Red Queen in *Alice in Wonderland* once said, "Fiddlesticks, I have believed as many as six impossible things before breakfast." Given that perspective, the Red Queen may be one of the few individuals who would be comfortable living in the world in which we now find ourselves. My own situation on September 11, 2001, fits that pattern of perplexity as I found myself on vacation traveling aboard a train some 150 miles north of the border of Afghanistan. Upon learning (a day later) of the great tragedy that had befallen America, I concluded that my best option was to continue on to my destination, Moscow, because I would be safe in Moscow—perhaps even safer than in my home in Washington, D.C. The irony did not escape me.

It was, of course, unreasonable to expect that human nature—or, more precisely, inhuman nature—which has evolved over millions of years had suddenly changed in December 1989 with the fall of the Berlin Wall. What one is more likely to find as one travels the world today is that deeply held religious, ethnic, territorial and other disputes have simply bubbled to the surface. What does seem to be new, at least in so far as America is concerned, is the manner in which these disputes are now evidencing themselves right here at home.

This should, of course, not have come as a surprise to anyone. In fact, America has been extraordinarily fortunate not to have faced major losses due to terrorist actions in our homeland long before September 11, 2001. A panel formed by the United States Congress and the Department of Defense under the leadership of former Senators Gary Hart and Warren Rudman, of which I was a member, issued a series of reports in the years 2000 and early 2001 in which its members, who span much of the political spectrum, unanimously concluded that, "America will become increasingly vulnerable to hostile attack on our homeland, and our military superiority will not entirely protect us. . . . States, terrorists, and other disaffected groups will acquire weapons of mass destruction and mass disruption, and some will use them. Americans will likely die on American soil, possibly in large numbers." The panel went on to say that, "Americans are less secure than they believe themselves to be. The time for reexamination is now, before the American people find themselves struck by events that they never anticipated." The report concluded that the first priority of the nation should be to "defend the United States and ensure that it is safe from the dangers of the new era."

As we now know, it is far easier to write reports stating such objectives than to make them a reality. But Charles Darwin offered some important advice in this regard when he observed that, "It is not the strongest of the species which survives, nor is it the most intelligent, rather it is the one most adaptable to change." Certainly change is all about us and nowhere is change more profoundly needed than in the composition and utilization of our national security apparatus. Even many of the fundamental principles which underpinned earlier thinking have been rendered obsolescent. For example, it is now necessary to deal with enemies who do grave damage to America's homeland—but in many cases whom we will be unable to find and in some cases will not even be able to identify.

As a technologist it is particularly disconcerting to realize that the tectonic change that is transforming our lives has been rendered possible in large part through unintended applications of relatively recent advancements in the fields of science and technology. For the first time in history, using technology, it is now possible for a very few individuals to significantly impact the lives of very large numbers of individuals. This is indeed a profound change—and it is this development that underlies many of the challenges that the world now faces in the national security arena. This imbalance, or lack of symmetry, makes it relatively easy for individuals or small groups of individuals to exploit the brittleness of modern society to deny others the ability to maintain order in that society. But at the same time, those embracing the technologies of terrorism will find that they, too, are unable to exert control, and that their role is reduced to that of simply being another disruptive force—albeit sometimes a monstrously disruptive force.

Fortunately technology also offers some promise in solving—or at least ameliorating—elements of this problem. But any overall solution will have to go far beyond the fields of science and technology. This will depend on improving the lifestyles of people throughout the world, reducing dependence on fossil fuels, enhancing understanding among peoples, and more. Not a list likely to be implemented next week.

In the meantime human-gathered intelligence will become a vastly more important companion to technical intelligence as we focus on the end of the national security spectrum where terrorism resides—as opposed to counting missiles available for a strategic nuclear exchange. Fighting terrorists in the traditional manner of conventional military forces is akin to fighting the drug problem in Washington, D.C., with airpower and tanks. Conventional forces are unquestionably a part of the solution to some terrorist problems—and still an important part of the answer to other very possible contingencies—but only a part. In fact, the world's state of readiness for dealing with terrorism today is probably about equivalent to where the world stood in dealing with so-called conventional warfare at the time the stirrup was invented.

While we have ample reason to regret our previous failures to adequately strengthen our nation's antiterrorism capabilities we, at the same time, have reason for hope that a number of positive steps can be taken in the near future. Some of these steps are simple and obvious, such as putting cockpit doors that are not easily penetrated on commercial aircraft, placing television cameras in aircraft cabins so that pilots can be aware of what is happening a few feet behind them, and so forth. Other steps will be much more difficult, such as sealing a nation's borders against the import of nuclear weapons. Those who doubt the difficulty of the latter, need only ask how well we would fare in stopping suitcase nuclear weapons if they were smuggled into the country in bails of marijuana—a proposition I had offered some three decades ago.

These and other equally compelling questions have been addressed by the group of authors who contributed to this book on nontraditional warfare. Until recently it has been aggravatingly "nontraditional" to write about nontraditional warfare—particularly in an understandable fashion. But the consequences of failing to comprehend the more unconventional forms of warfare not only increase one's vulnerability to major casualties but likely will also make a casualty of one of our most precious assets—our daily freedoms. It would seem not unlikely that America's citizenry, after two or three experiences on the scale of those of September 11, 2001, or greater, will be quite prepared to forfeit many of the freedoms our nation has enjoyed for over two centuries if it were deemed that doing so would substantially reduce the threat of terrorism.

On the heels of the relatively recent events in New York, Washington, D.C., and Pennsylvania, it has become commonplace to discuss such heretofore unthinkable actions as our government authorizing wiretaps of conversations between suspects and their lawyers, military trials of foreign persons in the United States, and even somewhat abstract discussions in the media of the possible role of torture in ascertaining from suspects plans for imminent terrorist acts. The truth is that we have *already* been forced to relinquish some of our freedoms as we stand in long lines to be searched at airports, remain confined to our seats for major portions of commercial flights, pass through security guards to enter public office buildings, detour around streets closed for security reasons, pass through metal detectors at schools, have our mail withheld while it is checked for dangerous substances, and so forth.

The most commonly expressed future concern is associated with the terrible triumvirate of weaponry, NBC—nuclear (radiological), biological, and chemical. Chemical agents have already been used in several conflicts as well as by domestic terrorists in the Tokyo subway attack. And although the world has long been aware of the dangers of nuclear weaponry, little has been done to counter those weapons in terms of implementing solutions. The explosive power unleashed upon the World Trade Center and the Pentagon was equivalent to that of very small nuclear weapons, yet it is enormously significant that no radiation effects were involved in either of these two occurrences.

The nuclear threat is of particular concern because of the magnitude of destruction such devices can produce, the large number of such weapons existing in the world, the number of countries possessing them, and the publicized attempts by terrorists to acquire nuclear materials. Not only will it be important to seek to preclude the use of such weapons by terrorists or others, it will be necessary to plan for recovery in the event such devices are in fact used. It is not an acceptable strategy simply to move out of Manhattan or Washington and wait a few thousand years before it is deemed safe to return. Hiroshima continues to be an active community, as is Europe, which at one time suffered a plague that cost the lives of one-third of its entire citizenry.

Our experience in America with biological weaponry, which as of this writing appears to have produced perhaps five fatalities, involved an agent that does not trigger a biologically communicable disease. That is, the introduction of this particular agent on a commercial airliner, for example, would not infect passengers who in turn would board other airliners and biologically spread the disease through large elements of the globe's population. In fact, it has come as somewhat of a surprise how readily anthrax *mechanically* spread itself through the nation's postal system. And, if the possibility of agents triggering highly communicable diseases does not raise concern enough, there are those who speak of the development of "designer-agents" that could be used to target particular groups of the populace. As difficult as the notion is to accept, it may yet prove fortuitous that this recent crossing of the biological barrier in America in a relatively primitive form may have given our nation a much-needed wake-up call.

The principal focus of defensive measures since our awakening concentrated, properly, on countering weapons of mass destruction. However, in so doing the impact of weapons of mass *disruption* must not be overlooked. The intent of the latter category of threat would be to shatter the economy; interrupt communications; shut down electric power; disrupt the banking system; or deny food, water, medical care, and other similarly essential resources to our society. The potential impact of such actions is suggested by the consequences of the attacks on the World Trade Center and the Pentagon, which produced aftershocks that resulted in large numbers of people losing their jobs not only in the United States but throughout much of the world as the economic ripple effect carried throughout the tightly coupled global economy.

Disruption on a massive scale can be produced by nonlethal attacks, such as an assault on the software that directs the telecommunications network upon which the world banking industry is dependent to transfer billions of dollars each day, or it can be created through the secondary impact of weapons of physical destruction. In this latter regard, we should not overlook more conventional threats, such as the use of shoulder-fired antiaircraft missiles launched at different airports every few weeks to make commercial aviation—and that significant part of the world's economy dependent upon it—no longer ·viable.

America has become a primary target for those who would seek to disrupt the world's status quo. In my own travels through perhaps 50 countries in the past decade I have observed, at least prior to September 11, 2001, much broader resentment of America than in any earlier period with which I am familiar. I have also been struck by America's profound influence around the world, whether it be in business, art, dress, music, entertainment, or simply the omnipresence of the American dollar.

But at the same time one cannot help but notice the genuine outpouring of empathy for America following the recent tragedies. That empathy will undoubtedly erode with time, as much of the world will continue to blame America for its problems—whether those problems be the shortage of water in a well in India or muddy roads in a part of Mexico, both of which recently received media attention when local residents criticized America for not resolving the problems.

The inescapable conclusion is that twenty-first-century America, no longer shielded by its surrounding oceans, is eminently vulnerable to major loses on its very own soil. This places a new priority on the defense of the homeland through actions both at home and abroad to counter enemies who would employ nontraditional as well as traditional methods of conflict.

But there is also opportunity in this tragic situation, for nothing unites like a common enemy. Today for the first time in decades there is a very real opportunity to build lasting bonds between the United States and nations such as Russia and China because of our shared interest in countering terrorism.

Unlike past conflicts in which America has engaged, there will be no clear end to this war. In fact, there likely will be no end at all. Perhaps the greatest danger is that we should simply become inured to the casualties of terrorism much as we have to the 40,000 fatalities we suffer each year from automobile accidents. That would be the greatest tragedy of all: for terrorism simply to become accepted as part of life.

And against this backdrop the gap between the haves and have-nots of the world continues to grow. Under such circumstances there can be no shortage of tinder on our planet for those who would seek to be a destructive or disruptive force. In the long term, reducing that gap is the most promising means of fighting terrorism and it is time to get on with that task, too.

Norman R. Augustine

The New Defense Challenge

As we begin the advent of the new century, the emerging threats, combined with the growing realization that technological development represents a primary engine for shaping the world, suggest that it is time, or past time, to consider some new approaches to the analysis of military affairs. This new analysis should be undertaken not only by military personnel and civilian experts and academics, but should also be open to interested and informed laypeople. Such laypersons are, after all, the ones who will have to eventually foot the bill, and whose sons and daughters may have to pay the ultimate price with their lives if bad policy choices are implemented. This issue has historically been one that rose above partisan politics, and it would be a very good idea to keep it that way.

The end of the Cold War confrontation between the Soviet Union and non-Communist West led by the United States has left much of the American national defense establishment, both civilian and military, somewhat at loose ends. The opponent that provided the central focus for all U.S. national security planning since the late 1940s has disappeared, and left the United States and its military as the only global superpower. The departure of the Soviet Union as an international player has also removed the main impetus for large-scale conventional warfare.

The history of the last 10 to 12 years amply demonstrates the inaccuracies of the fuzzily optimistic predictions of the shape of the post-Cold War world. The idea that the end of the Cold War would mean the end of formal human conflict, or at least of organized warfare, has proven entirely illusory. The removal of two great power blocs in international politics has, rather, permitted a host of once-dormant, or subsumed conflicts to bubble up, including a range of ethnic clashes in southeastern Europe and in sub-Saharan Africa.

A gradual realization that the twenty-first century is not necessarily going to be a politically stable and calm era has occurred in parallel with an interesting series of technological developments. Some of these are the results of long-established trends, such as the explosion of the Internet, and the prevalence of computers in everyday life, even in much of the so-called "third world" and certainly throughout the industrialized nations. It appears, at first blush, that the likelihood of major multinational conventional war is very low. Since that was the major focus of U.S. and NATO military planning between 1949 and 1991, some new approaches and reconsiderations are certainly in order.

Understandably, it will take some time for the world's political leaderships and military establishments to fully accept the new global politico-military environment. This is not a criticism of those institutions, either in the United States or abroad; it is a simple fact of life. Despite this caveat, it is certainly possible to begin the process of acclimatizing ourselves to the security risks and challenges of the new global political structure. Assisting in the accomplishment of that process, as openly and effectively as possible, is the goal of this book.

The authors of the essays that comprise this book constitute an impressive array of talent and experience, and they have approached the general issues from a wide range of viewpoints. Many contributors are engineers or research scientists, and the authors also include several defense analysts, at least one journalist, and a military historian. The contributors have each individually and collectively been working on issues of defense analysis, research and development, as well as defense policy and planning for some time. Not surprisingly, they do not always agree, and there is a considerable range of emphases and opinions contained in the essays. Some of them are current or former government employees or officials, while others have been associated with private industry or the academic community.

Characteristics of Nontraditional Warfare

A definition is in order at this point, before delving further into the term and concept *nontraditional warfare*. In employing this term, the authors collectively mean that they are primarily concerned with new, or at least heretofore ill-considered, forms of armed conflict. The essays in this book are concerned not only with the general characteristics of such "new" forms of warfare (some of which are, in fact, long established), but also with the utilization of new approaches to command, control, and information processing, and new management tools. The essays also consider, at least in part, the employment of new forms of technology, ranging from nonlethal weapons to advanced remotely piloted vehicles, improved sensor capabilities, and new weapons technologies. Particularly, the integration of this array of capabilities and risks provides the focus for the component essays in this book.

Essentially, nontraditional warfare is distinct from conventional warfare in two major aspects. First, it encompasses unusual forms of conflict, including terrorism and guerrilla actions; activities by international criminal organizations that constitute threats to the security of one or more nations; and the employment of various sorts of weapons of mass destruction (WMD), including chemicals, biological toxins and agents, and nuclear or radiation-based weapons. Strikes against computer and telecommunications infrastructure also fall within this category. Second, nontraditional warfare involves not just new or unusual types of action, but the employment of new sorts of technology, in both attack and defense. The authors here employ technology in the widest sense, meaning not only actual hardware, tools, weapons, and equipment, but also the development of methods and institutional mechanisms to employ these tools effectively.

Clearly, nontraditional warfare draws a sharp distinction between the general sorts of component conflict types, and traditional, formal warfare, as exemplified by the Kuwait War of February–March 1991, or World War II. Those conflicts, and other regular wars, involved a clash of arms between formally organized, regularly equipped, and trained national armed forces. Most armed conflicts since the end of the Soviet Union and the fall of the Berlin Wall, basically over the 12 years since 1989, clearly demonstrate that most military operations, and indeed the majority of actual armed conflicts, are of a different sort. The prolonged ethnic (if not tribal) conflicts in Bosnia, Croatia, Kosovo, and now Macedonia, pitted either haphazardly organized "militias" against one another, or militias against regular forces, comprising an assortment of international peacekeeping forces. U.S. military intervention in Haiti and Somalia has also comprised a similar pattern, and the experience of the recent past strongly indicates that such situations will prove the rule, not the exception, for at least the next several decades.

In a more specific sense, and within the context employed here, NTW or nontraditional warfare covers a range of contingencies, situations, and circumstances. Nontraditional warfare embraces a wide range of threats, operations, techniques, and weapons other than those outlined here. While the accompanying description is admittedly not exhaustive, it will at least provide a coherent guide to the sorts of conflicts with which the authors are concerned.

Perhaps the most readily discernible threat is terrorism, whether employed by states as an ingredient of more-or-less formal warfare, or utilized by nongovernmental organizations to achieve their own ends. Certainly, the events of September 11, 2001, emphasize the paramount importance of terrorist threats and actions. Terrorism, through assassination and bombings with conventional explosives, has become a depressing ingredient of the international scene over the last three decades. Fortunately, the employment of weapons or devices of mass destruction has been quite rare. Indeed, the primary example of such a terrorist action was the attack utilizing Sarin nerve gas by the Aum Shinrikyo doomsday cult against the Tokyo subway system. That instance was not an aggressive act committed against Japan by hostile foreigners, but was a religiously and politically motivated, purely internal affair, leaving 12 dead and thousands injured. The employment of almost fully fueled airliners as de facto guided missiles, employed to destroy the two towers of the World Trade Center in Manhattan, New York, and damage the Pentagon in Arlington, Virginia, produced explosive yields approaching several thousand tons of TNT and consequently, in the same order of magnitude as small "tactical" nuclear weapons, although (fortunately) without the radiation and fallout effects. These two sets of incidents demonstrate that we cannot depend on terrorists to either maintain a technological status quo, or to utilize only "normal" explosives and deadly devices.

In addition to the potential for terrorist attacks, other threats are also apparent, including weapons of mass destruction, electronic warfare, economic and industrial warfare, attacks with bio-weapons and biological agents, urban and guerrilla conflict, and a range of new and emerging technologies, many of them only now beginning to emerge into the open. Many of these threats have extensive nonmilitary dimensions, and indeed the military character of some of the threats is distinctly secondary to other aspects, especially technological or policy concerns.

The issues of nontraditional warfare also include the integration of a range of new techniques, new tools and weapons, and new approaches to both new and old problems. Employment of remotely piloted vehicles has only recently come to be appreciated as a means of achieving valuable operational goals at very little risk to human life. And this approach is being expanded to embrace a wider spectrum of devices than just aerial drones.

In a general sense, the purpose of these essays is to examine and begin an assessment and exploration process in order to promote greater understanding and appreciation of NTW issues and concerns. Some essays are relatively specific in terms of calling for policy initiatives or implementation of new technology, while others describe research initiatives to enhance understanding of old problems in new ways, or to thoroughly examine new problems. Still other essays are more general, describing emerging technological threats, or exploring the impact of new technology or broadly changing general conditions. While in part aimed at an audience of professional military personnel and senior government officials, the papers are also intended to be accessible to reasonably informed laypeople, who certainly have an interest in these issues.

Organizational Context

To help readers follow the intent of our presentations, and more completely appreciate the goal of this book, the thirty essays have been separated into six unequally sized groups. The essays are grouped into these subject areas according to their primary thematic focus. There is some overlap between these thematic groups, and several essays could arguably be placed within more than one such group without violating the spirit of this organization. The editorial staff has exerted considerable effort to effect the most suitable and coherent placements.

The text is divided into six sections: (I) Threats and Risks in the New Century, (II) Operations in the Nontraditional Warfare Environment, (III) Emergency Management in Hostile Environments, (IV) Models and Tools for Addressing Nontraditional Warfare, (V) Institutional Responses to Nontraditional Warfare, and (VI) Applying New and Emerging Technologies to Nontraditional Warfare.

Many essays contain photographs, graphs, and tables illustrating particular concepts or viewpoints. The graphics are not intended to replace the text of the essays, but rather to provide emphasis, and in some cases, to give clarification on particular points covered in the essay.

The essays progress from broader and more general aspects and approaches, to the more specific. Thus the first five essays focus on defining and exploring relatively broad-range issues of nontraditional warfare, defining threats and terminology, and laying some of the groundwork explored more deeply in subsequent essays. The sixth through eleventh essays explore several aspects of operations under nontraditional warfare conditions, including the emerging issues of terrorism and criminal activities that pose real threats to national security, along with the previously recognized but often-ignored issues of urban and guerrilla operations.

The third group of essays collectively comprises an examination of emergency management issues in the NTW arena. As such, they are primarily concerned with alterations in the institutions concerned with the relevant policy issues and, in a real sense, calling for a change in outlook and approach rather than looking for hardware solutions or exploring the effect of new technologies. Parallel to those essays, but approaching from a different orientation, are the sixteenth to nineteenth essays, concerned with the use of models and assessment tools for addressing NTW issues. Clearly, new types of warfare, and new threats to national security will require new approaches to assessing and understanding these threats, and for developing effective responses to them.

The fifth group of essays explores relatively detailed institutional responses to NTW threats, in terms of reorienting institutional approaches to handling problems. Most of these essays are, of necessity, in the nature of exploring such issues, examining a range of choices or a set of conditions undergoing change. The sixth and final group of essays survey more specific effects of a range of technological developments, including weapons, sensors, and other military equipment as well as the advent of operations in new environments.

The existing essays do not represent the last word on these subjects and related issues. Clearly, nontraditional warfare is an evolving subject area, and most of these essays constitute only a first approach to the subjects. This means that there will doubtless be additional essays, either expanding upon the material presented here, or substantially replacing it, as our knowledge and collective understanding of the general subject grows.

Role of the Essays

So far, most of the introductory material presented here has been concerned with outlining the philosophical and epistemological basis of the concept of nontraditional warfare, and providing a framework within which to comprehend and assess the ideas presented in these essays. As noted earlier, these essays are not intended to provide the final word on their subjects, by any stretch. In several cases, the subjects are too new, and opinions and views on them still too inchoate, for anyone to provide anything more than an introductory survey. Even for those subject areas where there is some existing corpus of knowledge and opinion, the essays presented here are not intended to provide a final viewpoint. It is the hope of the authors, both individually and collectively, that the views they have presented will spark some serious consideration and assessment of the issues, concerns, and problems examined.

In that light, this book and its component essays is intended as a starting point, or perhaps a "point of departure" for further research, discussion, writing, and evaluation. This intent may be more apparent with those essays that call for a particular path of research or development, but the general idea to spark more serious discussion permeates even those essays that may not explicitly spell out such a goal.

Collectively and individually, then, the authors look forward to comment, constructive criticism, and discussion about the concepts and ideas presented in these essays, and shared among them. Certainly, some of the materials produced in response to this book will not agree, either entirely or in part, with the views presented here. That is not a problem, and indeed it is something that the authors and editors essentially expect. They would be gratified if at least a significant portion of this newer supplementary material might be forwarded to them, in care of the Washington Institute of Technology, but they will additionally be gratified to see such material appear in a range of other venues.

Some of the essays included in this book have been available on-line, over the Internet, at the WIT website, www.wit-hq.org, since early 2000. Naturally, the newer essays have only been available for shorter periods. The primary purpose of publishing this book, though, is to gain a wider audience for these essays, and for the ideas they contain. Even among educated and knowledgeable professionals in the field of national security and policy analysis, access to the Internet is not universal. More, with the gamut of information presented on the Internet, a good deal of what is available varies considerably in quality. Books, being portable, and also generally producing reviews and comment, provide a more reliable presentation of information and views, and also ensure a degree of consistency not yet generally available in web-based material.

In conclusion, the authors and editors suggest that readers approach the essays in this book thoughtfully, and examine them in the spirit in which they were conceived and written. The ideas contained are not dogma, nor are the opinions expressed in any sense meant as definitive pronouncements. The contributors are urgently seeking to create a forum for exploring these and other related issues in order to help create a better, more stable, and more peaceful international environment. Although the issues raised in this book focus on the means and methods of armed conflict, the contributors are certainly aware that real progress in creating a true international community will depend not on creating new mechanisms for conflict, but on finding new and better ways to resolve disputes and differences before violence ensues.

William R. Schilling

SECTION I

THREATS AND RISKS
IN THE NEW CENTURY

One of the more obvious observations on global relations, military policy, and foreign affairs in the post-Cold War world is that many old presuppositions no longer apply. This situation poses some problems, especially for people who have spent their professional lives dealing with the Cold War and related policy implementations. The end of the conventional military threat from the Soviet Union and its satellites, largely directed toward NATO, raises some interesting and puzzling questions, as well as the need for some difficult choices.

First, the old equations and evaluation of geopolitics and international relations have been invalidated. The old scenario of two nuclear superpowers with loaded guns pointed at each other's heads has been replaced with a host of nations pointing weapons of mass destruction (WMD) in every direction. While there is only one real superpower remaining, the United States, there are a number of lesser powers, with access to nuclear weapons including Russia, Japan, China, India, Pakistan, France, and Israel and many other nations have access to non-nuclear WMD. It is not clear at this point, less than 12 years after the fall of the Berlin Wall and the symbolic end of the Cold War, exactly how this new international infrastructure will coalesce. Though one thing is already clear: international cooperation has assumed a greater role than in previous times in resolving and preventing conflicts. This can be observed in the new alignments organized to confront global terrorism.

Second, the new international or global geopolitical situation is not going to be marked by sweetness and light. Old and new rivalries that lay hidden or disguised under the armed truce of the Cold War have emerged, or reemerged, and markedly contribute to a major element of uncertainty. The end of the Soviet Union and the birth of 15 new former Soviet states significantly contributes to this situation. The removal of effective control over a substantial portion of the former Soviet nuclear arsenal creates a dangerous potential that a successor state may be willing to sell technology and systems to virtually anybody.

The likelihood of regional hegemons, rogue states, and terrorist organizations (national and international) acquiring WMD—chemical, biological, and nuclear—is one of the most disturbing and unsettling elements of the emerging post-Cold War world. Such actors on the international scene may gain access to or use of other systems as well, including sophisticated electronics and communications gear, long-range missiles, and advanced conventional weapons. The sarin gas attack on the Tokyo subway system several years ago as well as the September 11, 2001, terrorist attacks on the World Trade Center and the Pentagon indicate the potential for tragedy.

The armed forces of major powers, and especially those of the United States with its worldwide range of interests and commitments, need to consider carefully how they are going to deal with this new environment. The old rules do not apply, and so far no one has come up with a useful digest of the new rules. Conventional military operations between regular armed forces are relatively unlikely. Instead, the U.S. military must be prepared for a range of missions, including counterinsurgency and counterterrorist operations, peacekeeping and peacemaking operations, disaster relief, and law enforcement. U.S. forces must also be prepared to operate in a range of environments including urban terrain, WMD conditions, and asymmetrical conflicts.

That will be the major test for the United States over the next several decades. How long will it take to figure out how to function under the new conditions? How effectively will the new tasks be performed?

The essays in Section I address these questions and broadly examine the nature of the new conditions. Subsequent sections approach other major issues or groups of issues.

I

NONTRADITIONAL
WARFARE THREATS
William R. Schilling

An urgent response to the gathering storm from nontraditional warfare (NTW) threats must be quickly addressed with reasoned, feasible, economical solutions. This is the greatest military problem currently facing the United States and the Free World in the twenty-first century. Classes of NTW activities include the following:

- Weapons of mass destruction (WMD) proliferation (nuclear, chemical, biological)
- Electronic warfare (ECCM, ECM, C^4 vulnerability)
- Economic and industrial warfare
- Demining and chemical/biological (C/B) mine warfare
- Urban warfare
- Guerrilla warfare
- Terrorist operations

The basis for concerns about NTW threats to the continental United States (CONUS) and other nations evolves from the potential damage to populations and infrastructure that cannot be mitigated by existing U.S. civilian and military assets. Most approaches to the NTW threats are reactive and are applied under emergency response conditions. Deployment and employment of certain delivery systems by enemy nations using WMD can be disclosed and/or deterred by overwhelming U.S. counterstrikes. Other NTW threats are much more insidious and difficult to detect and contain using today's systems, technologies, and enforcement configurations.

One example of the emerging NTW threats that results in new development and user requirements is the potential terrorist and/or rogue nation attack against American territory and its citizens. These threats present challenges to national security never before addressed. On January 11, 2000, CNN presented a focus report that stated the weapon of mass destruction most probable for American cities is a chemical/biological threat, rather than a nuclear threat. Their report stated that, "It is no longer a question of 'If,' or 'When,' such an attack would occur but, 'Where.'" In the past year, the FBI issued four Level One alerts to chemical/biological threats planned against American cities. Currently, there is no accepted methodology for quantifying the effects from these threat employments. Therefore, countermeasures cannot be properly devised or assessed to counter the effects and save American lives and resources. Many Government agencies are involved (e.g., Department of Defense (DOD), Department of State (DOS), Department of Energy (DOE), Federal Emergency Management Agency (FEMA), Defense Threat Reduction Agency (DTRA), Department of Justice (DOJ), National Security Agency (NSA), Central Intelligence Agency (CIA), Department of Health and Human Services (DHHS), and others) but none have a specific charter to develop accepted approaches and methodologies to quantify the potential threats or the effectiveness of possible threat responses. There is an increasing urgency to address this mounting threat from within the United States and abroad.

Potential Threat Characteristics
Weapons of Mass Destruction

Weapons of mass destruction tend to be considered strategic weapons due to the potential damage and required responses. Most approaches to countering these threats involve identification of the perpetrators and their emphasis on missiles as the delivery system. Nuclear warheads can destroy very large cities as evidenced by the bombings of Nagasaki and Hiroshima. The technology for producing chemical and biological (C/B) weapons is available to rogue nations and provides a means to achieve massive damage against civilian populations (without using nuclear weapons, which require highly advanced technology and manufacturing capability). Even chemical warheads (2,000 pounds of Vx) can achieve 50 percent casualties against exposed personnel over a half-square mile region and biological warheads (2,000 pounds of anthrax) can achieve similar casualty levels over hundreds of square miles. Other delivery means besides missiles are also available for small C/B warheads and little serious attention is being given to many of these threats.

Electronic Warfare

Electronic warfare capability has been available to sophisticated nations for many years following the invention of nuclear warheads, lasers, radios, and radars. The technology for directed energy weapons (DEW) is well known in most of the world and off-the-shelf items are available to construct these devices. Without protective measures, many electromechanical devices can be impaired by individual engagements from DEW at modest ranges. Electromagnetic pulses (EMP) generated by nuclear explosions can negate the use of unprotected electronic devices, computers, and communications systems over thousands of square miles.

Computer Warfare

The widespread use of computers increases the risk of major damage or disruption through the use of generated viruses, worms, and trojan horses. These sophisticated computer programs can destroy programming codes and render them useless. Sophisticated computer hackers or terrorists can launch attacks against the U.S. economic and industrial base by infiltrating computer databases and destroying or changing critical data, algorithms, or formulas that are used to determine national policies and retain vital information.

Mine Warfare

Millions of previously emplaced conventional mines from regional and local wars cause thousands of casualties every year. The United Nations (UN) is undertaking broad demining measures to eradicate these threats, but the cost and time to clear the mines remains a challenging problem. Other new C/B threats from land and sea mines magnify the conventional mine threats. Critical vulnerabilities exist on land and sea from C/B mines because very little attention is given to either the requirements or means to detect, locate, and neutralize these threats. These C/B threats will have a major impact on the U.S. capability to execute current defense policies and force applications.

Urban and Guerilla Warfare

Conventional, C/B, and DEW weapons can be applied effectively in urban and guerilla warfare. These tactics allow small unit engagements in conventional warfare and permit perpetrators to close or wait for lucrative targets in DEW and C/B attacks. The Russians experienced severe difficulties and casualties in Chechnya in both 1996 and again in 1999 from a combination of urban and guerilla warfare tactics. Technologies are available to make this type of warfare even more severe (and unpopular) for sophisticated countries trying to limit collateral damage and friendly casualties. In fact, target acquisition is a severe challenge and better means are necessary for locating enemy groups or lucrative targets. Otherwise, different weapons and combat units will need to be conceived to match the urban or guerilla target spectrum. The guerilla warfare tactics in the Vietnam War were often effective in negating both the structured U.S. combat organizations and the available high technology assets.

Terrorism

Terrorist threats and actions are becoming almost everyday occurrences in the United States and the rest of the world. Easy access to information, explosives, and electromechanical technologies provides terrorists with new tools for widespread damage-producing situations. Terrorist threats have changed significantly over the past several decades largely because of the following:

- Centralization of critical elements of national infrastructures
- Concentration on civilian damage rather than military targets
- Training in technology and tactics to potential terrorist groups by elements of the former Soviet Union and other national governments
- Financial and logistical support by national governments or wealthy individuals
- Easy access to information and information technologies
- Easy access to technologies of mass destruction

The United States is becoming aware of the increasing vulnerabilities of the national infrastructure to terrorist attacks. In fact, terrorism may become the option of choice for hostile governments, transnational groups, and other militants. Because of its complexity and interdependence, the infrastructure presents unique targeting opportunities to terrorist adversaries. Complex infrastructures are vulnerable because they have critical nodes, or choke points, that can result in significant disruption or destruction. These infrastructure include: the national power grid, food processing, economic and financial structures, telecommunications, water supply, gas and oil, transportation (aviation, highway network, railroads, and waterborne commerce), continuity of government at all levels, and emergency fire and law enforcement.

The Department of State (Title 22, USC Section 2656) defines terrorism as "premeditated, politically motivated violence perpetrated against noncombatant targets by subnational groups or clandestine agents usually intended to influence audiences." Often the intent is to cause fear about the potentiality of future terrorist attacks.

More than 2,000 terrorist incidents have occurred in the last hundred years, producing casualties from the thousands to millions (depending on the definition of *terrorism*). The higher number includes intergovernmental actions to remove ethnic groups (i.e., Germany, Russia, Cambodia). Recently, the United States has become a target for terrorists seeking to influence political decisions internally and abroad (e.g., the Alfred P. Murrah Building in Oklahoma City, the UN building in New York City, U.S. embassies overseas, the New Year's Day celebrations for Y2K, the attack on the USS Cole, and the September 11, 2001, attacks on the World Trade Center and the Pentagon).

The potential for damage or disruption is nearly the same for perceived threats as for actual threats. The perceived terrorist attack on Y2K celebrations resulted in the cancellation of several events. The risk of terrorist attack on the White House closed a major traffic artery in downtown Washington, D.C., in 1995. Security at overseas embassies had to be reevaluated and reinforced after the 1998 bombing of two U.S. embassies in Africa. Whether or not these preventative countermeasures have actually averted terrorist threats is unknown. In fact, it may be argued that these measures emphasized and highlighted the vulnerability of missions abroad and the infrastructure at home.

Some Leading NTW Threat Issues

Nontraditional warfare threats must be confronted from a solid footing and with confidence and efficiency. The threats must be (1) defined in quantitative terms that permit response options to be measured and evaluated; (2) standardized to provide uniformity in comparisons; and (3) prioritized to husband resources and reduce damage consequences. Integrated consolidated movements must often be advanced to accomplish these objectives. Of course, certain items will be in the purview of a single Government department or agency. For example, military forces that deal with WMD threats outside the continental United States (OCONUS) are clearly in the domain of the DOD. Nevertheless, technology transfer from these defense initiatives could assist other Government agencies and organizations. A general sharing of intelligence and resources among the participating agencies would improve the nation's ability to counter and respond to the NTW threats.

Standardized scenarios for each class of NTW threat will be necessary to provide a framework for developing appropriate responses, countermeasures, and technologies. These scenarios must deal with the incident location, composition and posture of opposing units, resources available to respond, the conditions of threat employment, and the degree of warning and protection.

In defining and classifying the NTW threats, emphasis must begin with the means including intelligence, early warning, and sensor alerts for detecting, pinpointing, and sizing the attack. The characteristics of the threat must be known in terms of potential damage, the type of employed weapons, and preventive actions necessary to save lives and infrastructure.

As mentioned earlier, certain critical threats are not addressed since intelligence information on known terrorist or foreign country involvement is *not* available. Yet the consequences of clandestine acquisition or rapid development by a terrorist group or rogue nation could produce weapons, systems, and techniques for serious threats against the United States and the Free World.

For example, until recently, no attention was given to the possible application of high-powered microwaves (HPM) as a serious threat to military C^{4}I or civilian electromechanical devices. There is also a serious threat from the possible introduction of C/B sea mines that is still unaddressed by the DOD. Still another threat is the use of highjacked or chartered aircraft with loads of highly volatile fuel used as guided munitions.

One objective of terrorism is to create panic and fear in the populace to erode their confidence and trust in the Government. Even the use of limited chemical/biological weapons of mass destruction could undermine morale and confidence as demonstrated by the many anthrax scares during late 2001 and early 2002.

In short, NTW threats can be devastating to U.S. interests. Before suitable countermeasures and responses can emerge, the threats must be evaluated, not just the current or anticipated ones, but also others that could exist.

2

EFFECTS OF GLOBAL STRESS POINTS ON NONTRADITIONAL WARFARE

William R. Schilling

Since the end of the Cold War with the Soviet Union, the focus of international concerns has shifted to encompass a wide range of global hot spots. In general, these new "stress points" are less likely to trigger a large-scale U.S. strategic military response. The new problems arising from current world situations are more likely to be countered by a tactical or diplomatic response requiring international approval.

Many sensitive factors are involved in shaping policies and goals for alleviating these global stress points. First of all, interest and support from many nations are involved in settling hostilities or business disagreements caused by nationalistic fervor, religious intolerance, border disputes, trading irregularities, and criminal activities. Often, devising responses or applying foreign pressure to coerce involved parties to cease hostilities and negotiate a peaceful solution to disagreements or conflicts tend to involve approaches that can be ignored or involve threats that can be dismissed as not credible or realistic. Many times, the most effective response may be diluted by structuring the approach to include the interests of other nations.

Available options and instruments for affecting or relieving stress points can involve nontraditional force applications, united organizations, and international agreements. Selected response options must be consistent with the nature of the disagreements, the necessary resources to rectify the situation, and the perception of the threat as vital to U.S. national security. The characteristics of global stress points provide a basis for determining response option

Guided missile destroyer escorting the USS Dwight D. Eisenhower, CVN-69, and the USS Nimitz, CVN-68.

requirements. New research and development initiatives for nontraditional applications can assist in meeting these requirements.

Background

Six global stress points provide examples for exploring the nontraditional challenges and for developing initiatives needed to resolve differences or limit the escalation of threatening global conditions and instability. These six stress points and primary reasons for concern are listed in Exhibit 2.1 and are discussed in more detail in the subsequent sections of this essay. Other stress points caused by cyber warfare, drug trafficking, guerrilla warfare, and weapons of mass destruction are discussed in the following essays:

Essay 3. Military Forces Survivability in a Weapons of Mass Destruction Environment

Essay 4. Information Systems Survivability in Nontraditional Warfare Operations

Essay 6. Terrorist Operations in Nontraditional Warfare

Essay 8. Guerrilla Operations in Nontraditional Warfare

Essay 9. International Criminal Operations in Nontraditional Warfare

Essay 23. The Future with Nuclear Weapons

EXHIBIT 2.1   Global stress points.

Stress point	Concern
1. Taiwan-China	Taiwan's search for nuclear systems acquisition and independent nation status
2. India-Pakistan	Nationalism and nuclear weapon development
3. Middle East	Nationalism and religious intolerance plus oil reserves
4. Africa	Spead of HIV/AIDS
5. Rogue States	Terrorism and adventurism
6. International Business	Economic warfare and financial instability

Except for the topic of international business, each of the other five stress points chosen for discussion in this essay represent regional problem areas. Other NTW essays address certain aspects of these problems in terms of management information systems, countermeasures to terrorist and WMD applications, models and tools for evaluating response measures, and possible advanced technology initiatives. The intent of this essay is to recognize the serious nature of these problems and to provide a basis for ensuring that new NTW initiatives provide sufficient flexibility and resilience to deal effectively with these stress points.

Worldwide Stress Points

Taiwan-China

For many decades, the United States has had a mutual defense pact with the government of Taiwan. The United States is committed to protect Taiwan against the People's Republic of China's efforts to absorb the control and government of Taiwan. On the other hand, the United States is also committed to a single China policy that includes both regions. Parts of the political structure and many of the citizens of Taiwan continue to espouse independence from China. Others support recognition of China's ownership claim to Taiwan but want to have the freedom to operate autonomously, much like Hong Kong in the past. In addition, some political groups within the United States also espouse independent status for Taiwan. These differing positions between Taiwan and China exacerbate tension (stress) between the countries.

Another cause for global concern is the continuing Taiwanese efforts to gain nuclear weapon status through internal RDT&E efforts, acquisition purchases, or clandestine actions. Over the last decade, the Taiwanese have started and reduced nuclear RDT&E activities several times in response to

U.S. pressure. Nevertheless, the Taiwanese continue to seek nuclear technology as evidenced by their interrelationship with Wen Ho Lee of Los Alamos fame and perhaps others.

Taiwanese pursuit of nuclear weapon capabilities is seen as a means of gaining independence by achieving strategic balance with China. This nuclear capability could preclude or deter an invasion of their island homeland. If it appears that the Taiwanese could successfully acquire nuclear capability, the Chinese might decide to make preemptive attacks or invade the island. The United States could be drawn into the conflict by supporting the Taiwanese with counterstrike measures if peacekeeping negotiations prove unsuccessful.

India-Pakistan

Another potential nuclear engagement could arise from the conflict between India and Pakistan if one or both countries felt vital security interests or survival was at stake. This situation is especially critical and could occur since India's land and air forces are much stronger than the Pakistan elements.

Continuing strife and guerrilla warfighting between the two countries could lead to a more conventional force engagement if one side or the other decides to expand the intensity to bring the warfare to a conclusion and perhaps victory. This situation could set the scene for one side to counter with nuclear weapons. At a minimum, neighboring countries would be greatly affected by this release of nuclear weapons and the number of casualties in the region would lead to grave global concerns.

Middle East

Of primary concern for the United States are the hostilities that continue to flare and intensify between Israelis and Palestinians. The sharing or claims of ownership of holy lands and religious edifices by both groups as well as the establishment of Israeli settlements in previously held Palestinian regions, the prohibition of reentry of Palestinian refugees, and the desire of both sides to have Jerusalem as their capital complicate diplomatic discussions and peace negotiations.

The belligerence and aggressive actions, including terrorism, as well as a shared religion, incite Arabian nations to side with Palestinians while the United States and some European nations support the Israelis. The result of these disagreements and hostilities cause the situation in the Middle East to be very unstable. Furthermore, the area serves as a breeding ground for well-organized terrorist movements throughout the world and interferes with access to Arabian oil resources and with western trading opportunities.

Finally, these Middle East conflicts lead to arms races and competition for sales by the United States, European states, Russia, China, and North Korea.

Africa

Border disputes and quarrels over natural resources and land areas as well as uprisings by transstate groups continue to be points of concern within the African continent. However, the more severe threat and danger stems from the widespread HIV/AIDS epidemic throughout sub-Saharan Africa. In fact, over 20 percent of the population in South Africa, Botswana, Zambia, Zimbabwe, Swaziland, and Namibia are living with HIV and AIDS. These 25 million victims represent 70 percent of the known HIV/AIDS sufferers worldwide.

The African governments and health services including trained medical personnel, hospitals, testing units, and pharmaceutical dispensing programs are overwhelmed by the magnitude of infected people and are not capable of coping with the spread or treatment of HIV or AIDS. Private groups and world organizations provide some assistance but this support is insufficient to deal with the level of resources needed to arrest this problem.

If the cost of treating patients with HIV/AIDS could be reduced to only one dollar per day (a very optimistic goal), about $9 billion per year would be needed to treat the current number of patients. This $9 billion is equivalent to the money used by the Government to build the mass transit system in Washington, D.C., during the past 30 years.

In comparison to the possible $100 million per year promised by pharmaceutical companies, the shortfall in available medicine is about three orders of magnitude. Of course, the world community, charity organizations, and African governments are trying to fight against these overwhelming odds.

Unless measures are found and implemented to control this problem in Africa, countries may be forced to isolate carriers of HIV/AIDS, require health permits certifying absence of infection, and limit the birth rights of people by requiring testing to avoid spread to newborn children. Obviously, all of these measures are dehumanizing and certainly undesirable from a human rights standpoint. However, without strong control measures and technological breakthroughs that reduce the costs for treatment per person, threatened regions and countries may restrict the movement of peoples, the access to trading centers, and the economic development of nations. Therefore, the continuing spread of HIV/AIDS will become a destabilizing factor for many governments. It will require the training and use of military units to enforce travel restrictions and support medical resource security—new challenges for nontraditional force elements.

Rogue States

Rogue states or "states of concern" typically operate outside the norm of legit-imate, international standards or conventions. Of special concern are states that have been involved in nationally sponsored terrorist activities against other countries. These rogue countries reportedly include North Korea, Afghanistan, Iraq, Iran, Libya, and several others that have overtly or covertly sponsored or organized terrorist actions.

These terrorist initiatives can include providing weapons of mass destruc-tion (WMD), funding, training, or simply sanctuary. Deterrent measures to these activities are the NTW options of choice, but other actions to prevent initial applications are also necessary to avoid damage and capture potential perpetrators. Essay 21, Research and Development Planning Guide for Coun-tering Nontraditional Warfare Threats, describes some RDT&E initiatives for mitigating nationally sponsored terrorist threats.

International Business and Industry

Financial management and control has truly become a global enterprise with the widespread use of computer-based systems, the Internet, and the interna-tional business corporations. World banking establishments and linkage between nations, regions, and international lending institutions depend on each other for faithfully, legally, and accurately reporting and controlling financial assets and information.

These global business activities allow many nations to participate in the buildup of industrial development opportunities, access to financial support, and worldwide trading ventures. On the other hand, they also bring along financial risks, dependence, and trust on a scale not envisioned even a decade ago. Some characteristics of these business and economic concerns that affect the use of international enforcement measures and nontraditional approaches for ensuring U.S. resource security are listed next:

- Foreign nation lending practices, debts, and obligations to other nations and international banking organizations
- Unfair trading, lending, and labor practices
- Industrial espionage or sabotage
- Exchange rates validity and speculation
- Fraudulent financial practices (laundering and depositor secrecy)
- Formulation of economic consortiums to control resource markets and sales
- Stock market adventurism and investment risk taking

EXHIBIT 2.2 Aspects of global stress problems.

	World concerns	NTW implications	NTW initiatives
Taiwan-China	• Taiwan acquisition of nuclear weapons for deterrence • Chinese response to nuclear acquisition by Taiwan • U.S.-Taiwan commitment • Pace of Taiwan-China conciliation moves	• Naval support/blockades/ air strikes and interdiction • Chinese isolation/ preemptive attack • Russian involvement • U.S. force requirements/ structure/policy	• Options for response • Chemical/biological countermeasures • Containment of nuclear technology/transfer • Naval force requirements • Ship interdiction/ counterstrikes
India-Pakistan	• Tactical nuclear exchange • Guerrilla warfare • Terrorism/political insurrection • Destabilizing situation	• Pakistan-China alignment vs. India-Russia agreements • Collateral damage • Settlement conditions/ peace-keeping organization	• UN peacekeeping force • Lines of demarcation • Early warning sensors • Prevention of preemptive strikes • Emergency response measures
Middle East	• Continuing strife and killing • Control over religious places/symbols • Unwillingness for tolerance and acceptance of existence • Intervention of foreign interests and forces • Terrorist movements/actions	• Brokering peace negotiations • Employment of peacekeeping units and UN observers • Introduction of joint units including U.S. and others • Prevention of WMD usage • Capitalization/expansion of regional economies	• Prevention of WMD initiatives • Israel-Palestine hot lines • Less intrusive security management • Control of armaments • Reduction of civilian armament smuggling and new settlements
Africa	• 25 million with AIDS • Prohibitive treatment costs • Fears by noninfected population • Lack of training, education, and preventative measures • Isolation of AIDS carriers	• Protection of medical relief teams • Emergence of tribal and national boundaries to restrict movements of AIDS carriers • Isolation and identification of AIDS carriers	• Establishment of AIDS distance learning and network centers • Funding of AIDS immunization • Acceptance of birth control and prevention of sexually transmitted diseases • Pre-birth determination and termination
Rogue states	• Terrorism used to enhance national interests and extend favorable conditions • Access to WMD technologies • Fostering drug trafficking and criminal activities • Center for developing WMD	• Identification and countering of planned prestrike incidents • Tracking of known terrorists, training centers, and money laundering • Capture of terrorist leaders and resources	• Deterrence against WMD applications and incidents • Interception of rogue state weapon attacks • Utilization of HUMINT, standoff sensors, and smart sensor webs to monitor rogue state activities
International business	• Trade group monopolies • Economic warfare • Industrial espionage • Bribery and corruption of government agents/agencies • Human labor exploitation • Criminal management of financial centers	• Enforcement of international financial/ trading laws • Methods and organizations for monitoring international business • Collection of information to counter criminal activities	• Utilization of trade embargo and counterintelligence • Implementation of training and technologies to support law enforcement • Access and accountability for financial centers database • V&V for monitoring process

Nationalization of privately owned businesses, collapse or weakening of government controls allowing corruption and an increase in criminal participation in the economic infrastructure also affect the economic stability of a country. Civil war or large-scale rioting disrupts an economy through collateral damage to important or crucial industries.

The structure of international business and industry requires new approaches to resolve issues and balance economic forces. The only available tools at the current time are trade agreements, embargoes, negotiation, diplomacy, sanctions, and covert military (quasi-military) actions.

NTW Implications

In light of the situations generated from the six stress points illustrated in Exhibit 2.1, some nontraditional warfare implications and initiatives to address or alleviate these problem areas are listed in Exhibit 2.2 (p. 15). Many of these global stress problems require the tailoring of military-civilian activities and organizations to address these needs and responses. Most of these conditions are completely different from threats in the traditional battlefield arena or military missions. Obviously, adjustments and flexibilities in force sizes, composition, transportation, logistics supply, protection, countermeasures, and security need to be evaluated and tested. Likewise, no single or modular approach fits many of these circumstances, but concepts for ordering and mastering these types of conditions and support requirements need to be devised. Many actions require simple monitoring or assistance that must be derived from training and understanding the limits and constraints on possible support. Elements of the U.S. services have been participating in some aspects of these problems for many years, especially the units under control of Special Operations/Low Intensity Conflict and Special Operations Command. Nevertheless, continued attention to these problems is necessary to avoid surprises and obtain/retain the capability to respond efficiently and effectively.

3

MILITARY FORCES SURVIVABILITY IN A WEAPONS OF MASS DESTRUCTION ENVIRONMENT

Robert E. Bent

During the last half century, the national security strategy of the United States was committed to the containment of Soviet Communism. Following the fall of the Berlin Wall in 1989, and the dissolution of the Soviet Union 2 years later, world politics and the threat to the United States have been dramatically transformed. Changes in the international political environment have led many to believe that the likelihood of facing weapons of mass destruction on future battlefields is decreasing. However, the proliferation of both chemical and nuclear weapons technology suggests otherwise.

In 1998, Secretary of Defense, Bill Cohen, established the U.S. Commission on National Security, known as the Hart-Rudman Commission, an independent advisory panel charged with examining how the United States should ensure its security over the next 25 years. The report, *Seeking a National Strategy: A Concept for Preserving Security and Promoting Freedom,* issued a warning about the United States' lack of preparedness for an increasingly uncertain future. Furthermore, the current military strategy of fighting two major theater conflicts is a Cold War relic and inadequate for twenty-first century threats. The report suggests the following four high priority policy issues and five corresponding military capabilities for the next quarter century:

High priority policy issues

- Make nonproliferation a high priority.
- Strengthen cooperation with other nations against terrorism.

- Build domestic defense against missile attacks.

- Draw other nations, especially China, Russia, and India, into the emerging international system.

Required military capabilities
- Nuclear deterrence
- Homeland security
- Conventional weapons defense
- Expeditionary/intervention forces
- Humanitarian relief

With the onset of the new century, the nation faces an imperative need for creative thinking about the future security of this country. The Hart-Rudman report emphasized, "Americans are less secure than they believe themselves to be. The time for reexamination is now, before the American people find themselves shocked by events they never anticipated."

Survivability Policies and Factors
Nonproliferation Policy

The Hart-Rudman report's first key objective is "to defend the United States and ensure that it is safe from the dangers of a new era." Nonproliferation of weapons of mass destruction (WMD) is the highest priority U.S. national security policy for the next quarter century. The United States needs to seek international cooperation to combat the growing proliferation of WMD. This should include an effective and enforceable international ban on the creation, transfer, trade, and weaponization of biological pathogens, chemical agents, and nuclear weapon technology/materiel, whether by states or non-state elements. International cooperative and surety programs to deal with existing stockpiles of nuclear, biological, and chemical weapons present cost-effective and politically attractive ways to reduce the dangers of weapons and weapons materiel proliferation.

Should political methods of prevention and deterrence fail, the United States must have the military means to defend or fight in a WMD environment. Therefore, it is critical to the national interest that a capability to avert, or check, the proliferation of WMD be developed.

The potential use of WMD seriously threatens U.S. forces. Political realities and dwindling resources present enormous challenges. Recent nuclear testing by Pakistan and India makes it obvious that the proliferation of nuclear weapons among "rest-of-world" countries continues. Indeed, U.S. forces may face an opponent possessing a small number of nuclear weapons. Additionally, the prospect of the limited use of chemical agents, biological pathogens, and/or nuclear weapons by terrorists or tyrants trying to gain power through the ownership of such weapons or devices continues.

The WMD Environment

Former Secretary of Defense, William Perry, in his *1995 Annual Report to the President and the Congress,* highlighted the fact that "Military preparedness is the very heart of . . . the Department of Defense's (DOD) counter-proliferation initiative. In today's security environment, military forces of the United States will likely face the use, or threat of use of weapons of mass destruction (WMD)." Today, and in the foreseeable future, WMD poses the most formidable battlefield threat. These weapons are capable of inflicting devastation well beyond the scope of the average person's imagination. The means to avoid or minimize mass military, and/or civilian, casualties must be adopted. Delivery means for WMD range from complex missile systems to simple hand-carried devices as evidenced by the terrorist chemical agent attack on a Japanese subway in the mid 1990s. Continuing instability in the Middle East, Southeast Asia, and Southwest Asia only serves to reinforce U.S. concerns for possible WMD use by regional powers and third world countries.

Hostile forces may choose to use every weapon at their disposal to achieve their military goals. This could include any form of nuclear, biological, or chemical (NBC) as well as conventional munitions, delivered by aircraft, missile, rocket, or gun, and they may resort to the clandestine use of biological or chemical agents prior to as well as during hostilities. Initially nuclear weapons are likely to be controlled at the political level and chemical and biological weapons are likely to be controlled at the highest military levels. It is impossible to predict at what stage of conflict NBC weapons might be used, but it is expected that, once authority for the first use of chemical weapons has been given, hostile forces may regard them as acceptable as conventional weapons.

If deterrence fails in the present or future multi-polar world, the United States must be prepared to meet this monumental challenge. The threat of WMD continues to force corresponding changes in training, planning, and operations for military forces to achieve survivability on current and future battlefields.

WMD Battlefield Context

To accomplish its mission and defeat any aggression, U.S. military forces must survive and be prepared to continue to fight in a WMD environment. This is true in all forms of WMD environments and, as we transition into a nontraditional warfare environment, this precept takes on a special meaning. Classically the force must be able to perform critical functions in the unnatural (manmade) hostile environment. Systems include subsystems, support equipment, and facilities essential for accomplishment of the mission at all levels of conflict. The defensive measures outlined in this essay should limit the adverse effects of NBC attacks and help to ensure military forces retain cohesion and combat effectiveness. Two major aspects of survivability are discussed next.

Mission Survivability

Sufficient levels of personnel and vital equipment should survive long enough to perform the unit's mission. Survivability criteria including blast, thermal and initial nuclear radiation, electromagnetic pulse (EMP), transient radiation effects on electronics (TREE), ground shock and water shock effects should continue to be reviewed and improved. Protective features that meet survivability criteria should be incorporated into the design of future vehicles and equipment and existing vehicles and equipment should be modified as necessary.

NBC Contamination Survivability

Vehicles and vital equipment should be designed so NBC hazards cause the least possible constraint on function and operation. Equipment design should allow quick and easy decontamination; it must withstand any damaging effects of agents, decontaminants, or decontamination procedures; and it must permit unhindered use by operators wearing full protective equipment.

In general terms, sufficient numbers of military systems can survive in an NBC environment through a mix of the following initiatives:

- *Hardness.* The employment of design or manufacturing techniques that increases ability to survive the effects of a nuclear environment (e.g., shielding, robust structural designs, electronic circumvention, electrical filtering, vertical shock mounting)
- *Avoidance.* The introduction of measures to eliminate detection and attack (e.g., signal reduction or camouflage)
- *Redundancy.* The incorporation of extra components or methods in a system to accomplish a function so if one fails, another is available

- *Deception.* The employment of measures to mislead the enemy as to the actual system location in order to draw fire away from the target (e.g., decoys, chaff, aerosols)
- *Reconstitution.* The incorporation of design features into a system or piece of equipment to facilitate rapid repair and resetting of the affected items

Trade-off analyses are conducted during the acquisition process to determine the method, or combinations of the preceding methods, to minimize the life-cycle costs and provide the most cost-effective approach to survivability. The impact of system cost, performance, reliability, maintainability, productivity, and logistics support must be fully examined to ensure operational effectiveness consistent with program constraints.

Another critical component that must not be overlooked is crew survivability. The human component of a weapon system may be subjected to several types of hazards in a given engagement. The hazards include blunt trauma, blast overpressure, chemical and biological hazards, heat exposure, and fragment penetration among others. Equipment should be designed to remain operational for as long as the personnel serving it remain combat effective; should be easy to operate by personnel wearing full protective clothing; and should be easy to decontaminate. The application of agent resistant compounds to all surfaces and the provision of built-in decontamination aids should be considered in the equipment design.

Status of Nuclear Survivability Policy

Prior to cancellation in 1991, Department of Defense (DOD) Directive (DOD) 4245.4, "Acquisition of nuclear survivable systems," outlined the DOD procedures and requirements for acquiring nuclear survivable systems. In 1991, to streamline acquisition procedures and address post-Cold War issues, a new series of acquisition documents was published that combines numerous regulations and requirements into two major acquisition documents. These were DODD 5000.1, "Defense Acquisition," and DOD Instruction (DODI) 5000.2, "Defense Acquisition Management Policy and Procedures," both dated February 23, 1991. Although the 1991 5000 series documents were not as detailed regarding system nuclear survivability as DODD 4245.4 had been, they did outline the requirements and provided guidance on how to meet the requirements. However, the Federal Acquisition Reform Act of 1996, with its emphasis on commercial off-the-shelf (COTS) equipment and nondevelopmental items (NDI), eliminated numerous military standards (MIL STD) for the acquisition of hardware and equipment. All discussions of nuclear survivability requirements have since been deleted in the 1996 revision of the 5000 series of acquisition documents.

The current DODD 5000.1 states that systems should be tested to assure that they are "operationally effective, suitable, and survivable for intended use." The current DOD 5000.2-R (Section 4.4.1 "survivability") states that, "Unless waived by the Milestone Decision Authority (MDA), mission-critical systems shall be survivable to the threat levels anticipated in their operating environment. Survivability from all threats found in the various levels of conflict shall be considered and fully assessed." None of these words prohibit concern for system NBC survivability but the current acquisition documents, unlike their predecessors, no longer emphasize WMD survivability.

Survivability Needs

The Current Dilemma

The potential for limited use of nuclear weapons against U.S. military targets, especially those in forward areas, is the burning motivation for nuclear survivable systems. By fielding nuclear survivable systems, the United States can enhance nuclear deterrence by reducing large-scale destruction and collateral damage to our forces, and still retain the ability to fight back. However, the United States is not fielding and cannot field a truly nuclear survivable force. Even as our forces become more dependent on sophisticated electronics (e.g., the digitized battlefield), today's acquisition priority for developing and testing nuclear survivable systems is diminishing. The United States relies on a small, very sophisticated force to provide its security and cannot afford to lose a major portion of its overall fighting force. Today, "you fight as you come" (i.e., the equipment that you arrive with is what you fight with), with minimal backup for the very complex and expensive major fighting systems. The nuclear vulnerability of new systems is a growing concern because many new systems lack a requirement to be survivable and are not tested to define their vulnerabilities. For example, the performance of modern electronics is a major concern since unprotected, unhardened systems in an entire theater of operations could fail due to a single high altitude electromagnetic pulse (HEMP) event.

Acquisition of Nuclear Survivable Systems and Equipment

As indicated previously, the current DOD 5000.2-R, requires "mission critical systems be survivable to the threat levels anticipated in their operating environment." As U.S. forces become more dependent on electronic command, control, communications, and computers and intelligence (C⁴I) systems, HEMP effects present a large risk to the force. The facts are that (1) many mission critical systems are designed and procured with little regard to nuclear survivability; (2) U.S. forces may face an opponent armed with nuclear weapons; and (3) if a nuclear explosion occurs, critical U.S. equipment may be vulnerable. Thus any adversary possessing a crude nuclear device with the capability to detonate it at a high altitude of 30 km or more could threaten an entire theater of operations and present an asymmetric method of leveling the battlefield in their favor. And the perpetrator may not be vulnerable to a nuclear counterstrike since the high explosives primarily produce nonlethal effects.

Systems being acquired today, because of their costs and longevity, are destined to be retained in the field for many years. Thus, they need to reflect the nuclear threat 5 to 10 years out, not just today's threat. Also, if a system is nuclear hardened there are "bonus" effects since the system may be more survivable to conventional blast, near lightning strikes, electromagnetic interference (EMI), and electromagnetic radiation (EMR). The United States should not compromise the military capability of its forces by failing to consider and implement nuclear survivability measures in the acquisition of mission critical systems.

Nations possessing large numbers of high technology weapon systems stand to lose the most in future nuclear conflicts if these systems are not hardened against nuclear effects. Vulnerability to nuclear effects invites the use of those weapons. Mission essential equipment hardened against nuclear effects remains a critical element to support deterrence.

Test and Evaluation of Systems and Equipment

Nuclear weapons effects (NWE) knowledge is essential to the development of nuclear survivable systems and should be used throughout the development and acquisition process. Analysis plays an important role in nuclear survivability design and development. Computer-aided analysis helps engineers and scientists to estimate the effects of the various nuclear environments, design more accurate tests, predict experimental responses, select the appropriate test facility, and scale test results to the proper level and size. It also helps predict the response of systems that are too costly or difficult to test. Analysis is limited, however, by the inability to model complex items and to treat the large nonlinear responses encountered in nuclear effects and in digital electronics.

Since we are no longer conducting underground nuclear tests, all nuclear weapons effects testing is done by simulators. These simulators are usually limited to a relatively small exposure volume and generally used for single environment tests, such as x-ray effects, neutron effects, prompt gamma ray effects, and EMP effects. Free-field EMP, high explosive (HE), and shock tube tests are notable exceptions since they can test at system level. Full systems can be tested for neutron, gamma fluence, and total dose at the Army's fast burst reactors (FBR).

Implication of NBC Survivability Needs

Developing the Needs Process

Survivability requirements should be formally considered in the development of the initial requirements document, such as the mission needs statements (MNS). This document should address each of the threat categories (conventional, advanced technology, nuclear, chemical, and biological) in terms of the specific hostile environment as well as the preferred strategies (hardness, avoidance, redundancy, deception, and reconstitution) to achieve survivability for each environment. At a minimum, high altitude electromagnetic pulse (HEMP) protection is required for mission critical electronic equipment to preclude catastrophic theater-wide loss.

Systems designed to survive blast, thermal radiation, nuclear radiation, EMP, and in some cases TREE are said to be "nuclear hardened." Nuclear hardness is a quantitative description of the resistance of a system to internal (temporary or permanent) malfunction or degraded performance induced by a nuclear detonation. "Hardness" measures the resistance of a system's hardware to physical effects such as overpressure, peak velocities, energy absorbed, and electrical stress and can be achieved through a variety of well-established design specifications or careful selection of well-built and well-engineered components.

Key aspects of vulnerability reduction include affordability, a balance in system survivability improvement efforts, and joint activities. Affordability is measured in terms of initial acquisition costs, life-cycle costs, and weight and performance penalties. Affordable vulnerability reduction, testing, and evaluation must be started early in the acquisition program to identify and implement design changes at minimum cost. The costs of making changes increase dramatically as the system proceeds through its design, development, and production phases. If not identified early, some desired changes might become cost prohibitive.

Equipment Survivability

Since the 1996 acquisition reform and its emphasis on commercial off-the-shelf (COTS) and nondevelopmental item(s) (NDI), each service is finding it more and more difficult to acquire nuclear survivable systems. More importantly, few new system acquisitions are fully tested or simulated in a nuclear weapons effects environment to identify possible vulnerabilities. COTS and NDI systems, by definition, are not developed for military use and almost without exception are not designed to survive in a WMD environment. However, in many cases, COTS and NDI systems can be modified with simple inexpensive procedures to make them less vulnerable to nuclear weapons effects, but they must be evaluated to identify their intrinsic level of hardness. Some COTS and NDI items can be made survivable simply by placing them in a protective or hardened shelter.

In the development process, the cost of nuclear survivability has averaged around 1 percent of the total acquisition costs. However, the cost to retrofit nuclear survivability into an already developed system can be prohibitively expensive—possibly as much as 25 percent of the acquisition costs or more. As more COTS and NDI systems are acquired, some mission-critical systems are not tested to evaluate their inherent survivability.

Systems that initially have a sufficient level of intrinsic hardness may lose their hardness level when less survivable replacement parts are introduced throughout the system's life cycle. The ability to control the hardness levels of replacement parts is very difficult due to changes in markets over time.

After system vulnerability reduction design features are identified, trade-offs for improving system effectiveness, reducing susceptibility, reducing costs, and reducing weight must be considered. To ensure systems are survivable with an acceptable level of vulnerability, we must prepare operationally oriented performance specifications that are consistent with the requirements document, the test and evaluation master plan (TEMP), and the cost and operational effectiveness analysis (COEA). The system must be tested to ensure that survivability is achievable without sacrificing mission effectiveness.

Electronic Warfare Survivability

Electronic warfare vulnerability analysis (EWVA), which leads to a system electronic counter-countermeasures (ECCM) capability, is a key requirement of any weapon system. This requirement exists in all phases of the development, test and evaluation, and production of weapon systems and subsystems. As a process, it evolves through all phases of the acquisition process and should be verified at all milestone reviews.

The electronic vulnerability community has the responsibility for presenting a "realistic picture" of the "proposed" or "projected" system vulnerabilities. Program managers, however, have an obligation to ensure the conduct of an unbiased and adequately funded electronic vulnerability analysis that leads to the formulation of ECCM.

NBC Contamination Survivability

Broad implications of NBC threat dictate that even if the threat of NBC attack is low, all personnel may be obliged to wear part of their NBC protective ensemble and will have to contend with the inevitable effects of a buildup of body heat, psychological stress, and reduced mobility. If the threat is high they may be required to wear their full protective ensemble, in which case they will also suffer severe degradation of sight, touch, hearing, and speech. Immediately after attack the nature and extent of the contamination will have to be reconnoitered and monitored. Contaminated personnel, materiel, and areas occupied by critical facilities (e.g., hospitals and air bases) may need to be decontaminated.

Survivability from NBC contamination can be illustrated by describing the conditions required for crews of a main battle tank or an aircraft. Either description can be useful but for the purposes of this essay, the aircrew presents an excellent example of a fully integrated requirement to protect against a combination of WMD effects. The aspect of aircrew survivability that is generally overlooked is NBC contamination survivability. Aircrew survivability in a nuclear (fallout), biological, or chemical contaminated environment is enhanced through proper application of specialized NBC protective equipment. NBC survivability of aircrew equipment is achieved by strict adherence to three design characteristics: hardness, compatibility, and decontaminability.

While fixed-wing assets play a vital role in support of our combat forces, their potential exposure to NBC environments will generally be restricted to air and ground attacks against rear echelon support elements. Rotary-wing aircraft crews who perform low altitude combat missions near front lines have a higher potential for exposure than their rear area fixed-wing counterparts. Mr. David S. Paletta, in his "Aircrew NBC Survivability" article published in the Spring 1994 edition of *Aircraft Survivability,* discussed the hardness vulnerability that affects crew survivability of transparent material. If the cockpit windshield is "hazed" over, the crew will have difficulty seeing, thus hindering the crew's ability to pilot the aircraft. During night operations, this effect will be intensified and may increase the likelihood of the aircraft and crew being lost due to disorientation or other crew-related problems. These hardness vulnerabilities are addressed by selecting materials that are not significantly degraded by contaminants or decontaminants.

Containment vulnerabilities can affect aircrew survivability as significantly as hardness vulnerabilities. When the flight crew is required to wear NBC protective gloves and mask, their ability to operate critical flight/firing/targeting functions may be degraded. The pilot must be able to utilize night vision equipment in order to operate the aircraft during clandestine operations at night. If vision is degraded by the NBC mask/optical interface, then the possibility of the aircraft being targeted by the enemy due to slower and higher flight profiles is greatly increased.

Targeting can also be degraded while operating in protective gear because of the NBC mask/optical interface. This interface can cause the gunner to fail to target the enemy or require more time to do the targeting. Other critical tasks that may be of concern while in protective gear involve operating any dials, switches, or buttons while wearing the cumbersome NBC protective gloves.

Summary

During the Cold War, many survivable systems were designed and built. Both strategic and tactical systems programs devoted much time and money to develop the technology to protect and harden the systems (human and equipment) to the effects of NBC agents. During this period, the United States invested heavily in nuclear weapons effects research, the development of test facilities, and analysis methods that could be used to study nuclear effects to validate nuclear survivability. Following the moratorium on underground nuclear testing in 1992, nuclear survivability testing has placed greater emphasis on using nuclear effects simulators and/or computer aided analyses—modeling. Without question, the benefits derived from an active testing program will better prepare the U.S. military forces to survive on a battlefield under a threat of WMD.

Protection factors (PF) for combat vehicles and personnel continue to be a critical concern for chemical, biological, and perhaps nuclear attacks. Validation and verification using simulants are needed to expand our knowledge and generate new specifications for future developments.

Automated training models and simulations for chemical and biological operations are also sadly lacking. This paucity in models and simulations and our knowledge base restricts current capabilities to operate under the threat of these weapons.

For the tactical battlefield of the future, the potential threat is likely to be in the form of chemical or perhaps biological attacks rather than nuclear, except for the threat from EMP. The potential enemy would likely choose to employ a small nuclear arsenal as a strategic system against other nations or reserve it as a deterrent from outside attacks. Further, the enemy might forego the use of biological weapons on the battlefield due to collateral damage considerations. In short, the primary emphasis on the battlefield should be to guard against the enemy's use of chemical warheads by introducing appropriate survivable methods for personnel and combat vehicles. Then, possible means to enhance battlefield survivability from biological and nuclear weapon threats can also be considered.

Considered early in the development phase, survivability is achievable at a reasonable cost and should be addressed as a form of affordable "life insurance" for mission-critical equipment. The risk from weapons of mass destruction is increasingly more probable as time progresses into the twenty-first century. We must be prepared to survive any combination of NBC weapon effects on the battlefield as long as the threats persist.

4

INFORMATION SYSTEMS SURVIVABILITY IN NONTRADITIONAL WARFARE OPERATIONS

Michael D. McDonnell
Terry L. Sayers

The information age has penetrated every aspect of our modern society. It has engendered new ways of doing business, managing personal finances, and producing many improvements in our daily lives. It has also led to changes in the way warfare operations are conducted and weapon systems are managed.

In the rush to embrace this promising new technological behemoth, most users concentrate on the positives and fail to consider the negative consequences. Information can be a two-edged sword. When available, information provides a powerful planning tool. When denied, corrupted, or compromised by an enemy, it can become an overwhelming obstacle and can lead to failure.

The ability to rapidly process information has led to a new and nontraditional phenomenon—information warfare (IW). The development of offensive and defensive weaponry in this type of warfare has been largely fought in the commercial sector. The rapidity of changes in technology requires constant vigilance to defend information systems from attack.

The subtlety of information warfare lends itself well to surprise attack or covert actions. Current information systems operate at speeds too great to permit a considered response. The ability to identify an attack and the defense required to subvert it must be built into the system to enable it to instantly respond. The first step is detecting and recognizing an attack. In the time it takes to detect an unauthorized presence on the system, the intruder can insert a destructive program, corrupt the system, or steal valuable information.

29

The Software Threat

Information threats can be extremely sophisticated and devious. There are three basic types of threats to information systems: theft, destruction, and corruption. Any system, especially those connected to a network, is vulnerable. If the system can be accessed and read, then it can be compromised.

Information Theft

The most frequent attempts to breach information security are by "hackers" attempting to access, steal, or corrupt information. For the most part, these hackers are not enemy agents, merely talented and immature computer geniuses who enter a system simply to prove that they can. Common hackers are relatively harmless and seldom use the information they access. However, other hackers breach information systems for the express purpose of stealing critical information, usually of a financial nature such as credit card numbers. Using the same techniques employed by hackers, enemy agents can access and steal data from classified information systems unless these systems are adequately protected. Hackers can also breach networked communications and sensor systems using similar techniques. Any information can provide clues to the experienced and talented hacker that enable him to breach or spoof the system under attack.

More sophisticated and better financed enemies may access and use information for their own purposes, stealing designs representing millions of dollars of research, inactivating weapons or defenses, and crippling technological infrastructures. In fact, such financing would not be beyond the means of even small nations or terrorist groups that, heretofore, have practiced more conventional attacks against their perceived enemies.

Many of the attacks on information systems protected by a password use a brute force technique. The attacker simply tries a number of passwords and hopes to get lucky. There are password or character-string generator programs that can often run through combinations of letters and numbers until one is accepted as a legitimate password.

A more sophisticated technique involves the use of a "trojan horse." A program is inserted into the information system and remains hidden while it collects information about the system and the users. At some later point, the trojan horse program is triggered and the information collected is retrieved by the attacker. This collection process can be automated to send the data to the attacker without leaving an audit trail. These trojan horse programs are routinely used by unscrupulous hackers to collect usernames and passwords, credit card information, and other data routinely entered by users.

An example of such a trojan horse program has been used to emulate the sign-in program which asks for username and password. When the user enters the data, the program responds by transmitting the data to the intruder and launching the real sign-in program. The user is confronted with an identical screen asking for username and password. The user, assuming a typing error or simple computer error, reenters the data and, this time, is connected to the system.

A relatively new and sophisticated technique for information theft is the use of a "robot" program. This robot program searches networked systems and nodes for data streams. The robot program can be programmed to divert or echo the data stream to another node or system where it can be easily retrieved.

Information Destruction

Destruction of information is the easiest method of attack. These attacks can range from crude, physical assaults to sophisticated, covert insertion of destructive programs that can be triggered by future events. Hackers who are able to access systems at the operating system management level can destroy information or even the system itself, depending only on their level of access.

The most frequent method of destructive attack is to insert a program called a "virus" into the system. A virus program is a self-replicating program that "invades" and reproduces itself in other files. The virus program can be hidden in any file and transferred by floppy disk or by downloading from an "infected" computer. Some viruses have even been designed to retrieve other viruses from hidden locations in outside networks. The virus may also be used as a carrier for a "logic bomb" or other program designed to affect information systems operation. Logic bombs are executable programs designed to be activated by certain outside triggers. An example would be the "Valentine virus" which contained a logic bomb to be activated when the infected system changed the internal clock to read February 13. Another example of a particularly dangerous virus is a "mutating" virus. This virus program actually defends itself by changing its nature during replication. These attacks are generally designed to destroy mass data by erasing or overwriting the files stored in the information system memory.

Another, more sophisticated method involves the use of a "worm" program. A worm program is most likely a separate file or attachment which, when executed, disappears. The worm program travels from computer to computer until it reaches its programmed destination and executes its mission. The worm's mission may be to carry a robot, virus, trojan horse, or logic bomb program. Since the worm and trojan horse programs are camouflaged or hidden within other files, they are difficult to detect.

Information Corruption

The most sophisticated and insidious attacks involve deliberately corrupting information. This requires the attacker to have access to the system at a level that allows them to change information or have the ability to insert false information into the system. Such an attack might include altering or inserting a program that changes data or algorithms. An example might be to change the number "5" to "4" throughout the system. Calculations would then be based on false numbers and the system would be unreliable.

Similarly, the attacker may use a robot program to corrupt systems. The robot program is designed to search for data flows and then insert character strings into the data flow, making them unreliable and useless for computing purposes. Thus, you might send a 10-digit number to another system but the robot adds a digit or character string that renders the data flow unrecognizable.

The Hardware Threat

While all the usual threats of sabotage and willful destruction of assets can be applied to information technology resources, these usually require an opponent gaining access to the hardware. Precautions against such access are common practices. However, there are threats to information systems that do not require physical access to the actual systems. Attacks through the peripheral systems such as the electrical supply system or communication lines can also create disaster. Causing fluctuations in the current used to operate the information technology system can cause failure and disruption of the system. Other physical attack capabilities include the use of direct high energy radio frequency (RF) or microwave energy or the generation of electromagnetic pulses (EMPs) over limited areas.

The least threatening problem posed is by the time-proven "jamming" of signals. Jamming can be directed toward a transmitter or its emanated signal over a smaller area. Jamming is a relatively old and unsophisticated threat. The jammer is easily detected and can be destroyed if the threat justifies it. However, on the information warfare (IW) battlefield, time is critical and interruption of command, control, and communications (C^3) systems, even for short periods, can have serious consequences.

Directed energy weapons are newer and more difficult to defend against. Directed energy weapons generally aim high intensity RF energy at the receiver of a communications network or at a component of the network. The receivers are designed not only to receive these signals, but to amplify them. Since information technology software has become smaller and has relied on smaller electronic signals in the process, such attacks now have the capability to incapacitate critical communications systems.

Somewhere between jamming and the actual destruction of information technology hardware is the threat from an attacker intercepting and using electronic countermeasures (ECM) to decode commands transmitted to other unmanned systems such as satellites. The attackers could then issue their own commands to, for example, cause the satellites to move out of orbit.

The threat of EMP from nuclear weapons has been known for at least 40 years. The concern in this case is not the blast waves from nuclear explosions because, in the high upper atmosphere, or in low outer space, those waves are not propagated. Rather, the concern is that large fractions of the weapon energy will create very highly energized and ionized particles from the original weapon mass. These plasmas can create electromagnetic fields over continental areas that can destroy programs, memories, circuits, and so on. In recent years, research has resulted in the development of conventional munitions that are capable of creating EMP environments over much smaller areas (see Essay 29, Impact of Electromagnetic Impulses on Future Warfare Operations). Such devices, strategically emplaced, are capable of disabling or effectively destroying information systems in localized areas.

While critical military systems have been hardened against the EMP threat, civilian systems have not. Nevertheless, many civilian systems provide critical support to military systems. Such unhardened civilian systems present a weak link in the information chain upon which the Department of Defense (DOD) relies. Furthermore, the increasing dependence of even frontline equipment on commercial off-the-shelf (COTS) hardware increases the cost of hardening against EMP especially since retrofitting anything into electronics is more difficult and less trustworthy than designing it in from the start (see Essay 29, Impact of Electromagnetic Impulses on Future Warfare Operations).

A listing of potential threats to date is covered in Essay 12, Information Technology Applications to Counter Nontraditional Warfare Threats, while specific EMC threats are treated in more detail in Essay 21, R&D Planning Guide for Countering Nontraditional Threats.

Countermeasures

The fact that major disasters have not yet occurred is not because the required tools are not available. In fact, many new and improved tools are being developed every day. Most of the offensive tools are being developed and employed by hackers in attacks against commercial companies who, in turn, are developing and employing the latest defensive tools and measures. Some governments are also involved in the development of offensive and defensive tools but much less is known of their success.

There are a large number of private companies involved in the development of information system security. Many are members of associations dedicated to developing security standards and tools to defend information systems from intruders.

The U.S. government is aware of the dangers to our information technology infrastructure but has not adequately addressed the threats. Coordinated defenses against directed, intentional, financed, and dedicated information warfare adversaries whose targets are the national infrastructure and components of our warfighting capability must be further pursued and continually updated to keep abreast of the evolving threats.

The National Security Agency has been involved in the development of information systems security by developing secure computer systems. The Defense Information Systems Agency is involved in setting information system standards throughout the Department of Defense. Unfortunately, there has been no nationally concerted effort to defend against the known threats described in this essay much less those threats still under development. The problem must be treated as we are treating other threats. Certainly every organization should institute their own protection program against the threats to their information systems, and most have. However, just as no corporation would rely solely upon its own defenses to protect it against robbers, vandals, arsonists, and such physical threats, the threat to the information technology infrastructure must be similarly addressed. A certain reliance is placed on the established protectors of our society such as local and state police, the FBI, and the national security agencies for our defense against traditional threats. Unfortunately, there is currently no central government agency responsible for an overall defense against NTW threats in general, or the information warfare threats in particular. (See Essay 14, Emergency Response Management at the National Operations Centers, which addresses this problem and proposes some solutions to it.) Recently, a new director for cyber warfare has been designated at the National Security Agency (NSA) to assist in providing oversight and coordination for information security.

Software Defense

Most potential victims of information warfare attacks (defined today as those an adversary would use for "practice") are connected to the Worldwide Web (WWW). Many of these potential targets have the ability to detect attacks on their systems, and then to qualify and quantify their severity. However, the information warfare warrior is continually seeking and finding weaknesses in the technology that can be exploited with newer technology.

At present the normal software defenses for information systems are not only simple but obvious—the use of firewalls, encryption, frequently changed passwords, multiple layers of software to identify and nullify unauthorized access or operations, files which document and develop profiles of unusual activities, and programs that attempt to identify intrusions or, at least, document and record them. Even the relatively unsophisticated hacker can access poorly protected information systems and has access to programs that can damage or steal data in milliseconds.

Most defenses in information technology require user cooperation, and many users are not prepared, educated, or even sensitive to the nature and scope of the problem. Precisely because most people do not understand the technology they rely upon, they do not know how to adequately protect their information systems against unauthorized intrusion. The need is for approaches that obviate user involvement.

Serious information warfare adversaries will likely develop and test their weapons carefully and then attack first against poorly prepared targets—private sector and/or defense contractors having few rudimentary defenses and no history of informing government organizations of their experience with information warfare attacks. The adversary's goals would not be, necessarily, any serious disruption of such vendors. Their goal would be to merely test their attack mechanisms. Once success was assured, they would move on to more seriously defended targets employing more serious attacks. This escalation of targets would continue as they refined their information warfare methods. But they would always avoid their ultimate target until they were assured of the efficacy of their attack strategy.

Once the adversary was certain that his attack strategy was effective, once he had defeated the lesser foes, he would employ his proven strategy against his ultimate target. Such an approach could be disastrous when unleashed against even the most prepared current defender. It would be carefully orchestrated, tested at every level, and proven against, ultimately, the most capable defenses short of, or possibly even superior to, the DOD equipment and systems. The information warfare adversary does not factor deterrence into his equation; demonstrations of his prowess are counterproductive if they encourage defensive efforts. The information warfare warrior works in shadows and hides his very existence.

One possible solution would be to have these potential targets connected to a central processing activity that is then connected to the WWW. Such a connection could be transparent to the user with information on software attacks updated on a daily basis. Any attack against any user could be catalogued and ultimately sorted and collated to develop modus operandi (MOs), threat assessments, adversary psychological profiles, and threat projections. Essay 14, Emergency Response Management at the National Operations Centers, and Essay 15, Information Integration and Process Applications for Emergency Management Operations Centers, in this series outline the concept for an emergency management operations center (EMOC) that could provide these functions and processes on a routine basis. The threat to the information technology infrastructure surely necessitates coordinating this effort at the national level so that effective responses to this and other NTW threats can be undertaken.

It should be noted that high priority targets (national infrastructure, DOD) would need to be factored into this response scenario as well. Additionally, special consideration would have to be given to those government contractors who are under contract for "black" programs and companies with highly proprietary commercial material. Assuring the security of classified, proprietary, and privileged data would be critical to participation. While unable to share raw data, the participants would still be able to share details on attacks such as method used, detection tool, time of attack, and other information that would alert other participants to the attack and provide valuable clues on how to prevent future attacks.

Such a program would not need to be all encompassing to begin with. There is no "critical mass" for the success of such a concept. Certainly the more participants in the system, the more information would be gained on all varieties of software threats. With such information, the EMOC could develop threat projections and countermeasures and offer them to approved subscribers free of charge. As the value of this concept becomes more widely known, legitimate subscribers would participate.

Hardware Defenses

Countermeasures for the EMP threat are well understood but can be expensive to implement. Hardware can be shielded with metal enclosures to prevent EMP pulses from penetrating from the ambient levels produced by both nuclear and conventional threats and damaging hardware and software. Necessary connections to users and information sources can be protected from EMP pulses generated exterior to the hardware. External connections are actually a more serious threat since the currents generated by EMP are generally proportional to the length of the conductor subjected to the EMP environment. Therefore, connectors to information technology hardware can initiate a much greater EMP current than would be generated in even unprotected hardware. Such externally generated EMP pulses could be defeated by fuses designed to self-destruct at amperage levels that could damage protected hardware and software.

Unfortunately, hardware solutions to the EMP threat are even more expensive to retrofit into existing systems rather than to design into new ones. Designed-in hardening represents only a small percentage of the total cost of hardware. Retrofitting hardening can cost as much as 20 to 30 percent of the original hardware costs (for a more detailed discussion of EMP, ECM, and hardening, see Essay 3, Military Forces Survivability in a Weapons of Mass Destruction Environment, and Essay 21, Research and Development Planning Guide for Countering Nontraditional Warfare Threats). However, the expertise to date on EMP hardening for DOD hardware has been developed by a relatively small core of experts. If the need for such protection is more widely recognized, the possibility of cheaper hardware defenses designed by a wider spectrum of organizations can be realized.

The Emergency Management Operations Center

The EMOC discussed in Essay 14, Emergency Response Management at the National Operations Centers, could provide information to user/members on the latest protection mechanisms for all information technology threats. While this would not be its only function, it would provide all subscribers with readily available, and the most economical, defenses against information warfare adversaries. This aspect of the EMOC would have to be as silent and covert as the tactics of the adversaries it was intended to defeat. Even more silent and covert would be EMOC Red Team activities designed to emulate adversarial threats in order to develop countermeasures that could be proliferated among subscribers with appropriate protection against their compromise. Obtrusive releases of information on the state-of-the-art defensive measures would be counterproductive for the guardians of the nation's information technology infrastructure. The information warfare battlefield should not be open for public viewing and should not be reported on the daily news. It should be silent, unseen, and carefully protected from intrusion by both the offensive and the defensive forces.

The current course of warfare is toward the NTW threat. Asymmetric warfare concepts have been, and continue to be, developed. These attacks represent threats that have not been given the priority they deserve. Nations of concern, disenfranchised groups, self-proclaimed liberators, and even dedicated individuals with a mission represent real threats to the information technology infrastructure of the United States and its allies. Even a single dedicated individual can wreak havoc against the vulnerable information technology infrastructure that has grown to enormous size without adequate protection. The threat to our information systems represents an Achilles heel we cannot ignore.

Future Military Operations under Information Warfare Conditions

Currently, the U.S. military has an overwhelming dependence on the utilization of the electronic network and devices to carry out missions, observe and counter possible threat conditions, as well as transfer information and commands. Electronic warfare (EW) encompasses much more than information systems. Electronic emissions from other devices also convey information and are subject to attack or spoofing. Planning and development activities for future operations under EW conditions will need to know (1) what equipment will work and when will it work, (2) how effects from EW threats can be avoided or mitigated, and (3) where changes in processes and procedures can be made to enhance mission performance and survivability.

Test and Evaluation Initiatives

In order to operate in the new EW world, the United States needs to know how the electronic equipment will perform and how to use the electronics and information systems to their best advantage. To develop this information, both developmental and operational test and evaluation (T&E) exercises are essential. Of course, some T&E is constantly performed for all systems but new changes brought about by military applications, threat sophistication, utilization of commercial equipment, and access to advanced technologies or countermeasures, especially in the EW arena, make it imperative for the United States to continually upgrade its capabilities under these nontraditional warfare conditions.

Essay 21, Research and Development Planning Guide for Countering Nontraditional Warfare Threats, provides some research and development guidelines for new initiatives to counter EW threats. Some of the more relevant T&E concerns and issues are drawn from Exhibit 21.2 in that essay and are illustrated in Exhibit 4.1. While some efforts are underway to address the current deficiencies, limitations exist due to the lack of a comprehensive master plan for guiding the overall program, establishing the appropriate depth of investigations, and balancing investments in resources for full assessments.

EXHIBIT 4.1   Overview of T&E initiatives for EW threats.

Deficiencies	S&T initiatives/investigations
Commercial equipment unprotected from high electromagnetic pulses (EMP)	• Criteria and standards for critical commercial items • Tests and evaluation of commercial equipment to show compliance/ acceptance
Military equipment vulnerability to new nonnuclear generated ECM threats	• New tests to verify survivability of critical equipment from emerging DEW and nonnuclear EMP threats • Elimination of ECM sources before reaching effective range
Lack of built-in Faraday cages to protect equipment	• Testing to ensure no opening for electronic warfare environment penetration
Knowledge of phenomenology/coupling of electronic warfare energy to various types of targets	• Testing to determine energy coupling from electronic warfare source to targets and redundant protection techniques (e.g., shields, fuzes, hardening) • Determining sensitivity to counter-measures and engagement constraints
Built-in broadband/multiple frequency capability	• Viability of tunable frequency selection based on knowledge of EW source • Feasibility/security of randomization and management of frequency selections

Future EW Operations

As the world is advancing through the technology explosion and exploitation, the U.S. military has become increasingly dependent upon electronic systems, devices, and networks. In fact, nearly all the critical military items of equipment utilize some combination of electromechanical mechanism. This dependence on reliable electronics includes tracking and targeting, commanding forces, assessing threats, transferring information, warning of enemy actions, operating weapons and acquisition systems, providing light, computing and organizing data, and many other critical tasks. Without controlled, dependable electric energy, the military would probably look like an 1850 army without tanks, indirect artillery fire, aircraft, or radios. Certainly some particular losses of electronic systems can be expected from appropriate electronic warfare. Work-arounds and prior training can overcome these deficiencies by careful planning, awareness, and understanding of the consequences of electronic signals interruption or manipulation. Electronic countermeasures

(ECM) are the first counter to EW in the counter, counter-counter cycle seen in all offense/defense struggles.

While current critical U.S. military equipment is hardened against the effects of EMP, uncertainties exist on the vulnerability created by the emphasis on using commercial off-the-shelf (COTS) equipment to supplement or augment systems developed using Department of Defense specifications. In an EMP environment, protected equipment may perform as required while other electronic devices and information networks may not. This condition will lead to the need to have training and operating procedures in place for workarounds that allow missions to be performed and risks to personnel minimized. In this scenario, unexpected equipment losses and interruptions in critical information are certainly possible. So, alternative courses of action will need to be available to overcome confusion and support continuing missions and requirements.

Both ground-based and airborne platforms can be used to transmit electronic signals to jam other electronic systems using directional beams or area coverage techniques. Operating under these conditions affects the capability to perform missions and usually necessitates the employment of electronic counter-countermeasures (ECCM) from (1) high-powered standoff support systems, (2) switching to other electronic frequencies, or (3) applying antiradiation weapons to attack the jammers. These techniques are well understood and many countries in the world are adept at applying ECM and ECCM tactics. The United States has performed these tactics with a high degree of success in both Iraq and Serbia. While the EW environment will continue to change and become more sophisticated, the United States will undoubtedly keep abreast with continued attention and new technology enhancements.

Directed energy weapons (DEW) constitute new threats to some airborne and land systems from lasers, RF weapons, microwaves, and so on. Assuming targets can be acquired, the damage effects from these weapons are usually restricted by the normal considerations of range, power, and the mobility of both the source and the target. Accordingly, standoff distances, avoidance, and counterfire tactics are the best antidotes for these threats, as long as information on DEW systems location is available and accurate.

Because of the threat from electronic jammers, acquisition and communications systems, and knowledge bases, the United States will continue to need the very latest technology applications and operating concepts to counter the plethora of opposing tactical and strategic devices. These threats include radars for air defense, directed energy weapons, communications networks, command and control centers, weapons system, airborne and satellite surveillance systems, and many other electronic-based systems. To exploit these potential enemy vulnerabilities, the United States and its allies will need to have prior knowledge of the location and characteristics of static and mobile electronic devices/systems by using standoff systems from airborne and satellite platforms along with automated mapping updates.

Another concern for the future is the need for secure communications so missions can be coordinated and managed without fear of disclosure to hostile intelligence collection systems. Advances in automated data processing, computer analysis, listening devices, and ECM will continue to pose communications threats. User transparent protection through low probability intercept (LPI), burst transmissions, handshake verification between sender and receiver, frequency hopping, and so on, must be universally applied to one-to-one communications while similar protective techniques must be improved for broadcast communications in order to protect both the sender and the information being transmitted. These problems are exacerbated when joint and coalition operations are considered. The more communications are opened to diverse users, the more opportunities become available for enemy information exploitation, conventional targeting, and EW attacks. Field exercises, especially using joint and coalition forces, must include T&E aspects that realistically mirror the expected EW threat. The battlefield is not the place to identify EW vulnerabilities and ECM deficiencies.

5

VULNERABILITY TO BIOLOGICAL WEAPONS IN NONTRADITIONAL WARFARE

James J. Valdes

For a variety of reasons, nature, driven by evolution, has produced a diverse population of remarkably dangerous microbes, organisms, viruses, and plants that are lethal to humans and for which we have few early warning sentinels or countermeasures. Biological warfare (BW) agents derived from these naturally occurring mechanisms have been developed as weapons of mass destruction and could represent a primary strategic threat to the United States.

Unlike chemical or conventional weapons, BW agents such as bacteria and viruses are self-replicating; hence, very small quantities could be deployed in either military or terrorist operations and their effects would be amplified by secondary infection. Recently, infectious proteins called prions have been identified with mechanisms that defy the rules of biology as previously understood. The nature of these prions make them even more difficult to detect than conventional bacteria or viruses.

BW agents have been called the "poor man's nuke" and the assumption has been made that they are easy to produce and disseminate. While this assumption is not entirely supportable, it is true that they can be manufactured with commercially available cell culture and fermentation equipment by countries or transnational groups with relatively unsophisticated scientific capabilities.

We are now well into what some scientists refer to as the Biotechnological Revolution. The Industrial Revolution was ushered in by the steam engine and allowed agrarian societies to develop new methods of mass production and mechanized warfare, and the Information Revolution followed the invention of transistors and semiconductors and hastened a post-industrial "New Economy" facilitated by the Internet. Both gave humans a greater mastery of the physical world but the Biotechnological Revolution will allow mastery of the biological world.

The Industrial and Information Revolutions radically altered the warfare of the day, and the latter's impact is extensively reshaping both research and development and concepts of operation with the introduction of the "digitized battlefield." Recent biotechnological advances will be even more traumatic. The Biological Revolution goes hand in hand with the Information Revolution because it allows access to the vast information stored in genes, which will enable a radical reshaping of the biological world, including humans. With the tools of molecular biology and the completion of the Human Genome Project, potential adversaries will soon have the ability to tailor life forms to order, to manufacture microorganisms and their products in large quantities, and to design genetic weapons against human and agricultural targets.

Background

The use of biotechnologies, broadly defined, is literally as old as civilization. Beer, mead, and wine have been fermented for millennia, bread is leavened with yeast, bacteria are used to produce cheese and yogurt, and animals and plants are selectively bred for desired characteristics. The first systematic application of biotechnology to industrial manufacturing was in 1917 when pure yeast cultures were used to ferment cornstarch and produce the acetone needed for the manufacture of explosives. The fermentation or biomanufac-turing industry came of age after 1945 with the production of antibiotics. Both of these are examples of the "old" biotechnology that relied on trial and error.

The "new" biotechnology originated with the discovery of recombinant DNA by Cohen and Boyer in 1972. Developments such as DNA sequencing, synthesis and cloning, and macromolecular structural analysis now allow genes in yeast and bacteria to be reprogrammed, and these cellular factories are used to manufacture such BW relevant products as drugs, vaccines, enzymes, and high performance materials. The same developments have a dark side in that they can be used to produce recombinant pathogens and toxins.

The BW Threat

This dual-use nature of biotechnology cannot be underestimated for two rea-sons. First, the security of the United States relies on having an edge in the key technologies of the time relative to any potential adversary. Second, the ubiquitous availability of the tools of biotechnology make it virtually impossible to maintain this edge in real time. The Office of Net Assessment of the Office of the Secretary of Defense has sponsored two studies, including *Biology, Biotechnology and the Future of International Security* and, more recently, *Biotechnology and Human Enhancement*. More generally, the National Research Council is currently sponsoring the Committee on Opportunities in Biotechnology for the Army, which is examining a wider range of uses and impacts of biotechnology for the future army. The reason for this great interest is that, unlike nuclear technology, whose development is beyond the reach of individuals or non-nation-state groups, mastery of biotechnology is clearly within the capabilities of much smaller and more poorly financed potential adversaries.

Biotechnology has thus seriously complicated BW defense. Previously, BW agents were a threat on the battlefield, and force protection was based on contamination avoidance, physical protection such as masks and protective garments, collective protection of weapon platforms and facilities, decontamination in the event that these failed, and medical countermeasures such as vaccines and antibiotics. There was also the implied deterrent of nuclear retaliation against a battlefield foe that could be unambiguously identified and targeted. These relatively straightforward measures are ineffective against a perpetrator who cannot be identified and located with any real certainty, and against a BW agent that may have been deployed days or even weeks earlier, allowing the victims to travel far from the scene of exposure, and that may have been genetically manipulated to defeat detection or treatment.

Biological defense has been a triad of intelligence, arms control, and technology. In recent years, intelligence has been viewed as the base of the triad, with likelihood of use based on technical and doctrinal data. The result was an emphasis on arms control. It is clear in the aftermath of the Persian Gulf War that this approach failed since, despite having inspectors on the ground, the extent of the Iraqi BW program was vastly underestimated. The problem is compounded when dealing with ephemeral transnational groups or individuals whose capabilities and doctrinal approach may be—will be—radically different and largely unknown.

More recently, several people were exposed to anthrax during the month of October 2001 and it has been determined that the U.S. postal system was used to transmit the infection. These cases have produced major anxieties and concerns both nationally and internationally. In these types of anthrax incidents, it is extremely difficult to determine the source or motive behind such atrocities on the civilian populace.

Current Biodefense Situation

Before moving on to speculate about the future impact of biotechnology, it is instructive to review the present situation on biodefense. Nonmedical biodefense has several basic requirements. The first is detection. Since currently available sensor suites cannot run continuously because of power and reagent requirements, a sensitive biosentinel is required to act as a trigger. This biosentinel should respond in quasi-real time to BW agents, which may be masked, and should distinguish between pathogenic and benign organisms, whether or not genetically engineered, against a complex environmental background of biological chaff. Most current approaches are physical, rather than biotechnological.

A second requirement is to unambiguously identify pathogens at the strain level. This is an especially important requirement in a terrorist attack in which quality forensics data is needed. Current regimes of recognition and identification rely on criteria that may be shared by related nonpathogenic species. In fact, highly complex pathogens often differ from other species by only the smallest criteria, making accurate identification a very difficult diagnostic problem for even a microbiology laboratory. Completely sequencing a pathogen's genome and the development of probes for unique genetic sequences should allow for unambiguous identification of a pathogen. Similarly, developing probes for virulence factors should include a capability to detect genetically engineered "designer" BW agents.

A third area with vast potential for biotechnological solutions is in microminiature sensors. Current sensors rely on biological recognition sites such as antibodies, which identify specific surface features of a pathogen; others use gene probes to detect a particular genetic marker, and some have used receptors—the body's physiological targets—for more "generic" detection. The development of genetic arrays of human toxicology or stress response genes should vastly improve this area. Particular genes are often up- or down-regulated in response to pathogenic or toxic insult, and such changes often occur hours or even weeks before any morbidity is apparent.

Future Biodefense Directions

The recently completed mapping of the human genome's approximately 100,000 genes provides the basic blueprint for the identification of the functions of these genes. Near term applications abound in BW defense and toxicology. There is a limited number of "toxicology genes"—probably 2 percent of the human genome—whose expression is regulated by pathogen or toxic exposures, and these respond in an even more limited number of expression patterns. Examples include damage-specific genes, which respond to damage to DNA or the endoplasmic reticulum; metabolic-specific genes, which respond to intracellular homeostasis, such as ionic concentration; and redox-specific genes. It is now clear that genetic arrays, silicon or glass chips representing the expression levels of toxicology genes, can be designed as either high-density arrays used to identify particular genes of interest for a particular application, or subsequently as low-density, high throughput assays with a limited number of selected genes. This will revolutionize diagnostics, especially in the assessment of low-level, multiagent exposures, because changes in gene regulation sometimes precede gross physiological or histological changes by weeks, months, or even years.

Genomics can allow the selection of personnel based on genetic predisposition. While the concept of selecting for, or making genetic modifications to induce, a "super soldier" is still in the realm of science fiction, identification of genes involved in such functions as stress response, metabolic efficiency, or chemical sensitivities can be used to assess suitability for particular assignments. For example, if a gene related to enhanced sensitivity to organophosphorus pesticides and nerve agents has been identified, it could be used to preclude assigning personnel with this genotype from handling such toxic materials. Similarly, personnel exhibiting superior genetic disposition for immunological competency might be selected for tasks requiring this trait. As the functions of genes and gene clusters are identified, genomic techniques that combine genetic arrays with advanced bioinformatics will have ever expanding applications.

Another interesting area where genomics will have an impact is on soldier and emergency response personnel training. Humans process information in a number of sensory modalities (e.g., visual, auditory, somatosensory) and individuals appear to have differing preferences or aptitudes for using these modalities. Screening individuals for their favored information processing mode, or assessing the task for suitability to be processed in a given modality and then presenting the information accordingly, will greatly enhance training. Since the soldiers and emergency response personnel of the future will be in an information-intensive environment, using multiple sensory modalities will be critical to increasing cognitive "bandwidth."

A fourth area of application of genomics is in altering the body's immunological response to BW agents. Rather than targeting particular pathogens by developing vaccines, a strategy which is rather easily circumvented, it may be possible to augment general immunological responses and develop the "pan-pathogenic resistant" soldier (i.e., a soldier with improved resistance to a broad array of pathogens).

The above four areas are fairly straightforward applications of biotechnology to BW defense. It is more difficult and far more speculative to predict the "dark side," that is, offensive uses. The most obvious use is in biomanufacturing of pathogens and toxins. Fermentation and other bioreactor technologies are ubiquitous, and the molecular tools used to clone genes into efficient expression systems for production are off-the-shelf. The great efficiency of these systems means that large industrial-scale fermentation vessels are no longer required, and operationally relevant quantities, especially for terrorist applications, could be produced in small mobile systems.

It has been axiomatic that BW agents would be directed against people, but it is equally likely that economic targets such as agriculture would be selected. Various plant pathogens have been studied as potential BW agents, and the increasingly genetic homogeneity of crops makes them susceptible to disease with potentially catastrophic results. Agriculturally targeted agents, whether against crops or animals, have the additional advantage of plausible deniability, making attribution and retribution difficult. In Africa in the 1920s, foot and mouth disease killed several hundred million cattle and wreaked economic devastation, and the more recent outbreak of "mad cow disease" in Great Britain, now attributed to infectious proteins (prions) severely disrupted the British beef industry. Both of these were natural outbreaks, yet demonstrate the difficulties in containing agricultural disasters.

The world's total stored foodstuffs amount to barely what would be required to sustain its population for three months. Even a minor disruption in the regular flow of sustenance would lead to worldwide panic, starvation, and war.

Some have speculated that "super pathogens" could be genetically engineered, but nature has evolved pathogens of sufficient virulence and toxins of incredible lethality such that this is probably unnecessary. Even simple diseases such as smallpox, presently eradicated, represent a threat of 25 to 30 percent morbidity in a population that has not been vaccinated for a generation or more.

It is more likely that the tools used in gene therapy to design improved delivery vectors could be used to design more transmissible viruses. A variant on this strategy might be to design stealth pathogens by cloning virulence factors into otherwise nonpathogenic microbes. Finally, the same information from the Human Genome Project that enables the design of high density gene chips for such beneficial applications as toxicology screens could theoretically be used to target populations with unique genetic polymorphisms. Indeed, population-specific "Designer" BW weapons could target ethnic or race sensitive groups.

Summary

In the near term, the impact of biotechnology will be primarily on BW defense, particularly in the areas of improved biosensing, diagnostics, and medical prophylaxis and therapeutics. Conversely, improved biomanufacturing technology makes it easier for technologically unsophisticated groups or individuals to produce BW agents. Longer term, more complete genomic information creates the spectre of genetically modified and targeted BW agents that could elude defensive measures as they are now configured.

SECTION II

OPERATIONS IN THE NONTRADITIONAL WARFARE ENVIRONMENT

As the twenty-first century begins, one indication of the changing nature of military operations is the range of environments and conditions in which conflicts of all types may have to take place. These situations include not only the purely physical environments, like urban terrain, but also a range of operational conditions generally unfamiliar to military commanders, personnel, and commentators.

The end of the Cold War confrontation has removed the great "given" from military planning. No longer will the armed forces of the United States and its allies have the luxury of being able to clearly expect, from one year to the next, what the next conflict will hold for them. This uncertainty is due to the changing nature of global political conditions and the rapid evolution of national and international political structures. Among other elements, this lack of predictability will place a premium on strategic mobility. Rapid response task forces will be necessary to bring military forces to bear on a situation before it gets completely out of hand. Moreover, few Cold War-era armed forces, of whatever nationality, are prepared for that operational and strategic environment.

The experience of the multinational intervention in Somalia in the early 1990s demonstrated clearly that activities in urban settings will constitute an important part of military operations in the near future. This applies particularly in operations other than war (OOTW) situations. Increasing urbanization in the less-developed nations of the world only serves to emphasize the likelihood of such scenarios. The difficulties posed for regular armed forces conducting sustained operations in urban settings makes assessment of, and careful preparations for, such eventualities very important.

The military experience in Vietnam, coupled with other insurgencies in Colombia, Mexico, Rwanda, Indonesia, and elsewhere, have served to show that guerrilla operations will also form a significant element of military operations in the new century. Although much studied, the dynamics of guerrilla, insurgency, and counterinsurgency operations are at best poorly understood among the armed forces of many advanced nations. While many senior U.S. commanders are combat veterans of the Vietnam War, determined efforts to "unlearn" the lessons of Vietnam in preparation for an expected conventional clash with the Soviet Union has left the U.S. Army and Marine Corps, especially, with an incomplete and uncertain institutional approach to guerrilla and insurgency operations.

The relative low intensity of combat operations in insurgency and counterinsurgency operations should not detract from the professional dedication required for forces to succeed in these actions. This caveat extends to a range of other OOTW situations as well, including aid to the civil authority operations, a range of law enforcement activities, and counterterrorist operations, to name just a few.

The virtual demise of the Soviet Navy as a significant naval force over the last 10 years has left the United States Navy in the potentially enviable position of having no real blue-water opponents to worry about. This lack of serious potential opposition, though, also poses some difficulties, because naval support is definitely needed to project U.S. interests abroad as well as provide close air support, nuclear counterstrike capabilities, and protection from smaller opposing naval forces. Indeed, operations in the littoral environment (in coastal waters and in land areas near coastlines) have assumed great importance. However, few navies, with their blue-water and open-ocean traditions, have either developed effective doctrine and operational practices for such conditions, or begun to approach the issues of littoral operations in an orderly and rational manner. The U.S. Navy will have to do so, in order to meet the growing requirements for security of U.S. sea frontiers, especially in the Caribbean basin area.

Finally, both international terrorists and criminal activities pose grave threats and introduce new requirements to counter these threats with forces, technologies, intelligence gathering, information management, and financial controls.

6

TERRORIST OPERATIONS IN NONTRADITIONAL WARFARE

David L. Bongard
William R. Schilling

The goal of this essay is to provide a primer on the nature of modern terrorist operations. This includes establishing a historical framework and context. Within that context, several noteworthy terrorist "campaigns" are examined in some detail, and common threads and characteristics are established. The methods, types, and tactics of terrorist attacks are also assessed, partly with the objective of providing some realistic forecast of what actions may be directed against the United States and its allies over the next decade. Most of the selected terrorist campaigns introduce examples of counterterrorist operations undertaken by law enforcement and military units.

This essay further explores a range of options that can be employed to fight terrorists, terrorist organizations, and the phenomenon of terrorism, in general. Technology applications are explored as plans and new research and development programs emerge for countering and overcoming terrorist activities.

To further differentiate modern terrorists from other insurgency operatives who might oppose a current regime or policy, modern terrorists are proponents of a specified philosophy or belief that they wish to impose on others. In addition, many terrorist groups rely on one or more nations for political support, funding, and sanctuary, and do not place much personal emphasis or interest in material possessions, wealth, or long lifetimes.

Characteristics of Terrorist Tactics and Operational Style

Terrorist operations can be defined as the efforts of a small group using fear and disruption in an attempt to control the actions of a larger entity. Terrorism can range from the school yard bully who threatens weaker children for their lunch money to organized groups using weapons of mass destruction to threaten nations. Small-scale terrorism committed by individuals can usually be handled by standard law enforcement procedures, but modern terrorism presents difficulties unsuitable for traditional law enforcement responses.

Terrorists rely on concealment and subterfuge for success. Their operatives function in secret, wear no uniform, and generally move among the general population without calling attention to themselves. Their cause may be viewed with sympathy by a portion of the population that can be recruited for logistical support or new members (see Essay 8, Guerrilla Operations in Nontraditional Warfare).

The essence of modern terrorism, as practiced in the new millennium, lies in the nature of both the operatives and their targets. Terrorist operatives work in very small groups, sometimes even operating alone. Their plans rely on secrecy and surprise. The operatives may be involved in coordinated activities such as the bombing of the U.S. embassies in Nairobi and Dar-es-Salaam in 1999 or the terrorist attacks of 11 September 2001 on the World Trade Center and the Pentagon. Terrorists rarely strike directly at their enemy's military strength. Terrorists employ bombing, assassination, robbery, poisoning, or other acts of violence against symbolic targets designed to disrupt the social, political, and economic structure of their enemies. Terrorist targets may include judges, doctors, government officials, law enforcement and fire protection agencies and personnel, trade and economic centers, and random targets of opportunity involving ordinary citizens.

Historical Perspectives

Six terrorist campaigns have been chosen to illustrate the range of activities and goals pursued by terrorist organizations, some of which are still ongoing. Exhibit 6.1 presents an overview and comparison of the six campaigns.

Internal Macedonian Revolutionary Organization

The Internal Macedonian Revolutionary Organization (IMRO) had its origins in the southern Balkans in 1897. The IMRO's primary goal was independence from Ottoman rule and political self-determination for Macedonia. IMRO financed its operations through a combination of bank robbery and kidnapping for ransom. IMRO relied on a range of assassinations, bombings, and similar actions directed not only against Turkish officials (their primary target), but also against Christian Slavs who disagreed with their purpose, program, or methods.

Ireland and the Irish Republican Army

The Irish Republican Army (IRA) began as the clandestine revolutionary arm of the Irish nationalist movement in the late nineteenth century. The IRA's primary goal was political self-determination for a united Ireland. A campaign of sabotage, bombings, assassinations, and other actions helped bring about the 1921 granting of independence to the Republic of Ireland, with six northern provinces of largely Protestant Ulster continuing to be governed by English rule. The nationalist campaign to unite Ireland continues.

Palestine, 1936–1948

The Balfour Declaration of 1917 granted British recognition of Jewish-Zionist aspiration for Palestine as a "national home for the Jews." In the post-WWI delineation of the Ottoman Empire, the League of Nations granted England administrative responsibility of the Mandate of Palestine. Increasing Jewish immigration in the wake of Nazi anti-Semitism placed severe strains on the relationships among British, Arabs, and Jews, which erupted in a general Arab revolt in 1936. The three-way terrorist struggle convinced the British to abandon their League of Nations mandate duties in 1948. The resultant state of Israel was immediately attacked but managed to successfully defend its claim to Palestine.

Israel-Palestine, 1949–Present

Guerrilla and terrorist groups, many loosely organized under the Palestinian Liberation Organization (PLO), continued to attack Israel. During the Six-Day War in 1967, Israel conquered and occupied the West Bank and Gaza Strip, an occupation that continues today. The PLO launched terrorist attacks not only against Israel, but also against targets perceived to favor the Israeli cause. This conflict continues and the United States has become a target due to its support of Israel.

Colombia, 1960s–Present

The Marxist-oriented *Fuerzas Armadas Revolucionarios Colombianos* (FARC) is motivated largely by political and social conflicts with the government of Colombia. Complicating the situation is the support gained by the

EXHIBIT 6.1 Terrorist campaign overviews.

Terrorist campaign	Description of basic situation	Opposing strategies	Assessment
IMRO, Balkans	• Macedonian nationalist struggle against Ottoman Turks, and also against other ethnic groups between 1895–1930 • Area is patchwork of linguistic and ethnic groups, including Serbs, Greeks, Bulgars, Gypsies, Jews, Turks, Muslim Slavs, and others • Turkish administration had traditionally ignored ethnic alignments of subject peoples	• Mix of guerrilla military action, supported by assassination, bombing, robbery, extortion, and kidnapping • Directed mainly against Turkish authorities at first, but expanded to strike at others as well (Serbians, Greeks, Albanians) • Turks reply with arrests, deportations, military reprisals	• Goals of guerrilla action derailed and sidetracked through criminalization of activities, and "action for hire" • Settlement in wake of Balkan Wars and World War I does not provide anything better • Macedonians probably related to Bulgarians, in linguistic and religious terms
Ireland and the Irish Republican Army	• Irish nationalism on rise since late 18th century, coupled with rediscovery of Irish-Gaelic folk culture, music, literature led to 1941–1922 conflict • Irish Gaelic population largely disenfranchised from political establishment, and isolated from Anglo-Irish and English government • Anglo-Irish unwilling to accept compromise ensure a violent outbreak	• Irish nationalist failure in "Easter Rising" of March 1916 in Dublin leads to alternate strategies • Government relies on regular law enforcement and military forces • Local police and judicial structures notably sympathetic to IRA and its cause • IRA relies on cells and covert action, with effective PR campaign	• IRA successful against British administration, largely because or popular support • British effort hampered by war-weariness, and by lack of support among Irish civilian population • Anti-treaty IRA unable to prevail: they lack military power and popular support, but are also working against the war-weariness they had exploited against the British
Palestine 1936–1948	• Basic: Arabs vs. Jews vs. British • Arabs hostile to continued Jewish immigration, and suspicious of Jewish intent and "Westernization" • Jews determined to create and sustain "national home" within Palestine • British determined to maintain justice and internal order without utterly disrupting status quo	• Jews struggled to maintain and expand settlements, social structure, and polity • Arabs fought to expel Jews • British fought to maintain order and preserve balance among groups • Jews, backed by steady immigration and outside support, and better able to adapt to open conflict, are ultimately successful	• Jewish terrorism relatively infrequent: Bombing of King David Hotel, Jerusalem, and Deir Yassin Massacre outside Jerusalem; both were Irgun-Stern Gang operations • Arab efforts ranged from traditional raids and ambushes to flat-out terrorism • British and *Haganah* cooperated in suppression of 1936–1939 revolt: efforts of Orde Wingate and Special Night Squads • British suffered considerable loss of international support in aftermath of WWII

Terrorist campaign	Description of basic situation	Opposing strategies	Assessment
Israel-Palestine, 1949–present	• First stage: 1949–1967, involved raids across border into Israel • Second stage, 1967–1990s, involved terrorist strikes against Israeli and allied targets; this was popular with Arabs but gained little otherwise • Third stage, since early 1990s, involved largely nonviolent demonstrations against Israeli occupation	• Israelis able to restrict effect of terrorist attacks within Israel through security measures • "Allies" remain vulnerable to terrorist strikes • PLO and other Palestinians garner little international support before *Intifada* and largely nonviolent protests	• Despite heavy pressures, Palestinians have not suffered loss of national identify under occupation • Continued Jewish settlements, and abuse visited on Palestinians, has lost Israel much of support it once enjoyed • Israeli opinion has become harsher and less forgiving at same time • Political compromise is the only possible solution to the impasse
Colombia, 1960s–present	• Long-standing sociopolitical conflict between government and insurgents • Insurgents exploit cocaine trade to finance their operations, and thus erode U.S. and Colombian social structure • Colombian politics has tradition of insurgency and violence, dating back to early 20th century	• FARC employs assassination, kidnapping, bombing, and hijacking aimed at judges, government officials, army, police, tourists • Government gets notable aid from U.S. (Drug War), as well as for conventional security assistance • Pastrana initiative: cease-fire to produce negotiations with FARC and political settlement; may work	• Extensive U.S. military, technical, and economic assistance has provided little real advantage for government forces • Alienation of much of population (and support among peasantry and farmers for coca cultivation) gives pool of support for FARC • Criminalized orientation of FARC makes real political compromise difficult, but that may still be only real solution
Middle East radicals	• Grew out of radical pan-Islamic forces assembled to resist Soviet occupation of Afghanistan in 1980s • Sudden withdrawal of U.S. aid in 1989 solidified bin Laden's mistrust of and hostility toward U.S. • First instance of much-discussed "asymmetric warfare" for 21st century: strikes on 11 Sep 01 on U.S. soil	• Series of escalating terrorist strikes at U.S. evidently aimed at damaging U.S. position, and "bringing struggle home to U.S. people" • U.S. response includes financial, hi-tech, special ops, airpower, and especially allies • Bin Laden's support abroad muted: only Taliban in Afghanistan	• Bin Laden's international network of support, especially of sympathizers and intelligence assets, provides infrastructure • Roles of allies for U.S. efforts important, and not used before Sept. 2001 • Struggle will probably be long, and may involve several waves of terrorist strikes on U.S. homeland • Signs of parallel networks of terrorist agents on U.S. soil

FARC from the cocaine and criminal cartels that exert considerable power in the rural southern regions of the country. Tactics have included assassination, kidnapping, bombing, hijacking, and bribery. Targets have included judges, government officials, law enforcement, military, and tourists. The conflict continues (see Essay 8, Guerrilla Operations in Nontraditional Warfare).

Middle East Radicals

The perverted fundamentalist teaching of Islam with its distrust of nonbelievers has been reinforced by perceived slights against the Arab world. Particularly, the U.S. support of Israel, the U.S. support of the Shah of Iran, and Operation Desert Storm in 1991 reinforce the belief by Middle East radical elements that the United States is anti-Arab and anti-Muslim. Attacks against the United States and its allies have escalated, culminating in the 11 September 2001 attacks on the World Trade Center and the Pentagon.

Recent Terrorist Events

Since the Desert Storm campaign in the early 1990s, focus has shifted from conventional warfare toward global terrorist actions. Many of the more recent terrorist efforts have been directed against the United States and its interests. At the same time, the United States has also experienced a significant number of terrorist activities by disgruntled or deranged domestic groups or individuals using highly destructive methods to kill or maim many innocent civilians. These events are particularly troubling in a country like the United States where special emphasis is placed on individual freedoms and where attempts to moderate or eliminate these vulnerabilities may impinge on civil liberties and are contrary to the "American way of life." This section provides an overview of the recent foreign and domestic threats and identifies terrorist targets and tools for potential attacks.

External Terrorist Threats to the United States

Starting with both the first World Trade Center bombing in the United States and the tribal warfare campaign in Somalia in 1993, the United States has begun to lose citizens and soldiers to the actions of groups led by Osama bin Laden, a Saudi exile. These attacks have continued to escalate over the past 8 years and have become highly efficient through the use of the al Qaeda organization and other similar groups, now led by bin Laden.

Exhibit 6.2 shows some recent terrorist incidents that have been perpetrated against American interests. Many of these attacks are alleged to have been organized and supported by bin Laden and the al Qaeda group.

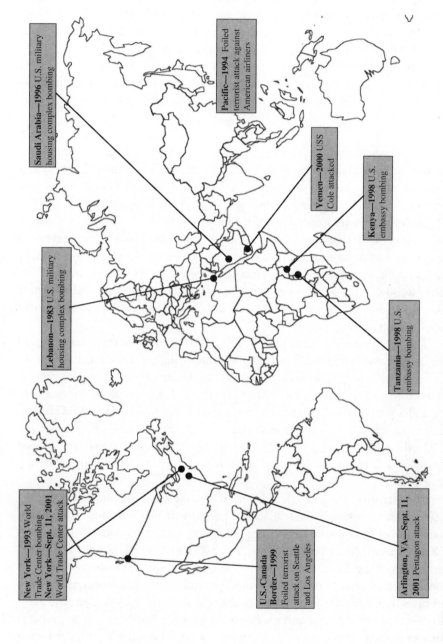

Saudi Arabia—1996 U.S. military housing complex bombing

Pacific—1994 Foiled terrorist attack against American airliners

Yemen—2000 USS Cole attacked

Kenya—1998 U.S. embassy bombing

Lebanon—1983 U.S. military housing complex bombing

Tanzania—1998 U.S. embassy bombing

New York—1993 World Trade Center bombing
New York—Sept. 11, 2001 World Trade Center attack

U.S.-Canada Border—1999 Foiled terrorist attack on Seattle and Los Angeles

Arlington, VA—Sept. 11, 2001 Pentagon attack

EXHIBIT 6.2 Recent international terrorist incidents against Americans.

As numerous U.S. government officials and news correspondents have pointed out following the tragic events of 11 September 2001, the United States has been catapulted into a new age. The attacks on the World Trade Center towers in New York and against the southwestern face of the Pentagon in Arlington, Virginia, represent an unprecedented escalation of terrorist activity. After those events, the full impact of the attack is not yet clear, and even the toll of human losses is not yet fully accounted. Current estimates indicate that more than 3,000 people died in these attacks and thousands more were injured.

Clearly, this attack represented the opening round in a new war, and in a new sort of war for which the United States is woefully unprepared. Some perceptive voices, including farsighted military officers, concerned civilians, and public officials, have been warning of the potentials of such a conflict for some years. Despite these warnings, it has been extremely difficult for most of the U.S. national security leadership, of whatever political orientation, to institute real reforms and reorientations to deal with the likelihood of massive and coordinated terrorist attacks. These attacks against the United States provide real, credible evidence of the impact and danger of asymmetrical warfare. Hitherto, such a conflict has been largely confined to theoretical and academic discussions, limited to some indefinite future time, as a conflict against some ill-defined and murky enemy.

The main problem in dealing with terrorists on a conventional military level is that they present a frustrating and annoyingly elusive target. They do not have permanent industrial or logistical infrastructures, they lack regular armed forces with their associated requirements for permanent training centers and arsenals, and terrorist cells can pack up and move within a few hours, or at most a few days. As a case in point, the training camps operated by the al Qaeda terrorist support organization in Afghanistan were abandoned within days of the terrorist strikes in anticipation of retaliatory strikes by the United States.

The terrorist attacks took place with notable sophistication and cunning ingenuity. This attack was in blatant disregard of the imbalance of conventional forces between terrorist organizations such as Osama bin Laden's el Khaida or al Qaeda (variously spelled and loosely translated as "The Foundation" or "The Base") and the massive, technically sophisticated conventional military arsenal of the United States and its allies. Mounting evidence indicates that some of the members of the operational cells (the men who actually hijacked the airliners and executed the attacks) had begun their preparations as early as 1996, more than 5 years before. The struggle that is taking shape, waged by the civilized world against international terrorism, cannot be

A-10A attack aircraft used in close ground support.

undertaken by utilizing the massive destructive power of advanced conventional weapons. Precision strike weapons, such as laser-guided cruise missiles guided by global positioning system (GPS) technology, will not provide the United States and its allies with all of the needed capabilities. Nor will the U.S. arsenal of tanks, fighter jets, aircraft carriers, nuclear attack submarines, and massed artillery provide the margin of victory.

The primary difficulties in attacking countries such as Afghanistan that provide sanctuaries for terrorist groups like al Qaeda lie in finding appropriate targets for air attacks. First, the Afghanistan government's Taliban military forces are dispersed throughout the urban areas and mingled with the civilian population. They can be quickly deployed in long trenches for combat and/or deployed in strategic areas to cover critical transportation nodes and in mountainous regions protected by inaccessible terrain features. Second, parts of the bin Laden organization are assimilated into the Taliban combat units or deployed in remote areas to protect the leaders hiding in mountainside caves or other areas outside the capability of normal sensor observations.

In summary, the difficulties of locating these terrorist leaders or punishing the Taliban forces for providing cover and protection using conventional means is less than satisfactory. While precision guided weapons and earth penetrating missiles or bombs can destroy caves, economic considerations do not allow massive attacks against a large number of suspected terrorist positions or targets. On the other hand, using conventional ground forces with supporting air power to locate the terrorists or negate the current Taliban government will result in significant allied casualties similar to those experienced by the Soviet Union in its 1990's war in Afghanistan.

Internal Terrorist Threats to the United States

The recent dispersion of anthrax as a biological terror weapon through the U.S. postal service during the months of September and October 2001 represents the culmination of a long line of domestic incidents during the past decade. Whether this crime against innocent people was the work of a foreign national or a deranged U.S. citizen, the impact was the same. Several people died and thousands were prescribed antibiotics. There was widespread panic as people rushed to buy gas masks and reports of "suspicious" substances increased tremendously. In addition, numerous high level government buildings were closed for decontamination purposes including the U.S. Capital, Supreme Court, and many post offices in New York, New Jersey, Virginia, District of Columbia, and Florida. Many other buildings had to be evacuated while tests were conducted on suspicious substances, and hoaxes were investigated.

Other recent domestic terrorist attacks or assaults include (1) a 17-year terrorist campaign of bombs sent through the mail by a single antitechnology fanatic, Theodore Kaczynski; (2) a series of bombings at abortion clinics throughout the United States, including one exploded at the 1996 Olympics, believed to be the work of antiabortion fanatics, many of whom are still at large; (3) assassinations of doctors and clinical workers by antiabortion fanatics; and (4) a high explosive vehicle bomb on the Alfred P. Murrah Building in Oklahoma City by antigovernment fanatics. Essay 20, Nontraditional Warfare Threat Responses, presents further details on some of these earlier domestic attacks.

These domestic attacks caused major disruptions in the "American way of life," generated substantial losses to the economy, and spread fear and apprehension to the population at large. In addition, these threats have diverted government and the national infrastructure away from the objectives of improving the welfare and education of the people in the United States and around the world. Due to these threats, many corporations are on the verge of collapse, including parts of the airline, travel, and recreation businesses; service industries; and mail circulation/advertising groups.

Vulnerability to Terrorist Threats

Traditionally, the United States has considered the primary type of terrorist threats to be from ballistic missiles with chemical/biological warheads, airplane hijackings, and vehicle bombs. Recently, this outlook has shifted to unforeseen methods leading to widespread fear and turmoil caused by mass damage effects, in particular, the attack using aircraft as guided missiles and anthrax deliveries through the U.S. postal service.

Likewise, new information has surfaced that indicates possible terrorist threats from "dirty" conventional bombs. These "dirty" bombs utilize radioactive materials from used nuclear rods, waste, and other uranium or plutonium by-products wrapped around a core of explosives designed to disperse the radioactive material over a wide area. While the area of weapon effects is likely to be only a few square kilometers, this dirty bomb threat is conceived as a means to cause panic to personnel that may have been exposed to the radiation as well as deny use of regions near the burst point. The likelihood of nuclear munitions being used in terrorist operations is described in Essay 23, The Future with Nuclear Weapons.

Moving from a reactive status to a proactive situation for terrorist threats involves a concerted, high level, systematic, organizational look at the nature of the threats, the concepts of implementation, and the type and vulnerability of intended targets. To date, the government focus has been on limiting the type of targets and terrorist tools by assuming low likelihoods of occurrence or no indications of terrorist interest in particular approaches. Of course, this saves money in the short run, but introduces unacceptable risks to the population and national infrastructure.

Exhibit 6.3 provides a brief view of the type of targets, the delivery mechanisms, and the possible damage mechanisms available for terrorist actions. While this exhibit is not all inclusive, it does provide an indication of the magnitude of the terrorist problem and lays the foundation for developing feasible and effective responses.

Lessons Learned

The experience gained from previous terrorist and antiterrorist campaigns over the last century provides some lessons. The requirements for and ingredients of a successful countereffort are not always clear though. Changes brought about by new technologies continue to offer more threatening situations and broader opportunities for other terrorist initiatives. For one thing, the terrorist will try to attack against least protected areas in unsuspected ways that produce the greatest damage to the projection of national power, prestige, and stature.

Attempts to rely on air power to attack terrorist groups in foreign countries are hampered by difficulties in finding targets, especially in remote areas. Under these conditions, the terrorist leaders disperse, hide in caves, or utilize

EXHIBIT 6.3   Dimensions of terrorist actions.

Delivery mechanism	Damage mechanism	Type of target
Vehicular (aircraft, boat, truck, car)	High temperature incendiary	Extremely high value targets—high profile buildings, nuclear power plants, national monuments, symbols of American way of life
	Chemical/biological/radiation	Urban population centers, agricultural storage areas, transportation nodes, business and corporation offices, military bases, and seaports
	High explosives	Government buildings, national monuments/symbols, schools and institutions, bridges, dams, power plants, transportation nodes, command and control systems, and communications systems
Man portable (suicide mission)	High explosives	Gathering points for small groups
	Chemical/biological	Gathering points for large groups
Manual covert implementation	Chemical/biological	Water systems, recreation areas, sporting events, Government operations, food supply, drug manufacturing, consumables
Sabotage	High explosives	Bridges, dams, power plants, transportation nodes, command and control systems, and communications systems
Delivery services (i.e., U.S. postal service, FedEx, UPS)	Chemical/biological	Delivery to Government, military, and civilian leadership
Mines and booby traps	Chemical/biological	All targets vulnerable
	High explosives	

cover and concealment. Even precision weapons have miss distances larger than many cave entrances and earth penetration is also required to damage deep underground hardened structures.

The oft-repeated doctrine "never to negotiate with terrorists" may have some justification in a moral and strictly law enforcement sense, but it is

EXHIBIT 6.4 Top ten rules for countering terrorism.

1	There is no substitute for human intelligence, either in terms of applying high technology, or of getting around the intelligence requirements.
2	A government struggling against terrorists on its own, without the assistance of allies, is virtually condemned to lose the struggle; terrorists by their nature are essentially "international."
3	Conventional military power, applied with however much skill and determination, cannot *alone* achieve victory over the terrorists due to the difficulties in finding appropriate targets.
4	Terrorists are often hard to distinguish from criminals, and their actions may be even harder to separate from organized crime.
5	It is essential for the antiterrorist forces to understand the motivations of the terrorists.
6	Victory will neither be achieved quickly, nor with a few decisive strokes.
7	Preventing further terrorist action, or frustrating efforts by infiltrating terrorist teams and assets is at least half the battle; terrorists who cannot strike pose less immediate threats.
8	Ending the terrorist threat cannot be entirely a military and law enforcement effort; the political and social dimensions cannot be ignored.
9	Terrorists must not be allowed to utilize sanctuaries provided by protective foreign countries.
10	Governments that protect terrorists must be encouraged to become stable, representative governments that will not tolerate the presence of terrorists within their country.

equally clear from historical evidence that compromise with the political causes and forces behind (or motivating) terrorists may be essential to achieve any permanent and meaningful resolution. It will be difficult to reach any accommodation with the array of shadowy radical Islamic fundamentalist groups that seek the elimination of U.S. power and influence in the Islamic world. The enthusiasm among radical fundamental Islam for martyrdom and holy war suggests that these two beliefs may be the greatest challenge of the entire dilemma. Nevertheless, it may well prove necessary to reach a negotiated accommodation in some other situations to end the struggle. The top ten rules for countering terrorism are listed in Exhibit 6.4.

Prognosis and Remedies

Until the United States and the international community show that terrorist actions do not lead to success for their cause or objective, the terrorist threats will persist. However, a number of modifications to conventional warfare concepts plus changes in processes and regulations and applications of new technologies can surely alleviate or eradicate this threat.

First, the military and political emphasis should be on capturing or eliminating the terrorist leaders and organizations. Punishment of nations providing sanctuary and support is also in order. However, care and caution must be exercised to make sure conditions do not worsen by creating more poverty and refugees, unstable successor governments, and additional foes to the United States and its allies. This means that prevention of collateral damage is a key concern in military responses. The military foes, especially the leaders, can avoid being targeted by using unknown underground structures and hiding places as well as vacating military positions. These same tactics can also be used to protect military equipment, personnel, and supplies until they are compelled to reoccupy military positions or engage in ground actions. Mingling their forces and equipment with innocent civilians and even children is another tactic used by terrorist groups. Targeting groups of military equipment and personnel that are co-located with civilians causes collateral damage that is quickly exploited as propaganda by the terrorists.

Likewise, miles of narrow, covered trenches do not make economical targets for bombers or costly missiles, especially when those trenches are unoccupied. Even using guided, earth penetrating warheads from aircraft to attack a reasonable number of suspected underground hardened shelters or caves is not feasible unless there is some indication of terrorist presence.

Air power alone is usually not effective for counterterrorist operations. A strong opposing ground force is required to cause the enemy to deploy or occupy defensive positions. Well-trained special operations units provide intelligence on terrorist locations and direct air-to-ground delivery of munitions and bombs. Finally, close-in staging areas for bombers, fighters, helicopters, and logistics are needed to deliver the number of sorties necessary to achieve damage levels required to destroy the terrorists' strongholds and hiding places. In any event, an extended campaign is to be expected when the enemy is dedicated and has very little to risk by continued fighting.

The lack of infrastructure and minimal physical resources that terrorist groups possess poses a problem for soldiers and military planners. So ephemeral are terrorist groups from the surrounding population and social structure, that unacceptably high levels of collateral damage to civilians could result from conventional bombing. The alternative is to pinpoint the actual terrorists and their immediate compatriots using human intelligence (HUMINT) assets, then really precise actions, either by special operation teams or by combat aircraft may be undertaken to affect only those actually involved with terrorist operations and their support.

For the second area, regarding changes in processes and regulations, the primary goal is to prevent terrorists from having easy access to (1) the United States or sensitive areas overseas, (2) supplies and resources critical to our national infrastructure and people, and (3) tools and mechanisms for carrying out their missions.

Terrorists should not be able to gain entry into the United States. Background investigations of visitors should reveal suspected terrorists or sympathizers and entry should be denied. In addition, national borders must be adequately guarded and intruders must be quickly identified, tracked, and apprehended.

The use of a national identification card may become necessary. At the very least, registration and tracking of foreign nationals should be mandatory. The Immigration and Naturalization Service will need to more rigorously enforce visa restrictions and work permits.

Standards and permits must be required for operating or gaining access to vehicles (aircraft, boats, trains, buses, trucks, and cars) that might be used to deliver explosives or weapons of mass destruction (see Exhibit 6.3). Also, access to control of vehicles must be denied by separating drivers or pilots from passengers or support staff. Currently, some commercial aircraft provide onboard security personnel and locked cockpit doors but this is insufficient to deter a determined adversary.

We will also require strict control and monitoring of access to important targets such as government buildings, national monuments/symbols, schools and institutions, bridges, dams, power plants, transportation nodes, command and control systems, and communications systems. Finally, to prevent terrorists from gaining access to tools and materials required to perform their missions, a careful monitoring of transportation nodes is needed to identify delivery or transport of lethal materials or mechanisms.

The current U.S. capability to respond to terrorist strikes with biological weapons is poorly developed. A 2001 essay by Jason Pate and Gary Ackerman of the Monterey Institute of International Studies entitled "Assessing the Threat of WMD Terrorism" suggests a number of major domestic policy initiatives to safeguard the U.S. homeland against such attacks. These include: (1) increasing funds and resources devoted to the U.S. public health system; (2) designing and implementing an extensive surveillance network for disease outbreaks; (3) applying Internet links for all health care providers with real-time data transfer capability to enable and coordinate rapid response to disease outbreaks before their dimensions grow unmanageable; (4) providing upgraded laboratory facilities and capabilities to identify pathogens, employing newly and specifically developed standardized procedures; and

EXHIBIT 6.5 Terrorist response objectives and initiatives.

Response objectives	Program initiatives/options
• Identifying and tracking terrorists • Ability to strike terrorists where and when they appear • Capacity to hamper terrorist actions and limit their capability to conduct terrorist strikes • Preventing or avoiding terrorist strikes with WMD (chemical or biological weapons)	• Create and sustain effective HUMINT network within terrorist organizations and in terrorist-friendly areas; promote rival nonterrorist organizations within passive supporting population • Weapons mix, with both lethal and nonlethal types, to control collateral damage and minimize effects on noncombatant population • Employment of advanced sensor suites and personal armor to limit casualties in friendly Special Operations forces, who will constitute the bulk of the "sharp end" of the antiterrorist military effort

(5) educating health care providers to recognize the signs and symptoms of "suspicious" diseases. In the near future, new technologies may offer a "silver bullet" for hampering and actually preventing terrorist actions. A fairly detailed look at the research and development (R&D) requirements, current deficiencies, and science and technology initiatives for countering terrorist operations is presented in Exhibit 21.3 of Essay 21, Research and Development Planning Guide for Countering Nontraditional Warfare Threats. One of the most important means for locating terrorist movements, positions, communications, and areas of operations lies in the concept of applying smart sensorwebs (see Essay 28, Development of Smart Sensorwebs for Future Warfare Operations). Efforts should be undertaken immediately to develop this concept, not only to prevent the use of remote areas by terrorists, but to overcome other counterinsurgencies as well. Other efforts to track the financial support, delivery of supporting resources, and communications with elements of terrorist organizations are mentioned in Essay 21. Briefly, a few ideas are extracted from Essay 21 and listed in Exhibit 6.5 to encourage further and more definitive review.

7

URBAN OPERATIONS IN NONTRADITIONAL WARFARE

David L. Bongard
William R. Schilling

The increasing urbanization of populations, especially in the developing world, suggests that warfare in urban areas will become more likely as the twenty-first century unfolds. Ironically, neither the former Soviet Union nor the NATO alliance has placed much emphasis on urban warfare with regard to operational planning, even though this possible zone of conflict is one of the most densely settled areas on the face of the Earth.

In the late 1980s, some officers in the Bundeswehr began to recognize the challenges imposed on mechanized operations by heavy urbanization in West Germany. One proposal was for the Bundeswehr to form several light motorized infantry brigades to defend urban areas. These forces would have been inexpensive in terms of equipment, and designed specifically to maximize the benefits of fighting a defensive battle in urban areas, especially against the expected heavily mechanized Soviet onslaught. Although this concept sparked some serious discussion, policy implications were ignored, and German reunification in 1991 and the end of the Soviet military threat to Western Europe removed the immediate need for any reform.

The relative lack of attention paid to urban warfare by the major military powers does not mean that such conflicts are unlikely, nor that the threat is inherently difficult to analyze and assess. Urban warfare is, however, marked by the following characteristics:

- Lines of sight that are often blocked by large buildings
- Density of infrastructure that includes roads, other transportation assets, and communications facilities

- Dense civilian population that causes more people to be exposed to collateral damage
- Entrapment of civilian populace to support and participate in enemy objectives
- Complexity of the landscape comprised of multistory buildings, multilevel roads, subway tunnels, elevated trains, sewers, subterranean shopping arcades, and parking garages that provide barriers and hiding places for people and materiel
- The sparseness of sufficient open areas that offer sound locations for weapons emplacement, force mobility, and battlefield observations

A distinction should be made between operations in fully urbanized areas, such as the core portions of major cities, and operations in less densely settled

Paratroopers rappelling from UH-60A Blackhawk helicopter.

suburban areas surrounding the urban core. In Western Europe, suburban development has typically progressed from small urban centers, whereas highly dense urban areas are the norm in the developing world, the United States, and Canada.

Historical Perspective of Urban Warfare

We have selected five situations during the past 60 years that demonstrate urban warfare situations. These incidents provide a framework for examining lessons learned and possible responses to protect U.S. interests and national security. Exhibit 7.1 briefly presents an overview of the historical situations,

EXHIBIT 7.1   Historical perspective of urban warfare campaigns.

	Stalingrad	Manila	Berlin	Jerusalem	Hue
Date	24 August 1942 to 12 November 1942	3 February 1945 to 4 March 1945	22 April 1945 to 2 May 1945	5 June 1967 to 7 June 1967	30 January 1968 to 25 February 1968
Opponents	German Army vs. Soviet 62nd and 64th Armies	U.S. 1st Calvary, 11th A/B, 37th Infantry divisions vs. Japanese 3rd Defense Group	Soviet 1st Ukr. and 1st Belo. fronts vs. German 4th, 11th, and 4th Panzer Armies	Israeli Central Force (3 brigades) vs. Jordanian 27th Infantry Brigade	NVA and VC (12 battalions total) vs. elements U.S. 2nd Marine and ARVN 25th Divisions
Forces	5–6 German infantry, 3 Panzer, and 2 motorized divisions vs. Soviet's 11 rifle divisions, 6 rifle brigades, and 1 tank brigade	5 U.S. infantry regiments with major artillery support vs. 6 battalions Japanese base security troops	Elements of 8 German divisions vs. 20 Soviet divisions with many supporting units	3 Jordanian infantry battalions (5,700 total) vs. 10 Israeli battalions (12,000 total)	NVA and VC had 3–5,000; U.S. and ARVN had over 6,000
Conditions	City 25 miles long, 2 miles wide; major resistance centered on factory complexes	Heavy destruction in old city of Manila; high civilian losses due to Japanese actions	Berlin damaged by air raids; German logistics breaking down	Israelis had ample armor and combat aircraft; Jordanians had neither	Superior U.S. firepower; VC resistance centered on Citadel
Outcomes	Germans unable to secure city by Nov. when Soviet offensive ended German assault	City fell after about 30 days of fighting	100,000 Soviet casualties; 120,000 German combat losses plus heavy civilian casualties	570 Israeli casualties; 660 Jordanian casualties	Heavy losses for both sides but NVA and VC forces destroyed utterly for little gain
Lessons	Open east bank of Volga aided Soviet defensive efforts; Germans missed chance to take city quickly in Aug.	Japanese resistance heaviest in Old City; U.S. tried to limit civilian losses and damage; U.S. lost 1010 KIA, 55670 WIA	Fear of Red Army prolonged German resistance	Swift action over 2 days in urban areas possible with heavy superiority of forces	NVA purge in city increased death toll; heavy physical destruction form U.S. artillery and air attacks

opposing forces, and some aspects affecting the outcome. Each of these situations has differences in terms of concepts employed by opposing sides and the size of forces used in the conflict. However, in every case, the opposing sides suffered very high casualty rates, not to mention the additional losses to the civilian populace and the infrastructure. Major damage to the landscape was the normal outcome wherever the attacker applied artillery and aircraft bombing strikes. For the most part, the defender utilized buildings and shelters for cover and protection against long-range delivery systems.

While many other instances of urban warfare over the last hundred years could be cited, several others deserve special mention from the standpoint of lessons learned and the overwhelming strength of the government forces relative to the insurgents or terrorists. These incidents include the Paris Commune uprising in 1871, the Algiers nationalistic revolt in 1956–1957, and the Buenos Aires insurrection from 1976 to 1982. In every one of these situations, the government used massive forces to brutalize and intimidate these radical groups that had sprung up to resist inhumane treatment and tyranny.

Factors Affecting Urban Warfare Concepts
Limited Visibility

Clearly, operations in an urban environment are directly and immediately affected by reduced lines of sight. Buildings are opaque, not only to visible light, but also to infrared detection gear and radar. This limited visibility has two primary effects:

1. Greater incidence for surprise and opportunities for ambush by the defenders. The dismal performance of Russian armored forces in both the assaults on the Chechen capital of Grozny were marked by heavy losses and general lack of tactical and operational success.

2. Short ranges of engagement, causing long-range weapons to be less effective but short-range weapons like submachine guns and rocket-propelled grenades (RPGs) to exert greater combat effectiveness. Returning to the example of Grozny, the bulk of Soviet armor losses, both main battle tanks (MBTs) and light armored vehicles, were due to the Chechen use of unguided antitank weapons.

These operational conditions alone mean that combat in urban areas will be slow, confusing, and marked by relatively high casualty rates, especially for the attacker.

Density of Infrastructure

By itself, infrastructure density may exert relatively little effect on the progress of operations. But the rate of advance will be very slow and the amount of urban damage could be unacceptably great and extensive. Obviously, the density of transportation routes may make relief and resupply comparatively simpler.

The relative absence of infrastructure, beyond the simple structure of residence units in most suburban zones in the developing world, will alter the course of operations. For instance, while the *favelas* of Sao Paulo and Rio de Janeiro are densely inhabited, their roads are mostly unpaved; their buildings are largely flimsy, wood-framed houses and shacks; and facilities such as schools, police stations, commuter railroads, and sewer and water lines are scanty at best. However, these areas should only be breached as a last resort since military actions are likely to perpetuate or produce massive fires, human suffering, disease, and further poverty.

Dense Civilian Population

The presence of large concentrations of civilian population in urban areas will certainly exert some effect, at least, on urban warfare. The desire of most civilians to get out of the way and avoid being killed or wounded will produce considerable disorder, not to mention panic. Certainly, the experience of civilian populations in cities bombed during World War II should provide some examples.

Further, in the case of terrorist and insurgent forces, the civilian population can provide a means of disguising their presence and precise location. While most guerrilla forces operate in the countryside, experiences of urban guerrilla warfare indicate that locating the actual combatants is akin to finding the proverbial needle in a haystack; this applies at least equally to locating terrorist units or forces in urban areas.

Finally, and even in the best of circumstances, urban warfare will produce heavy civilian casualties from collateral damage. Even a brief firefight with small arms may leave civilians dead and wounded, simply because they "got in the way." More intensive and larger-scale operations will produce proportionally higher levels of civilian casualties.

Complexity of Urban Landscape

Up to this point, we have been treating urban landscape as if it were uniform, in some way comparable to forest. In fact, that comparison has often been adopted solely in the interest of simplified presentation. Urban landscapes include a variety of buildings, ranging from apartment blocks through warehouses, factories, multistory office complexes, theaters, shopping areas, parks, and transportation facilities along with a variety of subterranean structures.

All of this variety in conditions poses considerable tactical difficulties for both attackers and defenders. Most structures, as comparatively hard targets, offer considerable cover and protection to inside personnel. This also applies to subterranean features such as subways and bomb shelters. Moreover, the presence of parks and recreational facilities provides extensive areas of essentially "natural" terrain such as Central Park in Manhattan, and the Rock Creek Park complex in Washington, D.C. These features drive engagements to near few-on-few conditions.

Certain other cities also have unique features. The densely settled Los Angeles basin, for instance, is marked by predominantly suburban-type development, with extensive parkland (especially on higher ground), and a more extensive roadway network than is typical even for most U.S. cities. Older cities, particularly in Europe, Asia, and North Africa, such as Jerusalem, Algiers, Lisbon, or Istanbul have extensive areas, like the Kasbah in Algiers, that are essentially impenetrable to motorized or mechanized forces under the best of circumstances. The streets in such areas are narrow, winding, and often blocked by sharp abrupt turns, and even by steps. Moreover, the buildings are low and sturdy, many of them hundreds of years old, and effectively form dense complexes of buildings in which many personnel, civilian or military, may be sheltered.

Urban Assault Tactics and Choices

The Military Response Dilemma

As discussed earlier in the historical perspective, urban warfare is rife with examples of major devastation to the in-country population, resources, economy, and infrastructure. Wars involving U.S. participation in foreign countries are reluctantly undertaken when the national security of the United States is at risk. If diplomacy or deterrence fails in these conditions, the preferred approach is to bypass cultural centers and artifacts, demonstrate the likelihood of an unfavorable outcome to the U.S. foes, and seek to gain surrender of urban areas to U.S. and allied control. This approach is always desired from a damage-limiting strategy and perspective.

In situations involving opposing sides with near equal strength, national disputes, rivalries, political control, or philosophical differences, the likelihood of urban warfare becomes more certain. In the conditions involving large-scale wars with participation by many nations or international organizations, the policy often shifts from military to political control in an attempt to achieve a favorable outcome since constraints are placed on allowable urban damage. Obviously, matching military plans and resources to achieve these damage-limiting objectives leads to longer warfighting times and higher friendly casualties. The bottom line is that structured combat forces on the open terrain are simply not compatible with the conditions in urban areas where military units, civilian populace, and materiel are intermingled.

U.S. forces could also be used to support other allied nations or developing countries involved in resisting internal or external aggression. However, the United States would seek to avoid military activities against urban areas for reasons cited in the previous discussion on infrastructure density unless suitable methods are imposed to limit collateral damage.

Another primary concern involves the application of U.S. military assets to provide homeland defense against terrorist or insurrection threats that might occur in our cities or urban areas. These types of situations might involve blackmail threats, electronic warfare, or the possible application of weapons of mass destruction (nuclear, biological, or chemical). Means to deal with these problems are addressed more fully in other Nontraditional Warfare essays, including Essay 21, Research and Development Planning Guide for Countering Nontraditional Warfare Threats; Essay 12, Information Technology Applications to Counter Nontraditional Warfare Threats; Essay 14, Emergency Response Management at the National Operations Centers; Essay 15, Information Integration and Process Applications for Emergency Management Operations Centers; Essay 5, Vulnerability to Biological Weapons in Nontraditional Warfare; and Essay 27, Impact of Radio Frequency Weapons on National Security and National Infrastructure.

Confronting the Landscape

The buildings that dominate urban areas offer considerable protection to any inside forces. Older and lower buildings, constructed primarily of brick and stone, are sturdier than modern glass with composite-walled, steel-framed concrete structures. However, even the latter type are largely resistant to anything short of concentrated artillery fire or high-explosive bombs/missiles.

When faced with serious resistance in an urban area, an attacking force has several alternatives:

- Bypass the urban area, thereby also foregoing any advantages from controlling the facilities or people.
- Enter the area and capture the buildings individually. This is time-consuming and may be extremely costly, as the Germans discovered at Stalingrad and the Soviets learned in Berlin.

- Simply flatten the buildings. This was substantially the approach taken by the Russians in Grozny, but has some of the disadvantages of bypass and brings along widespread condemnation from the international community.

- Apply weapons or systems that limit collateral damage and leave most of the infrastructure intact.

Clearly, no sensible commander or national control authority should commence operations in an urban area without carefully evaluating the risks, costs, and benefits.

Application of New Weapons/Systems

New weapons may exert a significant effect on combat actions in urban areas. The German Armbrust ("Crossbow" or "Arbalest") antitank weapon is just one such example. Developed in the early 1980s, the Armbrust may be fired from inside a vehicle, or from a small room inside a building. The weapon system eliminates the back blast common to rocket weapons by employing a mass of styrofoam "peanuts" that absorbs the ignition blast from the rocket engine to safely permit firing in enclosed areas. Firing other antitank weapons, from rocket-propelled guns (RPGs) and recoilless rifles to guided missiles (TOW, Swingfire, and others), in an enclosed area would be severely injurious to the weapon crew and anyone else nearby.

Some other current-generation antitank weapons may be fired from indoors, including the U.S. Army's Javelin system and the smaller, lighter SPIM/SRAW system. Both of those systems employ so-called "soft launch" capability, utilizing a low-yield neutral compressed gas charge to clear the missile from the enclosure before the rocket motor ignites.

On a more individual level, a variety of small lethal arms would be appropriate for troops involved in urban combat operations. Automatic shotguns, for instance, combine a high rate of fire with a wide impact area, but their short effective range makes them ineffective under most open-country conditions. Submachine guns, as noted earlier, would also play an important role in urban combat, and hand grenades (now largely relegated to a secondary or tertiary role) could also be extremely useful and effective. Naturally, these types of weapons are designed to ensure casualties.

Other weapon systems include a range of nonlethal devices and compounds that might be valuable in urban combat. Guns firing rubber bullets, pellet bags, loud noises, or other disabling agents could be effective at causing opposing personnel to cease and surrender. Deployment of "sticky barriers," normally intended for crowd control by civilian police forces, could be employed to deny enemy forces the use of streets or other thoroughfares. Other "instant barriers" may also be useful in a similar context. Nonlethal gas compounds, including lachrymatory (tear gas) and stenutator (choking) agents, might also be employed, especially to deny enemy forces use of or access to underground shelter areas such as subways and parking garages.

A number of advanced technologies are emerging that will greatly aid in the search and capture of personnel, buildings, and underground structures. For example, smart sensors (see Essay 28, Development of Smart Sensor Webs for Future Warfare Operations) to detect and observe people and activities can be inserted into any place where adversaries may be located. Other nonlethal concepts based upon directed energy applications like RF weapons, lasers, and nonnuclear EMP can be employed to disable enemy communications and information systems.

Based upon this type of information, robots and nonlethal munitions can be applied to clear the area of enemy elements. These types of technologies can result in major reductions in friendly casualties and change the way assaults are made upon suspected enemy positions in urban areas.

Observations and Remedies

As the preceding brief survey indicates, the issue of urban combat operations in the twenty-first century poses a range of potential problems. Urban combat has traditionally been costly in terms of casualties, and superior forces have encountered great difficulty in gaining a swift decision. This is reflected in situations as disparate as the battle for Hue during the Tet Offensive, or the ultimately successful French siege of Saragossa during the Peninsular War (20 December 1808–20 February 1809).

One reasonably clear conclusion that may be drawn is that dedication and perseverance on the part of the attacking forces is more important than sheer firepower or numbers. Swift action in urban areas is possible, as shown by the relatively quick Israeli capture of East (Arab) Jerusalem, including the walled "Old City," during the Six-Day War (5–7 June 1967). Such instances of swift success, though, are the clear exception rather than the rule.

More than in most other situations, combat in urban environments remains an issue for infantry. Armored vehicles are vulnerable to antitank (AT) and RPG weapons and can also exert only limited impact on the battle. Air strikes, whether by jets or helicopters, are similarly reduced in effect by the very structure of buildings. If the attacking force wishes to have any of the city's structures survive the battle, it is necessary to fight house-to-house, or at least building-to-building, in order to secure urban areas.

Such combat places a heavy demand on junior officers and NCOs, especially platoon and squad leaders. Also, the dreadfully close engagement ranges common in urban fighting ensure both high casualty rates and high levels of emotional and physical exhaustion on the part of the involved troops. German forces fighting in Stalingrad experienced this in particularly brutal form and German commanders soon learned to rotate tired soldiers into comparatively quiet sectors where they could get a few nights' sleep and several hot meals before returning to the close combat in the city.

After the urban battle, the winner is usually faced with a massive cleanup as well as restarting the utilities, food supplies, civil affairs, security, and other necessary living essentials. Thus, the eventual winner must keep these factors in mind as the urban battle is planned and executed.

Fortunately, some strides in advanced technologies can provide means to limit collateral and infrastructure damage. As mentioned earlier, new technologies for surveillance, early warning, and target acquisition using smart sensor webs, standoff sensors, and listening devices can be applied. These techniques will be available to locate and isolate small groups of terrorists or insurgents bent on creating incidents to glorify their organizations or gain recognition for their causes. Also, opportunities will exist to apply nonlethal weapons using indirect fire methods over the localized target area or the entire urban area to control all electrical, communications, and information exchanges. In short, these technologies and others (see Exhibit 7.2) will allow the United States and its allies to seek enemy control centers, isolate pockets of negligible importance, and provide communications control and blackouts to frustrate or eliminate enemy coordination and battlefield movement.

EXHIBIT 7.2   RDT&E initiatives for urban warfare.

Response objectives	Program initiatives/options
• Target acquisition and location of threat units and equipment • Pinpointing of enemy positions and strong points • Protection of friendly forces and equipment • Avoidance of surprise attacks, booby traps, and mines • Selective blackouts and interruption of enemy communications and conflict management • Minimization of collateral damage	• Smart sensor webs for acquiring concealed threats • Directed energy weapons for incapacitating personnel and equipment • Listening devices implanted in buildings and substructures for determining enemy capability and intentions • Lethal weapons with controlled area coverage • Nonlethal weapons for limiting collateral damage • Indirect delivery systems for general and focused nonlethal fires • Robots for detailed surveillance, removal of booby traps, and delivery of nonlethal effects • Light armored suits for personal protection

Finally, it is important to realize the existence of certain similarities and commonalties in urban and guerrilla operations. For example, both operations employ cover and concealment to avoid exposure and permit opportunities to utilize asymmetries in force strength and equipment. Thus, the United States and its allies must concentrate on target acquisition and means to overcome enemy resistance while limiting collateral damage.

The current group of combat models is built around structured battlefield concepts depicting large force deployments and movement in open terrain. New models and simulations need to be developed and evaluated in training support operations to assess urban warfare concepts and organization structure.

The U.S. Army and Marine Corps are beginning to appreciate the nature of urban combat, now made more important by the disappearance of the Soviet threat and the increased likelihood of combat operations in disparate parts of the world. This recognition requires not only new weapons and equipment, but perhaps most importantly, new approaches to training and combat doctrine. Failure to prepare adequately will be paid for, in blood, by American servicemen and women.

8

GUERRILLA OPERATIONS IN NONTRADITIONAL WARFARE

Terry L. Sayers
William R. Schilling

The concept of guerrilla warfare has existed since the dawn of civilization. The original, traditional role of guerrilla operations was comprised of irregular forces fighting small-scale, limited actions in support of orthodox military forces. Nontraditional guerrilla warfare has evolved to become a tool of revolution and insurrection. Almost every nation in the world has now experienced guerrilla operations in the form of strife or rebellion against the existing political structure, leaders, or programs.

This initial resistance usually forms within a country from dissident civil/military groups with limited resources and weaponry. The early phases of guerrilla operations involve small units hiding in cover and avoiding fixed battles until the combination of surprise and strength promises a favorable outcome. Thus, guerrilla groups are likely to be difficult to find and to remain small in unit size relative to the government military forces and assets. Accordingly, the strength of the guerrillas is derived by using tactics to minimize friendly casualties, create confusion, assassinate key people, support popular objectives, and produce violent incidents that undermine the popular support of the government. In short, guerrilla operations involve conflicts not efficiently opposed by conventional, structured combat organizations.

This essay addresses the nature of guerrilla operations, the vulnerability of opposing strategies and objectives, as well as some of the lessons learned for dealing with these nontraditional warfare threats. Six recent guerrilla insurgency actions are discussed. These guerrilla actions provide an overview of the spectrum and variations in conditions and problems that must be dealt with by applying nontraditional warfare plans, organizations, and approaches. The final part of this essay describes some concepts and technologies suitable for countering guerrilla operations.

Guerrilla Tactics

Guerrilla operations rely on surprise, cunning, deception, speed, and mobility. In addition to the traditional hit-and-run raids or ambushes against military targets, nontraditional guerrilla operations encompass a much wider range of tactics. Propaganda is often used as a tool to recruit new members for the guerrilla organization or engender support. Terrorism in the form of assassination or destruction of establishment infrastructure can also be used to demonstrate and strengthen the power of the guerrilla group and encourage harsh reprisals by the government which, in turn, lead to increased dissatisfaction among the civilian populace. By the judicious use of these tools, guerrilla groups can undermine the people's confidence in their government and increase their popular support base.

It should be noted that, while some of the tactics of guerrilla and terrorist operations are similar, the objectives have usually been different. Terrorists seek targets of opportunity to gain notoriety and support for a social, political, or religious agenda while guerrilla operations are focused on military objectives, nation control, and revolution. Another difference is revealed in the guerrilla group's reliance on indigenous popular support.

Guerrilla units require some minimal infrastructure. They must have safe retreats or hideouts where they can rest and recuperate between actions. Basic shelter, sustenance, and medical support are required although guerrillas are prepared to accept near starvation sustenance when mobility is the trade-off. Some form of logistics train to provide equipment and supplies is necessary. This logistics train may be minimal if the guerrilla group relies on capture and theft to resupply their needs. Most importantly, guerrilla organizations rely on intelligence resources. The group must have information on the terrain, the sociopolitical environment in which they are operating, the strength and location of opposing forces, the vulnerability of the targeted objective, and other information. This intelligence may be supplied by partisans and supporters or, if all else fails, it must be purchased. Most of all, the money for such operations must be obtained from some source, either by theft and robbery or contributed by supporters or a foreign government.

C Company, 1st Battalion, 20th Infantry Regiment.

Historical Perspective

Part of the material in this section is drawn from *War in the Shadows,* Vol. II, Robert B. Asprey; *Vantage Point,* Lyndon B. Johnson; *The Washington Post;* and *Operation Allied Force,* SBLM 99-2, Duane Schilling. We have selected six countries that, over the past 50 years, have experienced guerrilla activities that provide a framework for examining lessons learned and possible responses in the future to protect U.S. interests and national security. These countries are Cuba, Bolivia, Vietnam, Kashmir, Kosovo, and Colombia. Colombia is particularly important as the United States is determining how to meet the problem of criminally sponsored guerrilla operations in support of drug exportation. Exhibit 8.1 briefly presents an overview of the historical situations, opposing strategies, and an assessment of key factors affecting the outcomes.

Cuba (1953–1959)

Until the media (especially the *New York Times*) began to discuss and sympathize with the insurgency operation led by Fidel Castro in Cuba, little interest was observed in either the U.S. political or diplomatic circles. Even then, much

EXHIBIT 8.1   Overview of some recent guerrilla insurgency actions.

Country	Description of in-country situation	Opposing strategies	Assessment
Cuba 1953–1959	• Sugar-based, single-crop economy offers prosperity to landowners but only shortime jobs for workers. • U.S. government supports Batista, dictator of Cuba, due to U.S. corporate investments in sugar business and promises by Cuban government for social reforms and elections. • Some social reform underway but it is limited. • One-third of country lives in squalor with illiteracy over 40% in rural areas. • Disease, unemployment, and poor health services are rampant. • Corrupt government and Army elements cause widespread urban and rural dissidence.	• Cuban government relies on propaganda, Army brutality and torture, peasant injustice, insurgent isolation, and starvation or death. Several military skirmishes hindered by terrain, lack of intelligence and targets to attack. • Castro insurgence cause incidents and violence against government sympathizers in urban areas and organize peasants in friendly rural areas, remote from government intervention. Utilize U.S. media and propaganda to gain sympathy for insurgency. Avoid friendly casualties and focuses on very small military ambushes and surprise night attacks with high probability of success. • U.S. provides weapons and military/political advice to Cuban government. Access to reliable intelligence on insurgents' motivations and capability lacking in U.S. plans.	• Recognition of actual threat slow to evolve • Awareness of social conditions, magnitude of insurgency events, and erosion in government confidence hampered by U.S. diplomatic bias and Cuban propaganda. • Lack of support by populace for Cuban government and Army leads to civil uprisings in support of Castro guerrillas. • Political, environmental, and social factors become dominant over organized military events and outcomes. • Country becomes Communist due to U.S. hostility toward Castro's takeover and socialistic bent of key insurgents and participants.
Bolivia 1966–1967	• Cuban revolutionaries (Che Guevara and Castro) decide South America ripe for insurgency operations and select Bolivian countryside for exploitation. • U.S. government supporting land reform (Act of 1957), civic action programs, and training of ranges in counterinsurgency tactics. • Bolivian government receives loyal support of Indians representing two-thirds of population due to award of citizenship, land ownership, and civic action programs. • Indians suspicious of foreigners and have different dialect/language and customs • Communists have only limited support among miners and peasants prior to Che Guevara arrival in Bolivia. • Army in Bolivia assisting in rural areas in civic actions and security.	• Small cadre of Cuban guerrillas attempts recruitment of peasants to build revolutionary force and institute agrarian reform. Utilizes existing Communist infrastructure and terrain to provide logistics support and operational cover. • Indians hostile to insurgency mission due to rapport with Bolivian government and provide intelligence on guerrilla movements, location, and strength. • Bolivian government puts emphasis on applying counter-insurgency tactics by U.S.-trained rangers and intelligence from Indians on presence/location of insurgents to capture/kill guerrillas. • U.S. provides surveillance and military assistance to restrict continuance of foreign support or expansion of revolutionary activities.	• Recruitment of peasants by insurgents fails to materialize due to enlightened Bolivian government policies of land ownership and civic action programs. Indians remain satisfied and loyal to government and resist insurgents' propaganda. • Insurgents' lack of familiarity with terrain, culture, and language of Indians hampers recruitment and security. • Prior activity by U.S. government assists in improving Indians' acceptance and confidence in Bolivian government's promises and motivations. • Government counterinsurgency operations quickly overcome guerrilla movement in Bolivia due to training and Indian cooperation, support, and intelligence information.

Vietnam 1955–1973		

• Conditions in Vietnam degrade from increasing violence, corruption, and insecurity as well as misrepresentation, mishandling, and misunderstanding of responses to guerrilla operations.
• South Vietnam (RVN) under each government change continues to be corrupt oligarchy with limited support or confidence from the people.
• RVN agrarian people in abject poverty and harassed by government and Army with no freedoms or choices in lifestyle.
• Viet Cong (VC) and North Vietnam (NVN) guerrillas spend nights proselytizing peasants and promising land reforms. Also create numerous incidents and carry out assassinations of RVN supporters.
• Social reform by government very slow and pacification moves diluted over wide regions with insufficient police or security measures.
• NVN gradually escalates support to VC guerrilla warfare movement, providing leadership, volunteers, and direction.
• U.S. government begins support with military training assistance and insistence on social reform. Assistance escalates to include military operations pacification, and air and naval patrols throughout Southeast Asia (SEA).
• U.S. and RVN continue to attrit large numbers of enemy but lack of support/loyalty from RVN peoples continue to hamper efforts.
• Civilian and military casualties in SEA continue to increase far beyond limited objectives.
• Vast number of RVN peoples are conscripted but fail to press against enemy forces.
• At the close of the war, opposing forces begin to engage in organized combat and guerrillas suffer high casualties.
	• RVN government dedicated towards maintaining power structure, defeat of VC and NVN by building an Army and a pacification program, exploiting the agrarian economy, profiteering from U.S. financial assistance, and offering encouragement along with some promised social reforms for peasants.
	• VC and Peoples Revolutionary Party (PRP) concentrated on a three-pronged approach to the overthrow of RVN to include (1) political use of a united front or negotiated settlement, (2) social focus on instigation of class strife, and (3) military program of assassinations and other acts of violence to stimulate general uprising.
	• NVN strived to achieve control of RVN using surrogates comprised of VC, PRP, and volunteers from NVN, to avoid major military conflicts with the U.S. Army, and to provide support of the insurgency including supplies, leadership, organization, and command.
	• U.S. government approached RVN insurgency as a problem requiring military force, heavy enemy casualties, pacification of RVN rural areas, financial and intelligence support to the RVN, severe damage to NVN logistics support, and training of RVN forces with increasing attention to political negotiations after 1967.
		• There was no victory as all participants in the campaign suffered tremendous losses in casualties, world prestige, economic resources, and confidence in government/military decision making.
		• The U.S. lacked accurate, reliable, and secure intelligence. Expert advice was often wrong.
		• Primary U.S. attention devoted towards military rather than political solutions.
		• Entrenched belief in "domino theory" in SEA distorted other approaches for resolution.
		• U.S. overestimated impact of enemy casualties and damage to NVN infrastructure.
		• VC and NVN underestimated the U.S. resolve to support RVN with massive military and economic assistance.
		• U.S. lack of understanding and knowledge of culture, terrain, environment, dedication of VC and NVN with support by RVN peasants led to inability to force conventional military tactics on the opposition.
		• Losses from insurgency/guerrilla operations:
		  • NVN suffered 20 years of major degradation to agrarian, economic, and military resources
		  • Over 500,000 NVN soldiers killed in RVN
		  • Thousands of civilians died in NVN from bombings, disease, and hunger
		  • Over 1 million RVN soldiers killed, another 500,000 civilians wounded, more than 2 million civilians displaced in refugee campus/slums
		  • Over 50,000 U.S. soldiers killed, another 150,000 wounded, and nearly $50 billion in war materials and other costs

(continued)

EXHIBIT 8.1 Overview of some recent guerrilla insurgency actions *(continued)*.

Country	Description of in-country situation	Opposing strategies	Assessment
Kashmir 1987–1999	• Two of three wars between India and Pakistan fought in this area over control rights and religious disputes. • Both countries have nuclear weapons. • Insurgency skirmishes by both countries have occurred for last 10 years. • India applied air strikes and land forces to repel 600 Pakistani guerrillas in 1999 from region within assigned area of control	• Insurgents from both sides are fervently inspired to advance religious goals (India-Hindu and Pakistan-Muslim) and seek revenge for old incidents. • India seeks to reserve ownership of large part of Kashmir and prevent outside foreign involvement. • Pakistan wants to insure Muslim religious freedom, probably by making Kashmir a free state or integrating part of Kashmir into Pakistan.	• Unrest, insurgency, and strife for people in Kashmir likely to continue indefinitely. • Conditions in Kashmir could lead to nuclear strikes among participants. • Superiority of India's conventional military forces could cause Pakistan to respond with limited nuclear missile strike as means to protect Kashmir interests. • Encouragement of peaceful Kashmir settlement should be a worldwide goal.
Kosovo 1995–1999	• One of several loosely federated republics comprising Yugoslavia with a dissenting mixture of political, ethnic, and religious components. • Ethnic hatreds span more than 150 years. • Yugoslavia dominated by Serbian Republic. • Serbian Republic primarily comprised of Greek Orthodox followers which exercise intolerant control over Albanian Muslims in Kosovo. • Kosovo Liberation Army (KLA), seeking independence, begins guerrilla operations against small Serbian police units in 1995. • Serbian Republic responds to KLA with brutal oppression including ethnic cleansing, incarceration, and expulsion. • In 1999, the U.S. and 19 other nations, under NATO umbrella, enter civil strife to halt Serbian atrocities.	• Yugoslavia focuses on maintaining control of federated republics including the use of force to expel or remove any opposition. • Serbian Republic moves large force into Kosovo to protect Serbian civilians and overcome resistance. • KLA and supporters continue guerrilla operations against police units and Serbian military. • All attempts to negotiate a peaceful settlement to the conflict fail. • KLA provides some intelligence and military support to European and U.S. forces. • Large-scale air strikes by Europe and U.S. damage Serbian infrastructure and military units. • Europe and U.S. allies intend to force withdrawal of Serbian troops, install a NATO-led peacekeeping force in Kosovo, allow the safe return of Kosovo refugees, and establish a democratic self-government in Kosovo.	• Ethnic cleansing by Serbia in Kosovo approach levels unseen in Europe since early in WWII. • Retaliation by KLA and supporters after withdrawal by Serbia perpetuate ethnic hatreds. • Political future of Kosovo uncertain. NATO-led peacekeeping force maintains status quo. • Air campaign fails to find many Serbian military targets in Kosovo but does destroy much of the infrastructure in Serbia, including command and communications networks, transportation systems, oil depots, and military facilities. • A lot of time and money is needed to rebuild Serbian industrial and transportation complex. • Air campaign tactics and countermeasures eliminate European and U.S. casualties. • Communication deficiencies hamper close coordination between European and U.S. forces during air strikes.
Colombia 2000	• Colombia supplies 80% of drugs (cocaine and heroin) brought into U.S. • High profitability of U.S. drug sales corrupts Colombian institutions and peoples. • Antigovernment (FARC and ELN) guerrilla organizations exploiting widespread peasant discontent and suffering.	• U.S. launches major drug eradication program in Colombia with $1 billion in military aid and 230 million for social programs. • Communist/Marxist guerrilla groups support drug related economy and kidnappings to fund their effort to overthrow government and ruling class. • U.S.-Colombia striving to enhance government force capability, drug crop destruction, and peasant security and quality of life.	• Human rights violations, poverty, and refugees contribute to peasant support of Colombian drug economy. • A military solution to drug eradication needs support of peasants. • Emphasis on enemy casualties rather than social/economic conditions would likely widen war without achieving objectives.

of the intelligence and expert advice about the Cuban situation was very inaccurate. At the onset, the United States failed to correctly identify the seriousness of the threat to (1) a possible overthrow of the Cuban government or (2) the likelihood of Cuba ending up in the Communist column. In any event, the U.S. response was poor and inconsequential due to misunderstanding and lack of knowledge about the situation compounded by unreliable intelligence resources to counter the insurgency. Exhibit 8.1 offers further details on the Cuban guerrilla operation and success story.

Bolivia (1966–1967)

In Bolivia, the guerrilla insurgency led by Che Guevera forgot the lessons of the Cuban campaign and moved into unfamiliar territory with very limited support or interest from a weak in-country communist group. Also, under urging from the United States, the Bolivian government preempted the problem of Indian disenfranchisement with a Land Reform Act some 10 years before the arrival of the Che Guevera group. Accordingly and most importantly, the Bolivian government had the support of the Indian population as well as U.S.-trained ranger forces to deal with insurgencies.

Vietnam (1955–1973)

The guerrilla insurgency in Vietnam was probably the most divisive event experienced by the United States since our own Civil War more than a hundred years earlier. The primary U.S. emphasis was devoted toward a military solution based upon misplaced confidence in the overwhelming superiority of a conventional approach to warfare, plus dependence on intelligence data and expert advice that was inaccurate and unreliable. While the U.S. government realized the importance of peasant support and were backers of the pacification program, the Vietnam people never had confidence in the Vietnamese government promises to institute social and land reforms. The lack of protection or security for the peasants further doomed the pacification program. The U.S. unfamiliarity with the Vietnam culture and terrain, the unexpected dedication of the Viet Cong and North Vietnamese partisans, and a lack of suitable targets for the U.S. warfighting machines all contributed to the inability to win the "limited" war. Another poor decision by the United States was the emphasis on maximizing enemy casualties and damaging the enemy logistics/infrastructure—traditional thinking in a nontraditional situation. In guerrilla operations, many conflict situations become near one-on-one engagements and attempting to maximize enemy casualties leads to high friendly casualties as well.

Kashmir (1987–1989)

The United States has viewed the situation between India and Pakistan over the final settlement of the Kashmir situation with grave concern due to possible intense fighting between two nations that are considered friendly to the United States and its allies. The possible employment of nuclear weapons by Pakistan to balance inferiority in conventional warfare capability is of further concern. In this situation, the guerrilla insurgency groups have been comprised of opposing religious factions. While it is unlikely that the United States will take an active role on either side, further intensification of hostilities would cause instability in the region and could expand to involve other countries. Both sides are certainly vulnerable to guerrilla actions and further casualties are anticipated. The possibility of either or both sides employing WMD would be a serious escalation of guerrilla operations and is viewed with alarm by all nations. Recent counterterrorist activities in Afghanistan are also likely to destabilize government and political situations in Pakistan and surrounding environs.

Kosovo (1995–1999)

This conflict involved the use of guerrilla groups on both sides. In response to the Serbian movement of large military units into Kosovo to persecute and expel Kosovo Muslims, the United States and the European Union sought to quell the strife using conventional air warfare tactics combined with electronic countermeasures. Serbian military forces in Kosovo used cover, deception, and dispersion to minimize the value of the air strikes and protect their reserves. However, enough military targets and infrastructure were damaged in Serbia to bring the warfighting to a quick close. At this time, a political solution to the Kosovo-Serbian situation remains unresolved.

Colombia (2000)

The United States has renewed its attention on Colombia in an attempt to stop the production and exportation of drugs. Cartels have been formed that control large areas of coca production. The people living within these controlled areas are coerced by a combination of propaganda, bribery, and terrorism into supporting the drug cartel. Some of the enormous profits from the sale of drugs are used to fund guerrilla groups such as FARC who are promoting revolution and overthrow of the Colombian government. These guerrilla groups have become an entwined component of the drug war.

EXHIBIT 8.2   Top ten rules in countering guerrilla warfare.

1	Intelligence on guerrilla actions, plans, and capabilities
2	Government credibility to survive and meet needs of general population
3	Native peoples incentive to repel guerrilla actions
4	Understanding the indigenous cultural philosophies and beliefs
5	Familiarity with geographical/environmental conditions and factors
6	Local political support for foreign intervention (national security interests, economic considerations, and humanitarian interests)
7	Elimination of sanctuaries for guerrilla and terrorist operations
8	Availability of police protection for supporters (security)
9	Sufficient military force assets and structure to deny guerrilla objectives
10	Comprehensive and game planning (withdrawal, negotiations, follow-on support)

Lessons Learned

Successful revolutionary guerrilla operations are dependent on certain fundamentals (see Exhibit 8.2). The most critical requirement for success is popular support within or at least near the areas of operation. The greater the popular support, the greater the chance of success. Another important element of successful guerrilla operations is intelligence. The most valuable intelligence is garnered from sources familiar with the culture, terrain, environment, and local conditions. Without this critical intelligence, guerrilla or counterguerrilla groups cannot operate with any degree of success or confidence. This is a marked difference between a guerrilla operation and a terrorist operation. Of lesser importance, but still an essential element, is mobility to avoid entrapment by superior opposing forces. Other requirements are common elements of warfare operations such as a source of supplies, equipment, and materiel; safe havens for planning, recruiting, and recovering; and funding. Most of the difficulties faced by guerrilla groups have resulted from a failure to adequately fulfill one or more of these requirements.

Military superiority may not be sufficient to counter guerrilla operations. If the guerrilla group never allows itself to be entrapped into confronting a superior military force, another method of neutralizing them must be chosen.

Prognosis and Remedies

Residual problems after the conclusion of many guerrilla conflicts include the collateral damage and leftover mines in the battle areas. Antipersonnel and vehicular mines continue to be deployed in massive number in guerrilla operations and very little attempt is made to mark or clear the minefields. Accordingly, expensive, dangerous, and sophisticated demining efforts are necessary to clear these areas. Presently, up to 100 million land mines are candidates for demining efforts and are found in more than 70 countries. Essay 21 in this series presents research and development guidelines for mining and demining operations.

Another difficulty in dealing with guerrilla and counterguerrilla warfare is the lack of available, approved force models to treat these problems. As reported in Essay 17 on models and simulations, the current force models are based on traditional, structured, deployed combat units. This is certainly not the situation in guerrilla warfare. Essay 17 offers some area and point force model concepts that are more useful and relevant for guerrilla warfare.

In any case, intelligence on characteristics of enemy units must be available so organization, strength, and unit composition requirements for combating guerrilla operations can be determined. And the capability to locate and acquire these enemy targets along with weapon-target interaction data must be provided for unit damage calculation models.

A critical factor affecting the capability to defeat guerrilla operations is the need to acquire enemy personnel and materiel targets located in heavy vegetation, camouflaged, or poor visibility conditions. New data processing and computer automation technology combined with radar and imaging devices (IR/thermal) may lead the way for making guerrilla operations more visible. A key step in this evolving signature analysis arena is to combine data from different sensor types so false targets can be eliminated and real targets enhanced. Automated target recognition is the goal for this countermeasure. In addition, remote sensing devices and recoverable mobile robots will further aid guerrilla tracking and target acquisition and reduce friendly casualties. Exhibit 8.3 outlines some technology response objectives and program options for improving U.S. capability to deal with countermeasures to guerrilla operations. Further discussion of these technologies is included in Section VI.

For the United States, an immediate concern involves the attempt to stop the production and exportation of drugs from guerrilla-infested areas in Colombia. Previous military operations seeking to destroy the cocoa crops and capture or kill members of the drug cartels have been attempted with limited and erratic results. Any military action must be accompanied by a program to gain the support of the people in the coca growing regions. Drawing the people in the area into safe havens with human rights and social and economic rewards would deprive the cartels of their labor force. In fact, sealing the coca growing and distribution areas and permitting exodus of people wishing to accept a new life, with safety and opportunity, may be the best approach.

EXHIBIT 8.3 Technology responses.

Response objectives	Program initiatives/options
• Target acquisition of threat units and equipment • Pinpointing of guerrilla positions • Protection of friendly forces and equipment • Minimization of collateral damage	• Sensors for acquiring concealed threats • Lethal weapons with controlled area coverage • Nonlethal weapons for limiting collateral damage • Fast, lightly armored vehicles for combat operations support • Light armored suits for personal protection

Attempts to maximize casualties against guerrillas, cartel members, and coca growers will probably cause unacceptable collateral damage and expand the conflict with a concomitant expansion of U.S. military participation. Point and area force model concepts described in Essay 17, Models and Simulations for Evaluating Emerging Threats may provide a convenient basis to evaluate force and system requirements for preventing drug participants to enter restricted areas, burning crops, and allowing refugees to leave for the "promised land" and reform.

Additional efforts to combat drug trafficking are described in Essay 9, International Criminal Operations in Nontraditional Warfare.

INTERNATIONAL CRIMINAL OPERATIONS IN NONTRADITIONAL WARFARE

Joseph D. Douglass, Jr.

For two decades, the illegal drug problem has been consistently ranked in public polls among the five most serious problems our nation faces. Illegal drugs plague our society and threaten the entire globe. To better appreciate the magnitude of the illegal drug problem and what is necessary to cause change, consider, the "conventional wisdom" about this problem.

In September 2000, a four-hour investigative report on the war on drugs was aired on the Public Broadcasting System (PBS). The report accurately reflected the conventional wisdom and did not differ significantly from the dozens of previous treatments over as many years. The year 2000 material was just more authoritative, better packaged, more thorough, and quite compelling.

The following six points were unmistakable:

1. Massive amounts of money are spent in the war on drugs. The annual total in 2001 $20 billion, up from $1 billion early in the Reagan administration.

2. Notwithstanding all the money spent over the past two decades, illegal drugs are cheaper, higher quality, and easier to obtain than ever before. The more stringent criminal sentences imposed during the war on drugs have resulted in a massive increase in prison facilities and a quadrupling of the number of people in jail.

3. The lure of money is so great that little can be done. There is slight expectation of stopping the flow of drugs across U.S. borders. Customs

can hardly inspect 7 percent of the imports, and the problem gets worse each year. All the drug traffickers' losses to interdiction and pursuit of dirty money are *well* within the acceptable cost of doing business.

4. Education has accomplished very little. The only significant "blip" in drug-use statistics was in the late 1980s to the lethal effect of crack evidenced by the deaths of several highly publicized sports figures. The number of regular users has not changed over the last 20 years.

5. The only identifiable area where additional efforts might be useful is in the jails to cure or otherwise rehabilitate those prisoners with drug-use habits. Over 50 percent of the jailed population are drug users.

6. Notwithstanding the severity of the problem, there is still no federal organization in charge, no effective chain of command, and no strategy that is empowered with authority and resource controls to thwart the drug trafficking and usage. Of course, many organizations with resources (federal, state, and local governments as well as public and private organizations) abound to support elimination of functional areas of the problem but the activities are often fragmented or only partially integrated.

In brief, the war on drugs has been ineffective in decreasing supply or reducing demand. Few believe that even more stringent laws or police action would produce positive results. In addition, the drug problem is closely related to the process involved in other international criminal activities.

Dimensions of the Drug Problem

While the picture painted by PBS was devastating, it *still* underestimated the magnitude of the problem. For example, almost no attention was directed to (1) the true size of the drug-use problem, (2) the political and financial corruption that is tied into the massive amounts of money, (3) the accompanying growth and role of international organized crime, (4) the sub-rosa connections between drug traffickers and revolutionary/terrorist organizations, and (5) the implications of the growing presence of designer drugs manufactured by pharmaceutical companies.

The size of the annual retail sale of illegal drugs that is used in official statements is now $40 billion. But good numbers are hard to come by and this estimate is suspect because it is based on estimates of drug use that are believed to be notoriously low. They depend on household use survey statistics that assume (1) people tell the truth about their habit and (2) adults are knowledgeable about the use of drugs by minors in their households.

When the Emory School of Medicine tested the credibility of "self-report" statistics, they learned that a minimum of 70 percent, likely more than 90 percent, lied about their drug use. Actual use of drugs was found to be three times higher than what one would estimate using household use survey statistics.

Additionally, hardcore users are grossly underestimated; indeed, there are no known credible estimates. The results of 1999 efforts to estimate chronic drug users in Cook County, if extrapolated to produce a national estimate, also lead to numbers that are over three times higher than the conventional wisdom number of hard core users.

While annual drug-sale costs based on Drug Enforcement Agency (DEA) drug-use statistics are in the $40 to $100 billion range, costs based on drug production and money flows have been in the $150 to $200 billion range for over a decade. All these back-of-the-envelop estimates point toward a drug-use problem that is three or more times higher than the official estimates.

But even more important than the precise size are the implications. Regardless of whether the size is $40 billion or $200 billion, the phenomenon has been underway for more than a quarter of a century. All of the moneys are illegal, and there is no way an illegal business of this magnitude can continue, year after year, without extensive and expanding corruption of our nation's political, financial, judicial, business, law and order, and social systems. For example, there is not a major city police force that has not had significant drug-related corruption problems in the past decade.

Relationships between Drug Trafficking and International Crime

Integrally connected to narcotics trafficking is international organized crime, whose base is narcotics trafficking. One example of the linkage between the two is the money laundering apparatus that was designed to service narcotics trafficking and that also services international organized crime. International organized crime has its own narcotics production and trafficking branches. Narcotics traffickers are involved in other dimensions of organized crime, and there is cooperation and coordination between the traffickers and heads of organized crime. Profits are heavily invested in property and businesses, with both traffickers and organized crime bosses as silent partners, especially those businesses that can be used to launder money.

Another concern is the role of legitimate and illegitimate pharmaceutical manufacturers and what actions are appropriate to counteract this trade. Legitimate pharmaceutical companies are mainly responsible for the development of synthetic drugs such as ecstasy and methamphetamines. These drugs were intended for the treatment of health-related illnesses. The abuse of these drugs to create a heightened sense of awareness is prevalent among teens. Their use is especially serious in England and Germany, where the primary sources are illegitimate pharmaceutical manufacturers in the Netherlands. The plague has spread to the United States and Far East and even legitimate pharmaceutical manufacturers in Bulgaria, Hungary, and China participate in the trafficking. This is just the start. There are additional synthetic drugs already developed by pharmaceutical companies that are believed to be better than cocaine—better in the sense that they are cheaper to make, produce better and longer lasting highs, are more addictive, and have long-term side effects that leave users lacking in ambition. Most legitimate pharmaceutical companies have withheld these new drugs from the market. Other, less legitimate pharmaceutical manufacturers are just waiting for the right time to start production.

The size of international organized crime—that is, global criminal capitalism—was estimated by World Bank experts at $1.3 *trillion* per year in 1996. The UN *1999 Human Development Report* estimated the size of international organized crime at $1.6 *trillion* per year. Both of these estimates are likely conservative. Actual totals could exceed $2 trillion. Fifty percent of that is profit and the money launderers (banks, financial services, top law firms, investment houses) take 15 to 20 percent of the profit for their services. If we recognize the amount of corruption and influence *around the world* this amount of money can buy, is it any wonder that eight top law firms in London have been under investigation for money laundering or that no significant disciplinary actions have materialized?

As in the case of drug sales in the United States, whether the global crime total exceeds $2 trillion or is only a paltry $1.3 trillion per year is immaterial. What matters is the consequences: the millions of lives ruined and the corruption and influence that drug and organized crime money buys in police, intelligence, government officials, and the financial markets. At times, political doors open wide when the crime bosses come visiting. Organized crime money has become a large donor to political campaigns in many nations around the globe. Their largesse does not come without many strings attached. Less often recognized is the use of dirty money to buy elections for politicians who are organized crime bosses. They have learned the simple lesson: the easiest way to steal from the people is through the state.

Another reality that is rarely discussed is the close connection between organized crime and various intelligence services. In some operations, organized crime is viewed as a participant in state intelligence operations. Nation

AH-64A Apache attack helicopter.

states are in this game because of the connections between organized crime and politics and associated compromise and corruption—and blackmail potential—that is also present.

To understand what is happening to American currency, consider the growth in overseas dollars. Within a year after the Soviet Union disintegrated and possession of dollars was legalized in Russia, there were more dollars (currency) in circulation in Russia than in the United States! Or consider the flow of dollars into Latin America. Fifty percent or more of the deposits in Argentina today are dollars. In Bolivia it is 80 percent. In Colombia, the deposits have grown steadily and were reported at $34 billion per year in 2000. Why is it that U.S. one-hundred dollar bills have become the currency of international organized crime? The cumulative total of the narcotics traffickers over just the past 20 years exceeds $6 trillion dollars, and that does not allow for any investment capital growth. The cumulative total of all organized crime over the same time period probably exceeds $20 trillion—$40 trillion if capital growth is included. European intelligence estimates that 20 percent of the stock market is dirty money. This factor becomes extremely important should any country—including the United States—decide to start waging a real war on drugs sometime in the future.

Linkage between Drug Trafficking and Terrorist Organizations

Another rarely discussed issue is the connection between narcotics trafficking and terrorist organizations, as alluded to earlier. Until now, the war on drugs has involved independent bureaucratic efforts orchestrated to address some aspects of the problem. However, should the United States or any other nation find an effective deterrent to the flow of drugs into their country, will the drug traffickers simply capitulate? Hardly, because the connected terrorist and paramilitary capabilities are now an integral part of the drug trafficking and organized crime business. In the United States, we do not see that side of the business, nor do the Europeans, but it is there—just ask anyone in Colombia or Mexico what the life expectancy is of an honest politician, banker, police officer, investigative journalist, or military leader.

Seven years ago there was considerable concern about the Aum Shinrikyo cult that released sarin nerve gas in a Tokyo subway. Upon investigation, authorities learned that the cult had a war chest of slightly over $1 billion and was working on the development of anthrax and plague terrorist weapons. They had front companies in the United States. In fact, the United States was their next target. These findings caused people in Washington, D.C., to get serious about the terrorist threat.

What goes unsaid is that most of the illegal drug businesses make the Aum Shinrikyo cult look incompetent when it comes to war chests, delivery capabilities, presence in the United States, and serious political influence around the globe. Actually, the problem is much worse because some of the drug production and distribution networks were actually established with dual missions of moving drugs in peacetime and conducting sabotage or terrorist acts should war break out.

Implications of Drug Trafficking on Enforcement Counterthrusts

Over the past 50 years the United States has been engaged in numerous serious military actions around the world: Korea, Vietnam, Iraq, and Bosnia to mention the most obvious ones. In none of these cases was the United States under attack or even threatened.

In the case of drugs, the United States is directly under attack. Organizations (including foreign intelligence services) mounting the attacks have been identified, although public knowledge of the attackers has been suppressed. The damage inflicted on our country has been enormous. When the total cost of illegal drugs—sales, lost productivity, health and welfare, prisons, and the war on drugs itself—are added up, the total annual cost attributable to illegal drugs in our nation actually exceeds the total 10-year cost of the Vietnam War. This is also true of casualties as the U.S. fatalities from drug-related violence and overdoses each year are two times greater than the worst of the Vietnam War years.

In contrast to the previously mentioned military conflicts, in the case of illegal drugs, there has not been a single unilateral U.S. military action taken in more than 50 years. The only exception was the removal of the leader of Panama, Manuel Noriega.

What will happen if the United States decides to become a proactive participant in the war on drugs? This is becoming likely as drug trafficking and associated crime pose an increasingly embarrassing burden as, for example, in Colombia and Mexico. Combat involvement may be sooner rather than later for the United States because of the situation in Colombia.

The $1.3 billion in U.S. military assistance now flowing to Colombia is only the beginning of a package that could total more than $10 billion. Combat involvement of U.S. forces is now part of U.S. contingency planning and should be anticipated in 5 to 10 years, if not sooner. Troop increases are planned that will bring the number of deployed forces up from the present 1,500 to the 5,000 to 10,000 range. As in the case of Vietnam, the adversary will play to our weaknesses, not strengths. The implications will almost certainly involve devastating terrorism at home, which is the traffickers' normal response. One would be shortsighted not to consider terrorist responses that might involve financial terrorism and cyber warfare as well as the very real possibility of chemical and biological terrorism from groups such as the FARC.

The situation in Colombia cannot be assessed without an accompanying analysis of the enemy-coordinated activities now underway in Venezuela, Equador, Peru, Bolivia, Argentina, Brazil, and Panama. To approach military assistance to Colombia as a detached microcosm is to court disaster.

One of the reasons the war on drugs has been so limited is that too few have stopped to ask what is happening and why. As explained by Professor David Jordan in his book, *Drug Politics,* current thinking is conditioned by a set of assumptions, most of which are flawed. For example, explanations of the illegal drug business assume a simple supply and demand model. But only half the business is dominated by supply. The other half is dominated by demand, and the illegal nature of the trade brings in other complicating factors that invalidate normal supply and demand models. A second longstanding assumption is that the traffickers are ethnic or national gangs. This assumption does not give recognition to the active role of governments and their intelligence services that have dominated the drug trafficking business since 1950. In a similar manner, governments and banks are viewed as victims rather than active collaborators. This reality can not be overstated. Such a large industry as illegal drugs simply could not exist or grow as it has without the active, knowing, and willing participation of the banks and the political protection of governments.

Another main reason the drug war has been ineffectual is because of its focus. The war on drugs has been dominated by a law and order approach— that is, as a matter of enforcing the laws at the street level. This is why so many new jails were built and why there are now 2 million Americans in jail. You can jail all the peddlers and drug dealers that exist and they will be replaced within a week or two; the money available is simply that overpowering. In a different vein, top police intelligence officials in Europe have stated publicly that the problem cannot be solved by police work. The problems posed by the traffickers and their support network (including the best lawyers and all the high-tech equipment they need) has moved far beyond the capabilities of the police forces and courts.

We are told that crime is down and, thus, that drug-related crime is down. This, however, is an unjustified deduction. It also diverts attention away from a larger problem. One of the few studies of actual drug-related crimes was conducted by Professor James Inciardi 20 years ago. His report, "Heroin Use and Street Crime", appeared in the July 1979 journal of *Crime and Delinquency*. He was able to win the confidence of 356 heroin addicts in Miami. He learned that these addicts had perpetrated over 27,000 FBI-designated serious crimes during the previous year and that only 1 in 300 resulted in an arrest. Multiply these statistics by the assumed number of heroin addicts and the results are overwhelming: the number of unreported crimes by just heroin addicts nationwide alone exceeded the total number of all FBI-designated serious crimes by a factor of three or more.

The overseas aspect of the war on drugs is also approached in a highly questionable manner: it is in the hands of the diplomats whose more demanding tasks concern the needs of U.S. business and finance, which have a higher priority than stopping the flow of drugs.

Education and treatment, while necessary parts of the drug war, cannot begin to cope with the problem. The best hope is to somehow "hold the line," knowing the magnitude of the problem is growing faster than it can be curtailed. One of the mounting problems in education today is not teaching kids to "just say no." Rather, it is teaching classes where a significant percentage of the children have behavioral or learning problems due to ingesting drugs.

Formulating a Plan to Combat Drug Trafficking

Is there an answer? The message implicit in many investigative reports, such as the PBS special that triggered these remarks, is "No, there is simply too much money and no one wants to live in a police state, which is where we are inexorably led as more and more money gets thrown at the problem." This, however, is also based on highly questionable logic. There are many viable options that have not been tried and that do not lead to police state controls.

The fact that the war on drugs has been a failure is of little significance because there has been no effective war on drugs. Indeed, there has not even been a semi-serious law and order approach to the narcotics business. This business has grown and continues to flourish because it is protected. The war on drugs as conceived has been a bonanza to lawyers, accountants, banking and investment, and health services. The notion that government interest in stopping the flow of drugs cannot be effectively implemented without sacrificing individual freedom and liberty is simply not true if carefully constructed approaches are conceived and initiated.

The most obvious first step is to put someone in charge with the authority to reach across jurisdictional lines. The second step is to conduct a strategic assessment of the problem in which primary attention is directed to evaluate the seriousness of the problem. Until there is widespread agreement on the nature of the problem and its seriousness, programs to attack the problem cannot be meaningfully proposed or evaluated because this evaluation depends on the assessment of the problem and its seriousness. In addition, a concept must be conceived for effectively integrating and maximizing the available resources throughout the federal/state governments and nongovernmental organizations.

What a nation is willing to endure, or risk, is strongly related to the national perception of how serious the problem is. It cannot be viewed in a vacuum. What is acceptable if the problem is viewed as a $40 billion a year nuisance is quite different than what is acceptable if the magnitude and nature of the problem is perceived to represent a serious threat to our nation's institutions—political, finance, justice, government, education, and law and order, not to mention our families and children.

Today, as yesterday, there is little appreciation of the full nature of the problem and where it is leading us because of the reasons stated in this essay: drug use and costs are grossly underestimated, the top of the narcotics and organized crime pyramid is protected, and no accounting is given to the associated growing corruption and its consequences on government and civic institutions. The problem is additionally difficult because so much information on the principals and their support network has been incorrect.

The situation has become critical—not just in Colombia, Panama, Mexico, Canada, Russia, China, and so forth—but in America as well. The illegal drug chickens hatched over the past five decades might well come home to roost unless effective measures are identified and implemented quickly.

Essay 21, Research and Development Planning Guide for Countering Nontraditional Warfare Threats, describes some possible technology responses and countermeasures to terrorist drug operations. Essay 6, Terrorist Operations in Nontraditional Warfare, and Essay 8, Guerrilla Operations in Nontraditional Warfare, provide additional discussion on the nature of guerrilla warfare and ties to drug trafficking. Also, Essay 17, Models and Simulations for Evaluating Emerging Threats, and Essay 18, Factors and Considerations for Addressing Guerrilla and Counterinsurgency Warfare, discuss some aspects of models and simulations for addressing terrorist/drug-related problems.

IO

LITTORAL OPERATIONS TO PROTECT U.S. SEA FRONTIERS

David L. Bongard

As a nation with long experience in sea-borne commerce and naval activities, it should come as no great surprise that the physical dimensions of U.S. sea frontiers are considerable. The area within recognized territorial waters (out to 12 miles, or 20 km, from shore) covers an area of some 30,000 square miles for the continental United States alone. This increases to at least 50,000 square miles if Alaska, Hawaii, Puerto Rico, and smaller island possessions (Guam, American Samoa, and the U.S. Virgin Islands) are included. Considering the optional 24-mile contiguous limit raises that figure to some 100,000 square miles. This is clearly a large area, and effective control will require not only dedicated resources, but also could be made considerably simpler with some improved technology.

Historically, the security of U.S. sea frontiers has been the responsibility of both the U.S. Navy (USN) and the U.S. Coast Guard (USCG). Originally, the USCG's portion of this responsibility was borne by the Revenue Cutter Service, a part of the Treasury Department. The USCG was formed at the start of the twentieth century by merging the Revenue Cutter Service with the Interior Department's Lifesaving Service. Currently, in peacetime conditions, the USCG is responsible to the Transportation Department, but in time of war or national emergency, control passes to the Department of Defense (DOD). In some peacetime conditions, as in the ongoing efforts at interdicting the flow of illegal drugs into the United States through the Caribbean, local USCG assets and units may pass under operational control of other law enforcement agencies, such as the Federal Bureau of Investigation (FBI) or Bureau of Alcohol, Tobacco, and Firearms (BATF). Alternatively, USCG units may pass under command of local USN headquarters.

General Issues

One primary concern in assessing the vulnerability of U.S. sea frontiers is the long Caribbean "front." This zone is made more vulnerable by the relative proximity of offshore islands, including Cuba, the Bahamas, the Caymans, and others. The length of this frontier, and the proximity of offshore island "bases" for prospective enemies and lawbreakers combine to present significant obstacles to effective control of this frontier area.

Further complicating the situation is the political dimension. The memories of many of America's southern neighbors are long, and they do not generally recall past U.S. policies kindly, especially when those policies ran roughshod over local rights and sovereignty. Moreover, some of the nations around the western and southern rims of the Caribbean, and indeed on the islands in the sea as well, are either not politically stable, or are hostile to the United States and its national interests. The stormy relationship with Cuba is a prime example of this situation, but U.S. policy initiatives in Colombia, Venezuela, and Central America sometimes excite local opposition. Initiatives that are, to American eyes, straightforward matters of law enforcement become entangled in local recollections of past episodes of "gunboat diplomacy" and perceived American imperialism.

Essentially, the issue of controlling traffic and passage across American sea frontiers generally, and especially across the Caribbean-Gulf of Mexico zone, is focused on three major threats as shown in Exhibit 10.1. Clearly, the last

EXHIBIT 10.1   U.S. sea frontier threats.

Situation	Area of origin	Conditions
Drug smuggling	Colombia, Peru, Ecuador, often through Caribbean transshipment points	Substantial law enforcement issue, but little effort toward limiting demand
Illicit immigration	China, Latin America	Growing U.S. economy attractive, but significant humanitarian concerns
Weapons of mass destruction (WMD)	International terrorist organizations, often based in Middle East	Nuclear weapons are bugaboo, but chemical-biological (CBW) more likely threat

category in Exhibit 10.1 poses the greatest security threat to the United States. Traffic in illegal drugs, while a major contributing factor to criminal activity in the United States, could be substantially limited by reducing the market for these drugs within the United States. Legalization of cocaine (which was legal before about 1925) and marijuana would, at one stroke, destroy the massive profitability of drug smuggling. Admittedly, this is a radical step, and may be neither acceptable nor feasible for other reasons.

On the second threat, that of illegal immigration, rising economic prosperity, both among the nations of the Caribbean basin and further afield, will reduce the incentive for people to risk death, expense, and acute hardship for entry into the U.S. labor market and prosperous economy. Likewise, greater flexibility in work permits for Latin Americans may relax the illegal immigration problem. Movement toward a Western Hemisphere Free Trade Area (essentially an expansion of NAFTA into the Caribbean and Latin America), already a major policy goal of the new U.S. administration, will serve to support this development. Possible terrorist strikes against the United States, on the other hand, are unlikely to decrease, especially with the United States retaining its position as the sole global superpower and the world's largest and most dynamic economy. While radiation weapons (including EMP generators) and nuclear weapons are certainly possible terrorist methods, chemical or biological weapons are more likely. These materials are easier to produce, and

SH-3 antisubmarine helicopter on maneuvers with the USS Dwight D. Eisenhower, CVN-69.

especially in the case of biological agents, considerably more compact and easier to move.

In fact, since the September 11, 2001, attacks by terrorists on the World Trade Center and the Pentagon, stepped-up vigilance and patrols by the USN and USCG along the coastal areas of the United States have greatly increased.

Immediate and Short-Term Responses

The most obvious response to this three-fold threat comprises patrol and interdiction by sea-based systems. These systems include long-range, high-endurance cutters, as USCG parlance terms them. These are large vessels, typically displacing 2,000 tons or more, with crews of at least 150 or 200, and usually equipped with a helicopter for search-and-rescue and patrol tasks. In a crisis, USN frigates and destroyers could also fulfill these roles, although with fewer than 100 of such vessels available for worldwide commitments, any significant diversion would put quite a strain on USN resources.

Short-range, smaller craft would also be valuable for this purpose. Such vessels, usually displacing less than 1,000 tons (and often much smaller) are more lightly armed, and have smaller crews. They also rarely have any onboard aerial capacity. However, some of these vessels could be equipped with remotely piloted aerial vehicles (RPVs) for over the horizon (OTH) reconnaissance, and thereby greatly increase their patrol reach for a very modest cost. The main advantages of RPVs are that while they are less versatile than manned aircraft, they are also considerably less expensive to operate, and also much smaller; this last point is an especially important consideration for smaller seagoing vessels.

Such patrol and interdiction activities may be performed by land-based aircraft. Fixed-wing aircraft, such as P-3 Orion maritime reconnaissance aircraft have a long range, and can operate at great distances from their bases. They may also "loiter" in their chosen patrol areas for extended periods, a valuable capability in patrol work. Rotary-wing aircraft, or helicopters, have shorter operational ranges and more limited "loiter" times, but can operate from very small landing fields and from shipboard. Their ability to hover makes them especially useful for conducting close-in, nonintrusive inspections of vessels, as well as for search and rescue work.

The advent of effective tilt-rotor aircraft, such as the now-troubled V-22 Osprey, may serve to combine the advantages of fixed- and rotary-wing aircraft, combining the range and operational envelopes of fixed-wing aircraft with the versatility of helicopters. Second- and third-generation tilt-rotor aircraft would provide a valuable capability for such maritime patrol work, but any acquisition or deployment is at least two decades away, and probably not feasible before 2025.

A further capability involves the employment of lighter-than-air craft, such as blimps and dirigibles. Several private ventures into dirigibles for air transport are currently underway, making use of modern materials technology to increase lift capacity and endurance through the use of composites for both structural framework, and for the gas-bag envelopes. Both dirigibles and blimps can stay aloft for extended periods of time, even for several days. Medium-sized dirigibles, especially those equipped with a handful of RPVs to extend its operational area, would be a powerful patrol and interdiction asset. Such an aircraft would be able to cover large areas at higher rates of speed than any surface vessel, but would be much less expensive to operate, and would have much greater endurance, than any conventional aircraft.

Technological Initiatives and Applications

One technological tool that is as yet little developed, and little employed, for law enforcement operations over a wide area is the potential for real-time data transfer and exchange among units over a wide geographical area. The general success of wireless Internet technology in the commercial sector clearly indicates that real-time, or nearly real-time, data transfers over a wide area are well within current capabilities, and at comparatively modest costs. Some care would need to be taken to safeguard such communications links from "eavesdropping" by criminal or hostile foreign elements, but encryption software should be able to handle most if not all of those requirements.

The USN's new Cyclone-class patrol craft represent one major template for supporting sea frontier operations. While technically sophisticated, and seaworthy with considerable strategic mobility, the Cyclone class is by international standards extremely underarmed, with two 25mm cannons, and two mounts for Stinger SAMs, heavy machineguns, or 40mm automatic grenade launchers. European or Israeli vessels of similar size and, for that matter, the fast attack craft (FAC) predecessors of the Cyclone vessels, designed and built by the British marine engineering firm of Vosper, are much more heavily armed. Most comparably sized vessels carry a 76mm gun, four antiship missiles (Italian Otomat SSMs on the Vosper), and a twin 40mm antiaircraft gun aft. Other weapon options include four to eight antiaircraft missiles, as well as anti-submarine warfare torpedoes and/or rockets. Each such heavily armed craft possesses, at least in raw terms, 4.2 times the combat power of individual Cyclone-class vessels (this ratio comes from a first-blush estimate, with each Cyclone carrying 2x 25mm guns and 2x Mk.19 AGLs, and the Vosper

FAC's armament as given, with values per weapon derived from Col. T. N. Dupuy's QJM-TNDM methodology, 819 to 192). Further, while the Cyclone class has only simple navigation radar, the Vosper FAC has air- and surface-search radars, and radar-directed fire control systems for its guns and missiles. It is worth considering that as a general rule-of-thumb, smaller naval combatants carry considerably more ordnance than larger vessels like frigates and destroyers. This is due to one main consideration, rooted in the basics of naval architecture and marine engineering. Large ships, configured for blue-water operations, need to carry extensive supplies of food, water, fuel, and other supplies, while smaller combatants can rely on shore-based support.

A real-time data exchange system would enable close coordination between the patrol and interdiction efforts of different services and jurisdictions. Ideally, this would limit jurisdictional conflicts and disputes, generally by preventing them from arising in the first place, and enable disparate agencies and services to coordinate their efforts and resources when the need or opportunity arises.

Perhaps more importantly, a system of real-time information exchange would enable a USN patrol aircraft or blimp, or some other sensor platform, to pass on its intelligence. USCG, or state or local police forces could execute any actual search (and seizure, if necessary). Such a fully integrated concept could serve in part to circumvent the serious international legal questions associated with stopping vessels of any flag on the high seas, outside U.S. national waters. The USN would be able to track vessels or aircraft outside U.S. territorial waters, and then pass the information gleaned from such observation to the USCG and other U.S. or state and local law enforcement agencies. This procedure would serve to simultaneously sidestep the thorny legal issues of blockade, and the employment of the U.S. Armed Forces for law enforcement activities.

Another technological tool that is at least potentially available is the employment of remotely controlled sensor platforms. The use of reconnaissance RPVs, based on comparatively small sea vessels, blimps, or dirigibles has already been explored to a limited extent.

Static, floating (or ideally slightly submerged) "reconnaissance buoys" could be deployed along the outer edge of U.S. territorial waters to enhance sea frontier security and effectively extend the reach. Such reconnaissance and observation platforms could also be deployed in international waters without raising major international legal issues. Indeed, the mere presence of such platforms might discourage some illicit activities in some sea areas. In the right environment, especially in areas of comparatively shallow water, such platforms could be anchored to the sea floor, either floating in the depths or actually on the sea bottom.

Another technological tool, as yet unavailable but certainly worthy of some investigation and development, is the concept of very long endurance, very high altitude reconnaissance platforms. Through the use of extremely lightweight materials (i.e., aerogels), it should be possible to construct very light aerial RPVs for surveillance and reconnaissance work. Such platforms would ideally operate only at very high altitudes, at least over 10,700 meters (35,105 feet) and probably over 12,000 meters (39,370 feet), placing them above conventional air traffic. Moreover, at those altitudes they would also be above most weather. The fuel and endurance situation should be solvable by making such aircraft solar powered, utilizing large arrays in the wings. At high altitudes solar arrays would be more efficient, without the attenuation of solar radiation caused by dust and water vapor in the much thicker lower atmosphere. Furthermore, such an electric RPV would have virtually unlimited endurance and would be able to remain aloft for weeks or even months at a time. Indeed, the primary limitation would probably be the mass of batteries required to sustain even a limited operational profile during the hours of darkness.

The advantages offered by such a surveillance platform are considerable, not least their inherent capability to remain on station almost permanently. Tying such platforms into the real-time data network outlined earlier would provide all the involved agencies and services with a valuable "bird's-eye view" over a wide area, on a 24-7 basis, at very little operational cost and for a comparatively modest capital outlay per unit.

International Cooperation

In addition to the paramount need to address issues of interservice and inter-agency rivalries within the United States is the issue of cooperation with the law enforcement regimes of our neighbors, especially Canada and Mexico. This may become crucial. Maritime smuggling from Mexico and Canada has been prevalent for many years. While transporting drugs and untaxed products have been the smugglers' choice in the past, we must now be vigilant against weapons of mass destruction and other clandestine material. When a man entering the United States at Port Angeles, Washington, from Victoria, BC, was discovered to have explosives and raw materials for bomb construction in his pickup truck, this risk was emphasized. These materials could just as easily have been transported by a small boat. Later revelations that the man was part of a terrorist network in Canada associated with the nefarious Saudi Arabian renegade terrorist leader Osama bin Laden only emphasized our nation's vulnerability. Tightening direct entry into the United States and increasing surveillance along the shores and borders will discourage terrorists and other miscreants and evildoers from circumventing the barriers and trying for an "end run."

Growing economic ties with Mexico, and understandable Mexican demands for increased and easier access to American markets, will open another "window" for entry through Mexico. It would be politically more palatable, and probably easier in a logistical sense, to help the Mexicans improve their own immigration and international import controls. The reinforcement of Mexico's sovereignty would be popular, and would also satisfy the general public opinion in Mexico to open entry into the United States while at the same time improve Mexican law enforcement capabilities, and prevent Mexico from becoming a "terrorist highway" into the United States.

Cooperation and coordination with law enforcement agencies in areas such as the Bahamas, and throughout most of Central America as well, will also form a necessary adjunct to any effort to secure U.S. territory and citizens from such foreign dangers. Any activities in those areas will have to be sensitive to local concerns over infringement of sovereignty by the "big brother" to the north, whose past historical record on this score has not been marked by popular appreciation.

Internal and Domestic Cooperation

This dimension of operations encompasses a "gray area" between conventional if irregular military operations, and law enforcement activities. Traditionally, U.S. Armed Services have avoided law enforcement activities except in comparatively rare cases, such as John Brown's seizure of the Arsenal at Harper's Ferry, which stepped over the line into armed rebellion against the United States. While this attitude has spared the Armed Services from involvement in politics and prevented their politicization, it may no longer be possible to maintain as clear a separation between law enforcement and national security as existed in previous eras. Certainly, the founding fathers, or at least James Madison and the authors of the Constitution and the Bill of Rights, foresaw that the Armed Forces could be called upon for a range of situations that properly constituted law enforcement. The entire episode of the "Whiskey Rebellion" of 1798, where the federal government was compelled to call on unreliable state militia forces to help the tiny U.S. Army enforce its excise taxes on bottled liquor in the backwoods of Pennsylvania, illustrates that point.

Certainly, successful operations in this dimension will require careful consideration of issues of legal jurisdiction and constitutionality. However, the potential for serious threats to the lives and property of U.S. citizens and residents within the territory of the United States requires coordination among the several services, USN, Marines, USCG, and Army, that has not been required in the past.

The Armed Services collectively will also have to cooperate with a number of federal law enforcement agencies, including but not limited to the FBI, the Immigration and Naturalization Service (INS) Treasury agents, U.S. Marshals, and the Bureau of Alcohol, Tobacco, and Firearms (BATF). It will be impossible to manage effective control of the sea frontiers of the United States without a sustained and major attitude of cooperation and collegiality among the interested parties, not only at senior leadership levels, but also among the agents, officers, soldiers, seapersonnel, and airpersonnel in the field.

One likely avenue to help achieve such objectives would be the creation of "joint civil commands" for responsibilities associated with surveillance of traffic approaching and entering U.S. territorial waters and airspace. Such joint civil commands would have to include representation from all interested and responsible agencies and bureaus, and everybody involved would have to be conscious of, and sensitive to, the concerns of civilian and military, and federal and local, goals, intentions, and policies.

11

RAPID RESPONSE TASK FORCES FOR NONTRADITIONAL WARFARE OPERATIONS

William R. Schilling

New concepts are under consideration by the Department of Defense and the U.S. Army for improving our capability to deploy effective ground task forces under the severe constraints posed by allowable response times and transportability. In general, this need for a rapid response task force (RTF) translates into the deployment of a brigade or regimental-sized echelon within a few days. This RTF will likely be transported by ship using prepositioned sea-based supplies and equipment or by air transport systems.

Fast response task forces are necessary to achieve certain limited military and political objectives. Possible missions for an RTF include the following:

1. Demonstrate willingness to defend and protect regional or vital national interests (e.g., Bosnia and Kuwait)

2. Prevent overpowering of friendly nations from internal or external aggressive actions

3. Maintain distance separation between aggressor and friendly forces to improve opportunities for targeting enemy units and using long-range standoff weapons

4. Achieve delays in aggressor advances and provide holding operations to gain time for introducing larger, more survivable ground units

5. Support peacekeeping operations as part of allied forces

6. Provide homeland defense against terrorist operations and civil unrest using National Guard and Reserves

C-130H tactical transport.

Based on airlift capability, downsizing of combat and combat support vehicles to gross weights below 25 or 30 tons is necessary to meet the response time demands and to reduce the sustainability levels associated with larger size forces and combat vehicles. However, this vehicle and force downsizing can reduce survivability, target acquisition, and standoff engagement range capability. New technology applications may alleviate some of these weapon system shortcomings. Nevertheless, heavier vehicles represented by the Abrams Main Battle Tank (69 tons), the Bradley Armored Personnel Carrier (25 tons), and the Paladin Self-Propelled Artillery System (31 tons) will definitely still be required. These heavier vehicles will provide stability and combat superiority in certain regions of the world (e.g., NATO, South Korea, and the Middle East) thereby precluding challenges from well-armed countries organized to fight in structured force engagements.

Task Force Operational Concepts

Like most ground force operations, the rapid RTF capability and mission success will be governed by the firepower, survivability, and mobility of the fighting combat vehicles. Thus, the RTF will need to avoid situations of overmatching (e.g., meeting or attacking engagements against today's sophisticated

Blackhawk helicopters transporting M-274 light utility truck.

armored units). The RTF can be tailored with other units (i.e., airborne brigade and Marine expeditionary forces) to provide a rapid and formidable presence to confront enemy actions. In addition, the RTF must be compatible with other available allied fighting units to permit communications, joint operations, and integration of assets to maximize effectiveness.

Due to expected operating conditions, the RTF will need to utilize cover, concealment, and terrain to reduce threats from large antitank weapons and direct fires. These forces will also need protection (shielding) against nuclear, chemical, and biological weapons as well as a capability to operate in mine infested regions. They will need to operate in all weather, visibility, and terrain conditions; have good off-road mobility; and survive small arms engagements, direct fires from grenade launchers, and near hits or indirect fires from mortars and artillery.

For the most part, these forces will best be suited for defensive operations. However, some limited offensive capability can accrue from advanced technology insertions to increase survivability by (1) active armor, composite materials, and shielding; (2) advanced communications devices, computers, and target acquisition systems; (3) long-range guided projectiles plus brilliant munitions; and (4) mobility to reduce susceptibility to enemy guns. Standoff long-range guided/terminal homing missiles can reduce enemy capabilities to close with the RTF.

Task Force Characteristics

While the emphasis in this essay is centered on the nature of a fast RTF for early battle entry by the U.S. Army, it is recognized that a Marine expeditionary brigade and our Army Airborne Brigade could also be available. This combined joint force will contribute to the capability to match or repel high echelon forces, perhaps as large as two light enemy divisions. But this essay focuses on the characteristics and capabilities for possible main line elements of just the RTF.

Exhibit 11.1 postulates possible main components of a near-term RTF and indicates some future supplementary components that could be substituted for or added to the task force. Characteristics are described in terms of the principal vehicle/platform, the weight, main armament, and some relevant comments. For the RTF, the key driving factors or concerns are weight (transportability), armament (killing potential), mobility (deployability), and protection (survivability). So the future potential additions are directed toward providing an improved, lighter, direct-fire system as well as lighter personnel carriers, self-propelled howitzers and missile launchers, plus a new helicopter to improve armed rescue missions.

Task Force Capabilities

At the current time, the major deficiencies in capability to provide an early RTF evolve from the heavy weights of the U.S. Army main battle tank (Abrams) and self-propelled artillery (Paladin). Much of this heavy weight stems from requirements to survive highly accurate direct and indirect fires and to retain superior off-road mobility. These heavy elements make it nearly mandatory to employ ship transport from prepositioned stations, except where fully capable combat forces are already deployed (Europe and South Korea). In order to move by air wing echelons using C-17 and C-5 aircraft, the vehicle/platform weights need to be less than 30 tons.

An overview of near-term and future RTF capabilities is portrayed in Exhibit 11.2. By substituting an upgraded light assault vehicle (LAV) or armored protection gun system for the main battle tank, a greatly improved capability to employ an RTF by air can be quickly achieved in a few years. However, survivability and mobility in offensive operations may be greatly reduced. A future RTF could be operationally deployed by air in about 3 or 4 days. Strengths and weaknesses for near-term and future RTF operations are also noted in Exhibit 11.2. The future RTF combat units could assist the National Guard and Reserves in responding to terrorist incidents by the use of protected wheeled vehicles with nonlethal or lethal munitions.

EXHIBIT 11.1 Rapid response task force (RTF) characteristics.

	Key components	Notional type vehicle/platform	Weight (tons)	Armament (main)	Comments
Near term posssible RTF	Direct fire vehicle (DFV)	Upgraded light assault vehicle (LAV-25)	20–22	25 mm chain gun, TOW II	Need larger engine and armored blankets, etc., early battle entry vehicle
	Armored personnel carrier (APC)	Bradley (M2A2/A3)	25	25 mm chain gun, TOW II	Highly survivable to small arms and RPGs
	Self-propelled howitzer	Paladin (M109A6)	31	155 mm gun SADARM munitions	Highly survivable from indirect fires, 24–30 km range
	Light towed howitzer	M101A1	2.5	105 mm gun	Vulnerable to counter-fires, 11 km range, early battle entry vehicle
	Missile launcher	Multiple launcher rocket (MLRS)	26	Rocket pod, SADARM munitions, ATACM/BAT	Submissiles up to 40 km range, terminal homing missiles beyond 100 km
	Short range air defense (SHORAD) system	Avenger (M1097)	5	Stinger missiles, 12.7 mm machine gun	4.5 km slant range, supplemented with MANPADS
	Truck/utility vehicle	High mobility multi-purpose wheeled vehicle (HMMWV)	4–5	Small arms	Combat support tasks
	Close air support system	Apache (AH-64)	8	Hellfire missiles, 30 mm chain gun, folding fin rockets	Longbow radar for target acquisition and weapon guidance
Future potential RTF	Direct fire vehicle (DFV)	Fighting combat vehicle (FCV)	20–30	TOW follow-on, F&F missile or 120 mm gun	Well-protected, highly mobile, rapid target acquisition system
	Armored personnel carrier (APC)	Advanced combat vehicle (ACV)	8–10	TOW follow-on, F&F missile, 25 mm chain gun	Survivable to small arms and RPGs, external C³1 to avoid overmatching, highly mobile vehicle
	Self-propelled howitzer	Advanced combat vehicle (ACV)	10–12	105 mm gun, separate ammo supply vehicle	Survivable from indirect counterfires with RAP rounds for coverage to 18 km
	Missile launcher	High mobility artillery/rocket system (HIMARS)	6	Rocket pod or ATACMS/BAT	Wheeled fire support system, reach ranges beyond 100 km
	Armed reconnaissance support system	Comanche (RAH 66)	6	Internal carried Hellfire or Stinger missile	Stealthy high speed helicopter

Exhibit Acronyms:
ATACM—army tactical missile system
BAT—brilliant antiarmor submunition
F&F—fire and forget
MANPADS—man-portable air defense system
RPG—rocket-propelled grenades
SADARM—sense and destroy armor
TOW—tube-launched, optically guided, wire-guided missile

117

EXHIBIT 11.2   Rapid response task force (RTF) capabilities.

Factors	Near-term possible RTF	Future potential RTF
Force dimensions (approximate)		
• Number of personnel	6,000–9,000	5,000–7,000
• Weight of force	7,000-10,000 tons	5,000–8,000 tons
Force transportability (estimates)		
• Airlift wing (C-17 and C-5 aircraft)	115–165 sorties/5–7 days	80–135 sorties/4–6 days
• Sea transport (with 3 days for ground deployment)	4 days (500 sea miles) 10 days (4,000 sea miles)	3 days (500 sea miles) 8 days (4,000 sea miles)
Force sustainability (estimates)		
• Resupply levels	700–800 tons per day	500–600 tons per day
• Airlift sorties (C-17 and C-5)	15 sorties	11 sorties per day
Force vulnerability (lowest level threats)	Mines, RPGs, artillery fragments	Mines, HEAT missiles, top attack systems
RTF mission strengths	• Excellent indirect fire capabilities with Paladin and MLRS • Good mobility • Good point air defense systems • Good defense capability	• Good direct fire antitank capability • Improved recce capability • Reductions in manpower, material, and logistics support • Improved target acquisition, intelligence, and force control • Longer staying power prior to reinforcements
RTF mission weaknesses	• Limited direct fire capability • Reliance on standoff systems against heavy armor attacks • Area air defense coverage only from Air Force and Naval aircraft • Poor offensive capability • Reduced performance in heavy vegetation	• Weight reductions decrease indirect fire capability (smaller caliber weapons) • Main area air defense from Air Force and Naval air systems • Reliance on standoff systems to repel heavy armor attacks • Mines hamper mobility/offensive actions

Exhibit Acronyms:
  HEAT—High explosive antitank (a shaped-charge chemical-energy warhead)
  RPG—Rocket-propelled grenade
Note: Some information in Exhibit 11.2 derived from Rand report "Ground Forces for a Rapidly Employable Joint Task Force"
  (ISBN: 0-8330-2797-2)

Task Force Viability

Allies and other friendly nations will likely be hesitant to introduce new light- or medium-weight modernized fighting vehicles due to the cost and timing implications. So the United States must develop concepts to coordinate and integrate the use of forces with different capabilities, weapons, and communications systems.

The task force will need to depend upon the U.S. Air Force and Navy air superiority to provide protection from air strikes as the Patriot or other area defenses may be too heavy for early battlefield entry. Of course local air defense can be achieved with short-range point missile and gun defense systems. The digitized battlefield concept along with satellite and unattended airborne and ground sensors will provide necessary intelligence and indicators of enemy intentions and strength. Nevertheless, RTF operations in areas surrounded by heavy vegetation will greatly hamper intelligence gathering, reduce the effectiveness of long-range fires, and limit the availability of a venue (windows) for firing direct weapons.

In short, the rapid RTF will be capable of performing the missions described earlier for a limited time, perhaps as long as several weeks with air and logistics support, against enemy threats that do not exceed an augmented division sized force. But attrition will surely occur and must be expected.

Measure of Effectiveness

Missions involving rapid RTF should not be evaluated in terms of traditional measures of effectiveness (forward edge of battle movement and attrition rates). Instead, other measures such as mission capability, area coverage and control, recovery/replacement time, and protection factors should be considered as better indicators of combat value and utility.

SECTION III

EMERGENCY MANAGEMENT IN HOSTILE ENVIRONMENTS

A great deal of ink has been spilled in the last decade about the impact of truly portable computers and information technology on military operations and national security. It is not yet possible to draw definite conclusions on these points; however, it may be possible to begin to reach some determinations. It is not accurate to deal with these issues as strictly matters of warfare, although it is accurate to refer to them in terms of national security.

A recent simulation of a biological attack against the continental United States, undertaken in spring 2001, revealed that it was impossible to determine whether an attack was actually taking place until most of the time for the exercise had elapsed. Basically, there was too great a chance for "naturally occurring" outbreaks of disease to be certain an attack was in progress. Information warfare imposes the same hazards in determining whether an attack is actually taking place. In addition, the nature of the target of the attack must be identified. Is the attacker just "fooling around," or is this a serious threat to national security or infrastructure?

Information warfare has attracted a great deal of attention in the media. Issues of information and computer security deserve serious attention, both in terms of criminal activity and actual national security. Much of the emerging technology has been directed toward denying access to information through the use of firewalls, encryption, and passwords. Additional research is needed on detecting unwanted intrusions and tracking the perpetrators.

Of particular concern is the lack of oversight within the information technology (IT) community. There is no reliable threat response that can encompass both Government and industry. Every Government agency and commercial activity in the United States is dependent on information that is stored electronically. Disruption or corruption of these information sources will cause great personal and financial hardship. Information management tools are needed to protect and defend IT resources.

In responding to any attack or incident, information plays a key role. Determining available resources, directing those resources, and controlling collateral damage are key elements in responding to emergency situations.

Centralizing and integrating resource databases, providing overall direction to responses, and guiding R&D initiatives are critical elements in national policy. While the Federal Emergency Management Agency (FEMA) is responsible for controlling and directing the response to an emergency incident, there is no current provision or oversight of any proactive responses.

The following series of essays explore the need for a proactive initiative to establish a national emergency response center with prepared responses and information integration with other agencies to prepare and even prevent emergency situations from developing. This section covers information technology, enterprise management, emergency response management at/in the national operations center, along with information integration and process applications for emergency management operations centers.

12

INFORMATION TECHNOLOGY APPLICATIONS TO COUNTER NONTRADITIONAL WARFARE THREATS

Michael D. McDonnell

The Information Need

The United States and other industrialized nations of the world are currently vulnerable to a host of threats from many sources worldwide and for many reasons. These potential threats certainly include the usual nightmares of terrorist assassinations, random shootings, and conventional bombings but now extend to more extreme nuclear and overt or covert chemical and/or biological attacks. In fact, there have already been attempts or actual attacks with these characteristics here and abroad, including the following:

- *Attacking water/power supplies of major American cities.* A 1987 Federal Grand Jury indicted 14 white supremacists in Mountain Home, AK, accused of stockpiling 30 gallons of cyanide to poison water supplies in Washington, D.C., and Chicago. Attacks on power grids to disrupt electrical service to large population areas were conducted by a Black Muslim sect in Colorado.

- *Contaminating food or medical supplies.* Palestinian terrorists poisoned Israeli oranges with mercury in 1979. Followers of the Bagwhan Shre Rajneesh attempted to poison restaurant food in Oregon with salmonella to influence an election in 1984. Tamil guerillas claimed to have poisoned Sri Lanka tea shipments in 1986. An extortionist poisoned stocks of Tylenol pain relief medication in 1987, causing a nationwide recall. Chilean terrorists claimed to have poisoned exported grapes in 1988.

- *Dispersing poisonous chemicals in public areas or heating, ventilation, and air conditioning (HV/AC) systems.* A white supremacist "skinhead" group, the "Confederate Hammer Skins," planned to place cyanide in the HV/AC system of a Dallas Synagogue. The Japanese cult, Aum Shinriko, instituted repeated germ attacks in Tokyo in the 1960s; targeted the Japanese Legislature, the Imperial Palace, and the U.S. Naval Base at Yokosuka; and released sarin nerve gas into the Tokyo subway in 1995 killing 12 and injuring 5,500 (*New York Times,* May 26, 1998).

- *Indiscriminate, simultaneous bombings of crowded cities.* During February and March of 1993, Muslim terrorists allegedly instituted a campaign of 13 car and truck bombs in Bombay in revenge for destruction of an Islamic shrine. More than 400 were killed and over 1,000 injured.

- *Explosive attacks against religious shrines.* In 1984, two fanatic Israeli Jewish groups plotted to blow up the Dome of the Rock, an Islamic shrine.

Such threats do not have to actually cause casualties or even be carried out to have an impact. The mere threat of contaminated food, water, or medicine has increased costs to U.S. producers in the last two decades, estimated by some as in excess of $2 billion from destroyed products alone. There is no way to estimate lost sales due to erosion of consumer confidence. A letter purported to contain anthrax was received in a Phoenix office and an eight-block stretch of a major street was closed because ". . . in this situation we have to be pessimistic and go the whole route in our treatment of it and in our investigation" (*Reuters,* March 10, 1998). Again, the cost in lost productivity and law enforcement expenses might be calculable but the overall terrorist effect on the civilian population is not.

In the computer age, such threats have also extended to hackers attacking any and all computer systems and networks (including those sustaining the provision of basic services such as telephones, air traffic, water supplies, etc.). Examples include a series of viruses introduced over the past several years to destroy or modify software programs in Government and commercial institutions throughout the world.

Finally, such threats must include drug cartels which, in the international scope of their reach, ultimately undermine international relations and confidence in governments by crippling the economies, law enforcement organizations, mental and physical health support resources, and even lives of their citizens. The targets under threat of these potential attacks directly or indirectly include the Department of Defense, nondefense federal agencies, state and local governments, as well as the private sector through the national and international economies.

Fortunately, in the last few years security activity to identify and protect against these threats has become a high profile priority, resulting in the establishment of many programs and systems to gather and disseminate information on these threats. Unfortunately, because these threats are so wide-ranging and the targets so widespread, the systems currently developed are designed to protect only against specific threats on specific targets. A systematic, high level approach is needed to develop, coordinate, and integrate threat information across the various sectors of the United States and international community.

Part of the solution would be to plan for and develop both a system for identifying, organizing, and coordinating government and private databases and systems (federal, state, and local governments, open source publications, etc.) and a set of analytical methodologies and tools to use the resulting integrated database to do analyses and projections from the data. In short, the rapidly expanding capabilities of the world of information technology should now be brought to bear as a weapon against the terrorist threat.

The Information Management Plan

The "First Annual Report to the President and the Congress of the Advisory Panel to Assess Domestic Response Capabilities for Terrorism Involving Weapons of Mass Destruction" (15 December 1999) concluded that

> . . . much more needs to be and can be done to obtain and share information on potential terrorist threats at all levels of government, to provide more effective deterrence, prevention, interdiction, or response, using modern information technology.

Essentially, what is needed is a plan for integration of all efforts against this strategic (at least in the sense of being international) problem, initially starting out as a database creation project. The concept would be to establish a major virtual data warehouse with interactive links to all major databases and with a specialized search engine and tools to support data analysis, trend prediction, threat profiling, and decision making.

A detailed plan for developing, operating, and managing the data warehouse would be required. The plan would have to address questions such as the following:

- What data should be included in the database?
- How and when should the data be collected?

- How should the data be standardized?
- How should the data be classified?
- Who gets access and when?
- How should security be provided?
- How will freedom of information be addressed?

The virtual data warehouse would be designed to store and retrieve data efficiently and in a user-friendly mode and would include artificial intelligence (AI) tools to support data queries and decision making. Search engines would need to be surveyed and the most appropriate chosen for development as data retrieval tools. Data warehouses typically are built to contain enterprise-wide information collected from multiple operational sources. This virtual data warehouse would be magnitudes larger in scope and function than current databases. The data warehouse would be used by all levels of government and business/industry to examine threat problems, or possible threat problems, using data mining techniques and decision support tools across all relevant databases.

Some of the challenges for the data warehouse designer include determining the following:

- How to identify sources of threat information
- How to collect, maintain, and update the information
- How to standardize the data
- How to access the data
- How to analyze the data

The Analysis and Evaluation Process

Once the data warehouse has been created, the usefulness of the system would depend on how easily, quickly, and accurately it can access the desired data. Technologies such as the Internet and intranets, along with search engines, data mining systems, and AI tools would be employed to insure all users can get the information they need when they need it.

Middleware tools can be used to map and organize databases existing at supporting federal, state, and local sites into the proposed data warehouse. Such middleware tools can also provide current database users with graphic user interface (GUI) options to include existing federal, state, and local operations. Thus, users would not necessarily have to acquire new hardware or learn new interface techniques to access data.

Search engines and data mining techniques should also be examined for supporting AI tools to allow easy data analysis and integration. Such tools as Boolean Algebra key word searches can be employed to search data for trends across all source data. Preliminary tools should be developed in such a fashion that users who are familiar with the data retrieval search engines can easily learn to use the AI tools and form questions for the data warehouse. Questions posed to the database could identify areas where specific research might bear fruitful results. Such questions could be posed to the database to allow the following capabilities:

- Evaluation of excursions in efficiencies of law enforcement and NTW defense/deterrence efforts (i.e., increases/improvements in air/rail/bus terminal security, improved response times of law officers, improved effectiveness of SWAT teams, improved HAZMAT procedures and environmental cleanup)

- Evaluation of the efficiency of protective measures (i.e., shields and helmets for riot control missions, application of nonlethal munitions, Kevlar garments or body armor)

- Evaluation of extrapolations of specific NTW activities (terrorist attack rates, terrorist target types, computer hackings, CBW events, etc.)

- Identification of geographic and demographic trends (i.e., concentrations of incidents by geographic location, population density, socio/ethnic/religious/industrial target types)

- Improved psychological profiling of terrorists based on weapon of choice, target of choice, method of operation (MO), and other factors

- Improved information for undercover operations as to how indicators should be prioritized for investigation to develop a critical mass of incriminating evidence as soon as possible, to protect undercover operatives, and to time the initiation of forceful preemptive actions

- Monitoring purchases of uncontrolled chemicals and hardware necessary for creating terrorist conventional weapons and weapons of mass destruction

- Improved terrorist threat awareness for private sector security companies and security forces in industry

- Improvements in courses for law enforcement, private security forces, and "first response" teams

- Updating security awareness courses and improving distance learning

While some such approaches may seem Draconian, proper profiling and improved evaluation of suspected terrorist activities might have prevented the more publicized incidents in Waco, Philadelphia, and Ruby Ridge, not to mention numerous, less well-publicized incidents of BATF activities against individuals. Such evaluations would not, as envisioned, support decisions as to whether actions should be taken. Such decisions would be up to the law enforcement organizations involved. But such evaluations could be used to plan the reaction of the law enforcement organization so that response is strong enough to accomplish goals yet conservative enough to minimize not only collateral damage but also a posteriori charges of police overreaction and brutality.

Furthermore, such aides to the prediction, especially, of terrorist activities are sorely needed, not only to improve law enforcement but also to improve the public's perception of the law enforcers. Even those members of the citizenry who are not technically astute will lose trust in their law enforcement agencies, and, ultimately, in their government's planning and ability to deter threats and defend the people if future terrorist incidents are not resolved with the assistance of generally perceived improvements in IT utilization ("If we can put a man on the moon . . .").

Information as a Force for Deterrence

The knowledge among terrorists that sophisticated IT resources are arrayed against them, while not necessarily deterring all terrorists, especially dedicated fanatics, would complicate their planning and restrict their preparations in both scope and time. Terrorist actions would be complicated by the concern that obtaining the necessary hardware in "desirable" quantities would increase the likelihood of being detected. Timing of terrorist actions would be complicated by having to draw out the acquisition of necessary hardware, thus increasing the chances of detection.

Thus, some of the capabilities of the data warehouse should be made open knowledge. On the other hand, covert population of the database with inputs from classified sources would be kept from publication, not only to protect the classified sources but also to prevent the development of effective terrorist counterstrategies.

Data Warehouse Characteristics

It is quite likely that, given advances in the technologies and tools required, the actual data warehouse and supporting software could be established without any significant investment in physical plant. Furthermore, while source sensitive data should be restricted to approved users and real-time filters could monitor private and/or public access to sensitive but unclassified (SBU) or large volumes of data, the data warehouse should be generally accessible for remote data processing through the Internet. This would even reduce the hardware investment required to establish this important tool in the arsenal against terrorists.

The data warehouse should be designed using previous and current experience of existing, similar data warehouses such as the DOD Information and Analysis Centers (IACs). Data on initial, operating, and life-cycle costs can be generated from such IACs and a simple, generic cost model can be developed to estimate costs for the proposed data warehouse.

13

ENTERPRISE MANAGEMENT APPLICATIONS TO NONTRADITIONAL WARFARE THREATS

Lynne M. Schneider

The very freedoms on which America is based are being exploited to deliver terrorism to our shores. America is only starting to comprehend and understand what the terrorist threat really means and what preparations are necessary to respond, warn, and protect our citizens.

Until the bombing of the Alfred P. Murrah Building in Oklahoma City, emergency management at the federal level had focused primarily on responses to natural disasters caused by environmental abnormalities or extreme weather conditions. Most of the models and preparedness activities that have been developed to date have really looked at activities that happen in a geographic area or industrial plant or food type and with a specific exposure in terms of time. The methods are conventional in nature and do not take into account the existing technology derived management tools, knowledge base, or innovation strategies.

There are many types of nontraditional warfare threats. We have seen examples of biological terrorism with anthrax spores being sent through the U.S. postal system and suicidal pilots using commercial aircraft as guided missiles. In this essay, two types of approaches or processes are described to show how enterprise management integration and process modeling can assist in planning, modeling, and applying tools used to assess NTW threat-based activities and in supporting response training exercises. A major difference in this essay as compared to others dealing with emergency responses is the emphasis on enterprise management integration.

Whatever the nontraditional threat may be, emergency management response actions are essentially a series of processes, activities, and functions linking policies, data, information, and knowledge to achieve a particular outcome. The integration of these elements is the subject of this essay. In order to have a comprehensive understanding of the activities, issues, and solutions at hand, an enterprise-wide view is critical.

Emergency management (EM) involves a series of processes serving as triggering events for next steps in the response. Most processes can be modeled primarily as either functional or event-driven processes. Essay 15, Information Integration and Process Applications for Emergency Management Operations Centers, discusses process modeling in detail and provides some examples of functional and event-driven operations.

The following sections of this essay address enterprise management integration (EMI) in terms of these considerations:

1. Concepts and characteristics of EMI
2. Managing the enterprise process
3. Integration of the enterprise elements
4. Prognosis and initiatives for EMI

Concepts and Characteristics of EMI

To begin with, an enterprise is generally taken to be any complete operation that encompasses a group of activities in support of a product, service, or mission. In short, an enterprise consists of all the elements necessary to achieve the goals of an operation. Recently, information technology in the form of computer software and hardware along with valid databases has been utilized to automate many aspects of enterprise management. In these situations, emphasis has been placed upon the transmission and utilization of information to expedite and control the enterprise output.

EMI consists of the management of the elements that enable and maintain the enterprise as a means to ensure and enhance the integrity of the operation or endeavor. Information technology has emerged as the enabler to allow the elimination of many aspects of the manual tasks in the management process. Through the adaptation of the EMI approach, a number of benefits accrue to include the reduction of operating times, cost containment, constant awareness of the status, and productivity of assets, plus record keeping and performance of critical items.

With regard to emergency management, a new philosophy and integrated approach needs to be undertaken. This approach must *integrate the enterprise process, people, time, organization, and element interfaces.*

In order to implement an EMI concept for emergency management operations (the enterprise), the characteristics of each element in the operation must be addressed to treat the interrelation or relationships between people, missions, resources, and Government constraints. Then, measures like time, cost, and productivity/efficiency must be used to evaluate the concepts and strategies consistent with the emergency management needs and threats. Integrating all these facets, dimensions, and aspects of the problem is the essence of the EMI concepts. The next two sections of this essay address the details of the management process and enterprise integration.

Managing the Enterprise Process

For this discussion of enterprise management, emphasis is placed on the characteristics and implications of two types of processes applied to the needs of emergency management evaluation and response.

The first is referred to as a *functional process*. Functional processes are usually initiated by a single event such as a tornado, terrorist bomb, or building fire which generates the need for a task to be performed. The initiating event is constrained in time and place and its effects can usually be contained by prompt action of the response team or unit.

The second kind of process is referred to as an event-driven process. Event-driven processes are usually occurrences which evolve over time with a series of events, beyond the control of the emergency manager. These processes involve some sequence that is largely unpredictable. Event-driven processes would include such things as a terrorist hostage situation or a forest fire. The event sequence may be guided by some human intelligence, as in the terrorist case, or may be the result of random or semi-random factors such as wind, terrain, forest floor tinder, and so on. The main point is that "events" occur which are not readily predictable or within any control of the EM personnel.

The organization responding to the event-driven processes is not, however, completely at the mercy of the entity initiating them. Experience allows the responding organization to prepare alternative courses of action and institute them as the events outside their control evolve. What is needed for this kind of flexible response is an information technology capability that stores preplanned alternative courses of action and responses, then retrieves them as the events develop. In some cases, with the aid of artificial intelligence tools, the responding organization can even position themselves ahead of the event drivers. In such cases, the responding organization can predict the probable course of events and develop, and even implement, actions that nullify or at least seriously ameliorate, the course of events.

An example of a functional process could be an explosion in a metropolitan area with possible linkage to a terrorist group that might have placed other chemical or biological agents in the area. This type of management process might involve units created to respond to emergencies requiring search, rescue, medical, law enforcement, and fire department actions. The second example could be for a terrorist-driven event involving the taking of hostages in the waiting area of an international airport.

Such process models can also be generated for other emergency situations. Their first level is the simple laying out of the process elements. Usually this pictorial display is in itself instructive since the response personnel can see, at a glance, what process elements are necessary and which are redundant, superfluous, or followed in an order which is counterproductive.

At the second level, the computer tool, based on a commercial off-the-shelf (COTS) program can track performance measures (PMs) such as time or cost, and accumulate or aggregate them to give overall times to accomplish individual functional processes or the entire process.

At the third level, the models can easily be modified to replace process elements with new elements. This allows desktop planning and testing of other functional process elements developed by others with more experience in such EM problems.

Lastly, the models can be utilized for training, exercises, and "what if" scenarios. Necessary changes derived from these activities could lead to improvements in the process element descriptions.

As long as the functional and event-driven processes are understood and the IT software is in place, such equipment can be used for any management purpose. Although its primary responsibility is EM, the capability of the software to incorporate the results of training will permit the mission record of the EM to be recovered and used as required.

A broad discussion of managing emergency responses is presented in Essay 14, Emergency Response Management at the National Operations Centers. Essay 14 describes in more detail the management and analysis models and the characteristics of possible emergency management operations centers.

Integration of the Enterprise Elements

How do we fundamentally and effectively manage such a process that is rooted in tradition in order to transfer and leverage the knowledge? A new philosophy and integrated approach needs to be taken—an approach that integrates the processes, people, time, organization, and push/pull (interface) aspects.

How does one really integrate the EM response capability, rapidly, accurately, precisely with all of the different viewpoints, responsibilities, variable solutions, and responses? How does one sort the layers of complexity? Factors to consider in developing this integrating concept include the following:

- *Process.* A concurrent process with numerous feedback loops, not a linear process
- *People.* A continuous process of human interactions, not discrete deliverables
- *Time.* A real-time process that occurs at the source, not a sequential process from A to Z
- *Organization.* A networked, interdependent collaboration
- *Push/pull.* A complimentary push/pull process of mediating and interfacing with military and civilian capabilities to match needs, not a push phenomenon of directions emanating from a control

Integration, interdisciplinary cooperation, and innovation will be the basis for the new EMI models of the twenty-first century. These models for the future will be based on the concept of holonic enterprises.

Arthur Koestler first created the word *holon* in his book *The Ghost in the Machine* written in 1967. Briefly, a holon is the operation of systems within systems or processes within processes.

A *holonic network* is a set of companies or organizations that act together and organically, constantly reconfigured to manage each presented situation. Each holon in the network provides a different process capability and contributes to the outcome. Each node in the holon understands and contributes to the core processes and core competencies of the holonic enterprise, in this case, EM.

As more and more of private industry and governments at all levels begin to outsource support and management functions and activities, the issues and complexities of managing a business will become even more critical. Developing a holistic enterprise view with performance and cost indicators will be challenging but possible. Each of the nodes in a holon that contributes to core processes and their outcome is able to continually improve and change to meet the new or changing measures of performance.

In a holonic network, the organizations must develop a new level of trust. This implies developing a capability to operate without rigidly defined hierarchies and predetermined times. Large and small entities are equal, and no one gets a free ride because of size or reputation. Within the holonic network, any entity, large or small, can exploit its core competencies by linking them with complementary core competencies of others. This occurs in virtual companies. The virtual company creates the best core business process possible and manages the critical path in real time.

The advantages of the holonic approach for EMI are as follows:

- *Leverage.* True synergy achieved by combining the best capabilities of many operations
- *Speed.* Decision making streamlined and rapid
- *Flexibility.* Ability and agility to change the service, product capabilities, or companies within and external to the holonic enterprise
- *Shared risk.* Several nodes form a holonic network and a shared risk and reward plus a reduction in fear of revisions as each holon is confident in capabilities and will change for the good of the whole

For this brief introduction, several types of holonic networks or arrangements are listed next:

- Vertical
- Horizontal
- Regional
- Out of necessity
- Self-promoted

Each of the networks are configured to maximize particular benefits or specialties derived from the characteristics of the enterprise, the organizational stength of the process sequence, and the existing resource constituents.

In 1993, when Paul Allaire was CEO of Xerox Corporation, he said:

My view of speed is that it is clearly the source of competitive advantage and along with knowledge, is probably one of the key sources of competitive advantage for our industry for the future. What it means is you have to change all of your management processes—make them simpler, more customer focused, less bureaucratic and less centralized. And have a process whereby the people closest to the action can make the decisions and implement those decisions quickly.

Prognosis and Initiatives for EMI

In the holonic enterprise, computers support information processes for the core processes. The purpose of the computer in holonic networks is for immediate distribution of data. Information management allows for data to be organized to support processes, and knowledge management is really linking the information to form a knowledge network.

Knowledge networks have many characteristics that distinguish themselves from traditional systems networks. They can be used to obtain knowledge rather than simply supply information or data. They contain data from many sources external to the organization, and they are maintained by systems and people who capture and structure information for later operational application.

An enterprise model is such an integrating framework that can be applied at any level to facilitate integration, cooperation, responsibilities, and adaptation within the enterprise. Further, it is a coherent management strategy for the future that balances the competing priorities of the enterprise while optimizing support to the EM situation. The value of the enterprise model lies in the ability to understand the relational value of the components to each other and how the interdependencies must interact if the enterprise is to be able to truly respond with flexibility and timeliness.

The enterprise model is a dynamic framework. It allows for integration of views, which cut across multiple organizations, and links vision, strategies, requirements, and resources to the execution of both business and response operations. The architecture is designed to optimize utilization of resources—financial, human, and technical.

The benefits of enterprise management derived from integration of elements and the accompanying complexity lead to the requirements for a framework to guide the construction or linking of systems or holons that produce timely and efficient management of resources, especially for emergency responses.

The great challenges to the implementation of EMI for emergency response operations are threefold. First, the governmental organizations involved in EM extend over a large number of agencies where no single group has the overall responsibility for linking or integrating the functional areas or nodes (security, recovery and response, health and medical support, terrorist investigations and databases, environmental conditions, fire control, transportation, etc.). Second, the scarcity of knowledge about the characteristics and value of EMI or information technology operations within the participating organizations is pervasive and leads to concerns about job security and responsibilities. The third challenge revolves about the need to commit resources for the development of EMI and the need to demonstrate software feasibility for program automation.

Finally, the development of the EMI program requires the integration of a number of disparate items (the communications and information and decision flow, the people in the endeavor, the time to implement, the organizational structures, the interface between participants, and the governing constraints on responses). Validation and verification of the processes, software, and hardware must be accomplished prior to acceptance and certification of such an elaborate but important program.

14

EMERGENCY RESPONSE MANAGEMENT AT THE NATIONAL OPERATIONS CENTERS

Michael D. McDonnell
William R. Schilling

With the end of the Cold War, the world supposedly became a safer place. Unfortunately, this supposition has not been borne out by experience. During the Cold War the greatest threat to world peace was the Soviet Union. However, since the fall of the Soviet Union the internecine rivalries within the area previously under Russian domination have, without the control of their previous Soviet masters, flared up as they had in previous millennia.

The wave of freedom rarely stops with the successful liberation of one country. The American Revolution of the eighteenth century undoubtedly fed the European revolutionary fervor, which first swept France in the 1790s and then ran across Europe deposing most of the monarchies by the last half of the nineteenth century.

A new wave of revolutionaries, liberators, call them what you will, is sweeping the world. But the revolutions of the twenty-first century are not to be fought on easily demarked battlefields by soldiers wearing uniforms of identifiable causes with weapons similar to those of the past or against targets previously defended. Faceless people will fight these revolutions in the shadows, using non-traditional weapons against targets of opportunity. This is terrorist warfare.

Context for Emergency Management Operations

Emergency management (EM) is a term that has more commonly been applied to natural disasters such as earthquakes, tornadoes, and flash floods, or to large-scale accidents such as industrial explosions or hazardous materials spills. The commonalities among these events were largely unpredictable, sudden, and involved large-scale damage and/or loss of life. These disasters severely stressed, or even overwhelmed the organizations that usually handled emergencies, such as the local or state fire, rescue, and police resources as well as the indigenous medical treatment facilities.

Terrorist threats are now being classified as an EM problem because they have the same factors in common with the historically considered emergencies, and their management, in most cases, is quite similar in terms of the principal functions to be performed.

Integrated Terrorist Database Concept

In the management of previous emergencies, one of the principal tools at the disposal of the emergency managers was a comprehensive knowledge of the nature of the emergency. Years of study and hundreds of millions of dollars have been invested in determining the nature of earthquakes, tornadoes, floods, forest fires, and other natural disasters. The results have been far reaching. Structural engineers have designed buildings that better withstand earthquakes. Tornado warning centers track and provide early warnings that save lives. Hurricane watch programs classify the storm severity, predict tracks, and decide what level of reaction is appropriate (boarding up windows, strengthening levees and dikes, evacuation). Forest fire prediction codes take data on the area and dimensions of the fire, the strength and direction of the prevailing winds, the local terrain features, and the forest fuel load so the course of the fire and the best use of resources can be surmised.

No one questions the value of the investments made in basic research into natural disasters; the ongoing costs of warning centers; remote weather monitoring devices; the millions of lines of code used in predictive analytical tools; or the specialized equipment designed, built, and maintained at great cost when they are only called upon for use in relatively rare instances. All of these are perceived as good investments that save lives and property.

Yet the growing terrorist presence, certainly likely to become an EM threat to human life perhaps more serious than forest fires, has only been studied in sporadic fashion. In fact, no concerted effort has been made to characterize it using an analytical approach consistent with earlier initiatives for natural disasters.

True, there are databases on terrorist individuals and groups, on terrorist events of the past, on terrorist weapons and capabilities. These are resident in databases at the State Department, Department of Justice, FBI, CIA, DIA, and others. Databases at Immigration and Naturalization Service (INS) and state and local law enforcement agencies contain information on individuals and groups who may also be considered potential terrorist groups or supporters. However, these databases are not connected, cannot communicate, and are even frequently unknown within the terrorist response community.

The situation at present is similar to that with earthquakes 30 or 40 years ago. Geologists discovered the plate tectonics theory and knew, generally, what happened as the plates moved against each other. Geophysicists could predict how different types of soil would react under the vibrations of an earthquake. Structural engineers knew how to strengthen buildings. But there was no central management function that tied all these groups together to determine where earthquakes were likely to occur geologically, how strong they were likely to be, what soil types were most dangerous, and what kinds of structural improvements might make a difference. It was not until an EM function integrated the disciplines and their information that any real advances in earthquake EM occurred.

If there is to be a credible capability to "manage" terrorist emergencies, a similar management function must unite the information sources for both intelligence and damage predications. Thus, an integrated, all-source capability to treat the threat and identify and address the gaps in the data and management approach can be envisioned. Essay 12, Information Technology Applications to Counter Nontraditional Warfare Threats, in this series addresses information integration of databases to support management decisions in response to terrorist activities. This essay concentrates on the threat management aspects of the problem.

Emergency Management and Analysis Concept

The Washington Institute of Technology has described an emergency management and analysis model (EMAM) to support an emergency management operations center (EMOC). Exhibit 14.1 shows the decision support model (DSM) elements of the EMAM. Exhibit 14.2 expands on the characteristics of

EXHIBIT 14.1 EMAM for operation centers: decision support model.

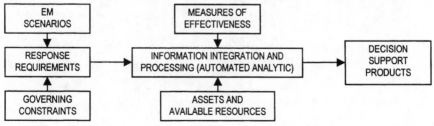

EXHIBIT 14.2 Factors bearing on decision support model dimensions.

Model elements	Purpose/utility	Element features	
		Input	Output
NTW scenarios	To describe the situation surrounding the threat incident to provide a basis for understanding the danger, engagement dynamics, and response variables	• Information transfer from data warehouse • Routines to prepare damage predictions according to substance type or explosives, C/B agents • Real-time data transfers form national weather bureau, NIMA, etc.	• Historical/relevant data • Threat characterization predictions • Damage prediction • Substance characteristics • Physical/geographical environment • Perpetrators' resources/modus operandi • Meteorological factors
Governing constraints	To disclose relevant policies, command authority, environmental conditions, communications, data processing, and exposure guidelines to protect response teams and comply with governing regulations	• Missions and duties of participating agencies and support groups • Official information transfer process • Telecommunications and ADP resources • Federal, state, and local regulations pertaining to type of threat incident	• Commanding authority • Support operations and management • Evacuation guidelines • Exposure limitations • Protective equipment regulations • Communications/ADP utilization
Response requirements	To prescribe the appropriate remedy to meet the threat incident in accordance with the given scenario and governing constraints so plans can be generated to limit dangers and expedite response in a cost-effective manner	• Organization and integration of incident facts and governing constraints • Characterization of incident in terms of engagement dynamics	• Response task definition and allocation • Specification of response dimensions • Translation of requirements to command authority/operations center
Measures of effectiveness	To provide a baseline for assessing merits of each possible response option so the best choice can be made for saving lives and reducing waste	• Formulations to translate desired outcomes into parameters for measuring capability and progress • MOEs expressed by time, rates, cost, and efficiency	• Quantitative expressions to indicate/measure outcomes of response alternatives • Aggregated MOEs/PMs for alternative processes/scenarios
Assets and resources	To produce a real-time list of indigenous and external assets/resources available to respond to incident	• Available trained personnel/equipment with locations • Location of vaccines, antidotes, and medical supplies • Skilled inventory lists (MOs) • Communication links for obtaining real-time assets/personnel • Specifications on equipment performance/availability	• Development of list of available assets and resources as function of time to respond to incident • Transportation and logistics support factors

EXHIBIT 14.3   National terrorist database and analysis center concept.

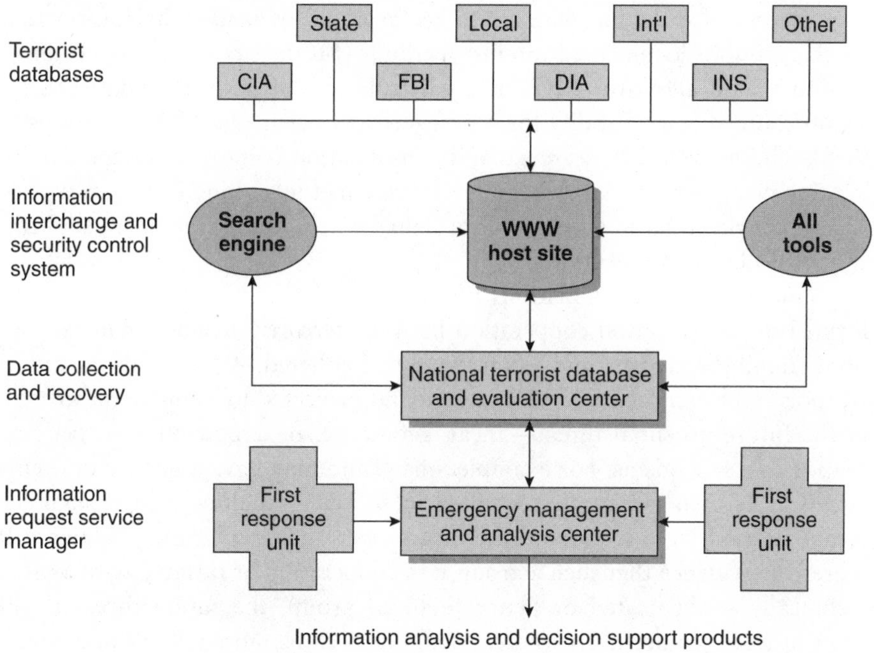

Information analysis and decision support products

the elements of the DSM. Exhibit 14.3 depicts, in part, the overall information integration concept represented by the DSM element, information integration and processing (again, for a further discussion, see Essay 12 in this series).

However, Exhibit 14.3 goes beyond the information integration concepts of Essay 12. Information integration is depicted in the top half of Exhibit 14.3. The lower half shows a national terrorist database and evaluation center and an emergency management and analysis center. These may be either a single or separate centers. For the present, while allowing for these to be separate entities, there is no clear division of roles and responsibilities between them so this essay refers to a single EMOC that subsumes all of the functional responsibilities discussed next.

The EMOC has a terrorist and terrorist event evaluation function. This function includes a routine examination of terrorist trends, activities of terrorist organizations, and the psychological profile development of individual terrorists through searches of the terrorist databases and the use of artificial intelligence (AI) tools to collate data, weed out duplications, and crosscheck information. In addition, damage predictions can be included for various types of terrorist weapons according to logistics constraints and target vulnerability.

Past terrorist events would be examined. If a terrorist group claimed responsibility for the incident, comparisons could be made with information on the group's documented modus operandi (MO). Any new, derived information would allow the MOs of a particular terrorist to be updated. If no group claimed responsibility for a past terrorist event, the MOs of groups in the databases would be searched and identification tentatively assigned to an existing group if sufficient criteria levels were met (e.g., kind of target, type of weapon/device used in event, level of damage achieved or intended, sophistication of plan and execution).

Similar routine examinations of terrorist group activities would be performed. Information on cooperation between terrorist groups, financial support, training activities, and so on, would be collated. Again, with the aid of AI tools, such trends would be analyzed and projected to estimate the growth in the future potential threat—linear, geometric, or exponential—depending on possible synergisms. For example, one group may have a history of events aimed at civilian targets that resulted in serious casualties even though the weapons used were crude and the targets were geographically contained. If there was evidence that such a group was cooperating or training with a more technically sophisticated or better financed group, the future threat might grow at least geometrically as their weapons became more reliable and devastating, and financial assistance allowed expansion of the geographic area of their operations. Similar routine examinations of terrorist individuals would also be performed, especially with the objective of developing psychological profiles on the potential perpetrators.

EM Analysis and Evaluation Utility

The EMOC terrorist and terrorist evaluation function would also have *real-time* EM response aspects. It would affect how assets and precautions are brought to bear on the problem in a cost-effective and timely operation.

The first of these would be preventive, provided there were warning indicators that international tensions were increasing, that terrorist group rhetoric was becoming more vehement, and that small-scale, isolated terrorist events were possible precursors to a major event. The EMOC would institute a multipronged correlation of the warning indicators with the data available on terrorist groups, past events and targets, individual terrorist psychological profiles, and so on, to provide tactical warning to nations, industries, and individuals perceived to be at risk. Such warning would not be a simple alert. Threats would be prioritized, types of weapons likely to be used would be identified, and likely MOs would be presented. Warned individuals and organizations would be able to establish better defenses and prepare for damage control and casualty treatment if defenses failed. At the same time, international, national, state, and local reaction forces would be able to concentrate their information gathering and intelligence operations against a narrower spectrum of usual suspects and prepare possible preemptive actions.

The second of these real-time aspects would include analysis of ongoing terrorist actions such as events involving hostages. The MO of the terrorist group would be generated for the ongoing event, refined as the event unfolded, and matched with the file of known MOs to identify the group and predict likely courses of action. If photos or voiceprints identified individuals in the group, their individual psychological profiles would be accessed and added to the group MO to predict likely courses of action.

Essay 15, Information Integration and Process Applications for EMOCs, discusses COTS software that allows the development of prepackaged processes for responding to, or even preempting, terrorist events in real time. However, the number of such events is myriad. Group MOs and individual psychological profiles can narrow the likely number of events in a particular incident so that preemptive actions are more likely to succeed and responses can be more thoroughly prepared. It is a well-known fact that if terrorists are faced with responses that rapidly nullify their activities, or even thwart the activity before it can be initiated, they are more likely to abandon their activities.

The third of these real-time aspects would include analysis of an isolated event such as an individual terrorist bombing. Here, the event would first be compared with past events of a similar nature to compare the MO with the existing file. The most immediate interest would be to consider if the present MO matched with MOs that indicated the possibility of follow-on or ancillary events and what the likely nature of such actions would be. Targets likely to be threatened by such events would be warned, defended, and/or evacuated. A less immediate but still pressing interest would be to identify the instigating group or individual(s) and examine the stored MO(s) and psychological profile(s) to predict escape alternatives so that early capture possibilities would be enhanced.

Support Products for EM Decisions

The final element depicted in Exhibit 14.1 relates to the decision support products of the EMAM. Exhibit 14.4 discusses these in more detail. Decision support is useful in the full range of activities required for EM response, including planning, training, management, and execution. The EMOC is viewed here as a national asset although, as noted earlier, suitably linked regional EMOCs

EXHIBIT 14.4   Management decision support products.

Functions	Utilization
Planning for threat response	• Explore alternative asset allocation concepts to match hypothetical scenarios • Develop information protocols and communication and management strategies
Training for threat response	• Identify critical issues for threat situation • Determine MOs and training exercise parameters • Apply TRAM to evaluate sensitivities to external conditions and available assets • Generate improvements in training process
Management of threat response	• Define critical information nodes and communication transfer methods • Establish methods to control and direct resource applications • Track, monitor, and adjust response to match changing needs and dangers • Record and maintain statistics, resources applied, and cost incurred
Execution of threat response	• Nominate and allocate resources to meet threat incident (best approach) • Modify selected option to match changing conditions (flexible response) • Advise operating center managers on potential problems, status of resources, and location and costs for additional resources • Provide new information affecting lives and resource utilization

are possible. Again, as in the discussion of Exhibit 14.3, the present interest is to identify the functions to be performed by an entity or entities like the EMOC. How these functions are divided between or among entities will depend on how they relate to roles and missions of existing or planned organizations.

As a national asset, the EMOC would provide assistance to at least the next lower level EM organizations on a regular basis and to even lower level EM organizations as needed and approved. As a national terrorist database and evaluation center (Exhibit 14.3), the EMOC would not only store and evaluate data on terrorists, it would store, and in some cases evaluate, information on activities of all EM organizations nationally and internationally. Trends in hardware, software, special equipment, and so on, to assist any of the four functional activities depicted in Exhibit 14.4 would be stored and made accessible to EMOC users/members down to the first response unit (FRU) level (shown in Exhibit 14.3).

To take the first example in Exhibit 14.4, "Explore alternative asset allocation concepts to match hypothetical scenarios," the EMOC would not only search its accessible databases for such information, it would use AI tools to assess the capabilities and responsibilities of the requesting user/member. This would ensure that, for example, if an FRU initiated the request, it would be provided with information primarily applicable to the positioning of equipment, medical stores, and so on, likely to be of interest to the FRU and not to the allocation of information technology (IT) assets, which might be of primary interest to a state level user/member.

Similar examples could be elucidated for all of the functions and utilizations presented in Exhibit 14.4 but space will not permit such exhaustive treatment. However, it should again be pointed out that Essay 15 in this series covers COTS software that can model processes. These processes could be prepared for any or all of the four functional areas of planning, training, management, and execution of EM functions. Processes could be stored and retrieved by any user/member to examine and compare with their own existing processes. Also it could have some preliminary process in place for an emergency that would be possible but unlikely in their location but relatively common somewhere else (e.g., Pennsylvania is unlikely to experience tornadoes but it is possible. Pennsylvania could access processes for tornado response submitted by Plains States). Essay 15 of this series takes the EM concept further by providing emergency managers with a tool set that can assist in the planning, training, and real-world application of processes designed to address terrorist threats and actions.

In summary, the EMOC would provide a valuable coordination role and information source for planning and treating threat responses. It offers a cost-effective process for automating many aspects of the elements, resources, and information available to meet nontraditional warfare threats.

15

INFORMATION INTEGRATION AND PROCESS APPLICATIONS FOR EMERGENCY MANAGEMENT OPERATIONS CENTERS

Michael D. McDonnell

Effective emergency management (EM) requires the integration of information from many sources and at many levels of federal, state, and local government resources. Some state and/or even local government response units have extensive experience and data regarding certain EM situations. Certain California-based units have extensive experience in earthquakes and disastrous mudslides. Plains States units have greater experience in dealing with tornadoes. While other state and local EM response units can respond to earthquakes, mudslides, tornadoes, and other natural disasters, their experience may be more limited due to geographic and climatic conditions. Terrorist threats from conventional explosives, hostage situations, and potential chemical and/or biological (C/B) weapons are not related to geographic locations or prevailing weather conditions. They are sporadic and threaten targets of opportunity as perceived by the terrorists and are not necessarily predictable by the EM response units. The purpose of this essay is to present an overview of a tool set that can assist emergency managers in the planning, training, and real-world application of processes designed to address emergencies.

Context for Information Integration and Automation

No EM response unit can train and exercise for every possible EM contingency. An effective emergency management operations center (EMOC) must have access to integrated information on how to deal with most EM possibilities, even if they are statistically improbable. Obviously the more remote the

EM threat, the less training the EM response unit is likely to have. Therefore the requirement for more detailed directions, and truly integrated information, on how to respond to the emergency grows directly in proportion to the unlikelihood of such an event.

What an EMOC needs is a "library" of processes designed, and proven in the real world, for handling nearly all emergencies. Such a library would contain details of the required processes at every level from the topmost federal level to the first response unit (FRU) of the local government. FRUs are designated to respond to emergencies in the first hour when most of the victims that can be saved will be rescued. Each responding level could access the library and extract details on what processes had to be performed, and in what order, and in coordination with what other organizations (e.g., local fire, rescue, and police; National Guard; Environmental Protection Agency; Federal Emergency Management Agency; the Defense Coordinating Office).

The EMOC is not only responsible for this information library, it is also responsible for establishing the necessary communications with all of the involved organizations and providing the response units with a principal source for communications, coordination, and information integration. The response units have enough of an information-handling problem in collating the data at the site and providing it to the EMOC. Ideally, the EMOC will provide this coordination function as part of its integration role to transfer information to supported organizations.

Data transfer, and to a certain extent data integration, has been extensively researched in recent years. It is not the purpose of this essay to refine the current state of those arts. This essay explores the problems arising when the elements of data transfer, integration, and evaluation are applied to the problems of dealing with processes. Essay 12, Information Technology Applications to Counter Nontraditional Warfare Threats, and Essay 14, Emergency Response Management at the National Operations Centers, in this series deal with these other aspects of the overall problem.

Process Modeling Concepts

EM is basically a process. Keeping this in mind, we will digress into the concept of managing processes.

Most processes can be modeled primarily as either functional or event-driven. In most cases functional processes are embedded within event-driven processes.

Standard processes that are usually performed in a rote fashion are generally referred to as functional processes. Event-driven processes tend to be governed by events outside the control of the organization responsible for dealing with them.

Functional processes are familiar in concept. They include manufacturing processes, training processes, and office management processes.

Event-driven processes are more complex conceptually. Examples of event-driven processes include responses to natural disasters of a continuing nature such as severe storms or fires and responses to interactions with individuals or organizations or states. In such cases, there is a continual interaction between the organization responsible for responding to the events and the entity, natural or human, initiating and driving the situations.

The organization responsible for responding to the event-driven process(es) is not, however, completely at the mercy of the entity initiating them. Experience allows the responding organization to prepare alternative courses of action and initiate them as the events outside of their control evolve. What is needed for this kind of flexible response is an information technology (IT) capability that stores preplanned alternative courses of action and retrieves them as events develop—a library of processes. In some cases, with the aid of artificial intelligence (AI) tools, the responding organization can even keep ahead of the entity event drivers. The responding organization can predict the probable course of events and even implement actions that nullify, or at least seriously ameliorate, the course of events.

In the real world, of course, the situations are not so clear-cut. Some processes involve both functional and event-driven situations. The methodologies at present can still manage such emergencies. There is, however, a requirement for more real-time information integration (preferably automated and with assistance of AI tools plus human intervention) to meld the two process models together.

For the purposes of the present discussion, however, we will discuss examples of functional and event-driven processes individually. Examples will be used that are fairly diametric in their situations. Both process models are supported by commercial off-the-shelf (COTS) software.

Functional Processes

The first example is one of a functional process that has been developed for the Washington, D.C. National Medical Response Team (NMRT), formerly the Metropolitan Medical Strike Team. This is one of four teams intended to deploy to major emergencies (others are in Los Angeles, Denver, and Winston/Salem). There are also over a dozen similar FRUs, which are not considered deployable, around the country in areas such as Atlanta, New York City, and Seattle. These have been created to respond to emergencies requiring search, rescue, medical, law enforcement, and fire department actions. The NMRT includes units that supported the responses to the Oklahoma City bombing, the earthquakes in Armenia and Turkey, and other national and international EM situations.

The scenario deals with a bombing of a building (see Exhibit 15.1). It is suspected to be a terrorist incident. The model covers the usual functional activities such as processing the initial report. This includes the possibility that the initial report is from the entity instigating the event and that the call is traced, the caller is researched, and existing databases are used to identify the caller, his method of operation (MO), and to initiate a psychological profile of the individual and his associated group. Other functional activities are also modeled as the FRU transits to the scene of the initial event, cordons off the area, treats victims, and so on. The model also allows for the possibility that the terrorist/bomber has placed secondary explosives or released chemical or biological agents into the area of the initial event.

However, this is still a basically functional process. The NMRT has procedures in place to handle all expected threats outlined earlier. The terrorist/bomber does not instigate any further events after the initial set. The FRU and later responding units can follow preplanned and exercised functional processes without further influence from the terrorist/bomber.

The utility of the model has been in developing a pictographic outlay of what the NMRT plans, trains, and exercises. It allows the NMRT to review its functional processes in a quick overview to identify subprocesses, which might be scheduled inappropriately or redundantly. It also allows the compartmentalization of subprocesses into activities that can be trained and exercised individually and with limited resources, rather than conducting full-scale exercises that cost significantly more. Finally, the model allows immediate replacement or addition of new, previously developed processes as the NMRT responds to a real-world event. At any point the model can be run to determine performance measures such as time to achieve a set of related functional processes and cost expended. The ultimate capability envisioned would require the library of processes proposed as a responsibility of the EMOC so that there would be a large database of detailed functional processes for FRUs to study and evaluate in light of their resources and training.

As the COTS software is more widely employed by organizations such as the NMRT, more functional processes and subprocesses will be coded and shared among FRUs. This will lead to a better sharing of knowledge and experience, nationally and internationally, and continuous improvements in all functional processes modeled. Obviously the resources of any FRU are limited

EXHIBIT 15.1 First response unit functional processes.

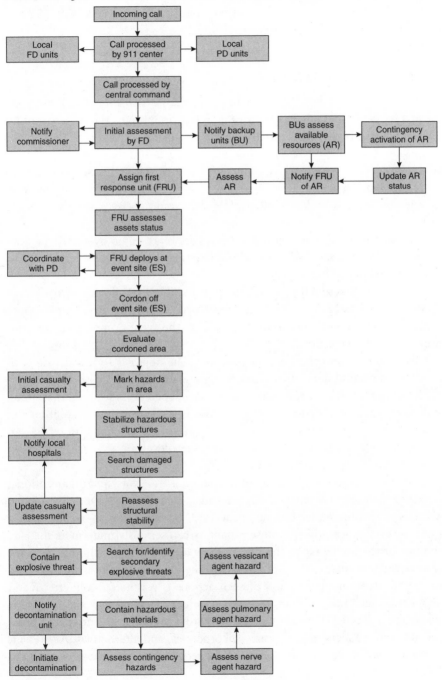

while the possible number of functional processes and subprocesses is, essentially, unlimited. Only a more centralized, and better resourced, EMOC could populate and maintain the library envisioned.

Event-Driven Processes

The second example has been developed for the Federal Emergency Management Agency (FEMA). It deals with the initial response to the takeover of an airport waiting room by terrorists (see Exhibit 15.2).

Assuming that the terrorists are initially successful, there are several possible event-driven processes. Exhibit 15.3 shows the response processes to some of them. Threats to destroy an airplane or other property, kill hostages, or release chemical and/or biological agents would follow the same general response process.

Another possibility is that the terrorists are represented by a national government. The international political ramifications dictate a process similar to that outlined in Exhibit 15.4.

Unlike the functional process shown in Exhibit 15.1, not all of the events shown in Exhibits 15.3 and 15.4 necessarily occur. However, the event response processes must be available so that, as soon as the event occurs, it can be connected into the event flow.

Event-driven processes must be flexible. The object is to identify all conceivable events and develop alternative actions to them. In this instance, multiple events are foreseen and responses are developed at least to the first order. Again, preplanned functional processes can be called up from the library in real-time response to terrorist actions. Organizational elements (in ovals) can be defined down to the individual member level to execute functional processes with appropriate expertise.

The COTS software allows all of these processes, events, and organizational elements to be predefined and copied and pasted into the computer model. In cases where the entity driving events is a human agent or agents, such a rapid, or even preemptive response capability can seriously undermine the psychology of the human(s) to the point where he ceases to pursue his intended course of action since every first order event he instigates is almost immediately frustrated. Real-time frustration of such actions is psychologically effective in terminating such events. And, again, the number of events that are possible is effectively unlimited. Furthermore each event has another, undetermined number of possible functional processes, subprocesses, and alternatives. At present, even an order of magnitude scoping of the requirements for the library would

EXHIBIT 15.2   Terrorist airport event—stage one.

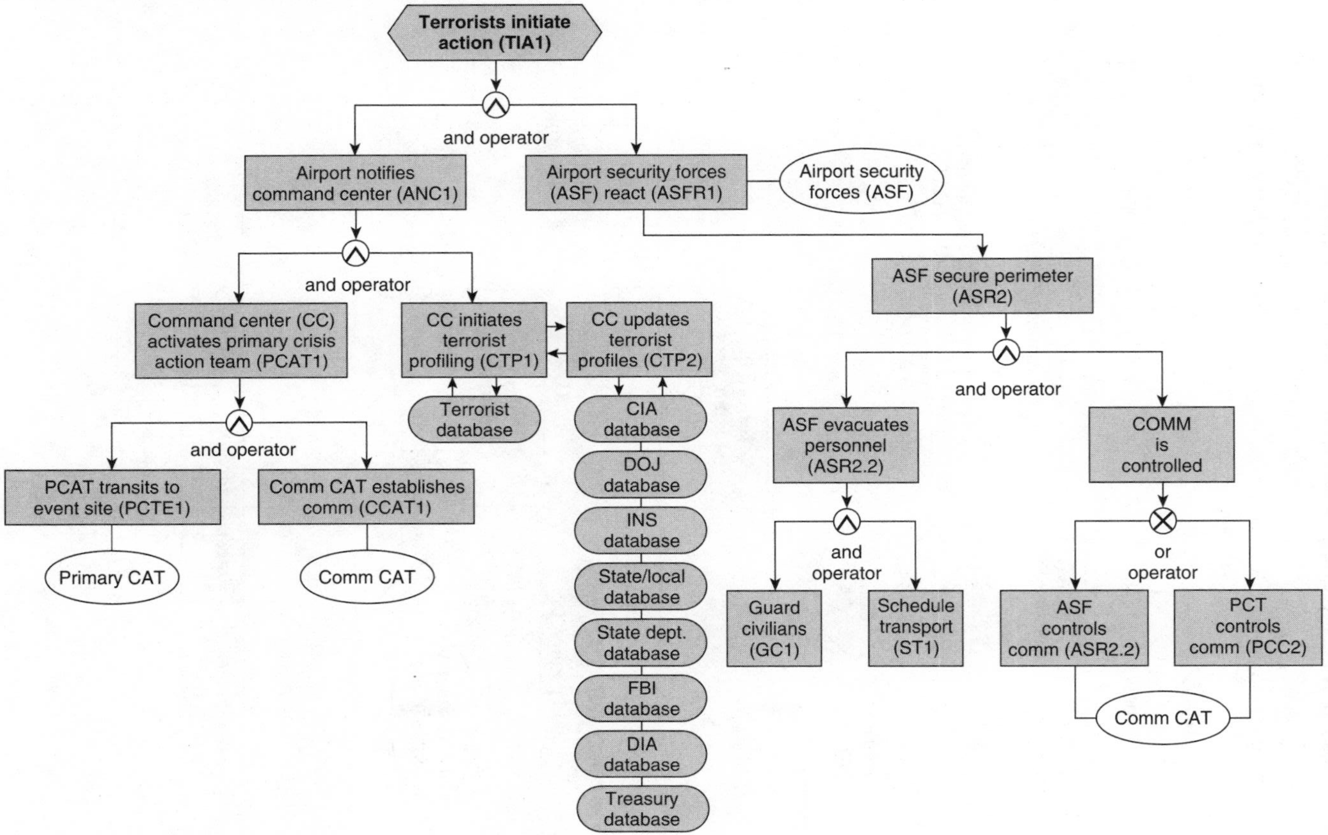

155

EXHIBIT 15.3 Terrorist airport event—secondary stages.

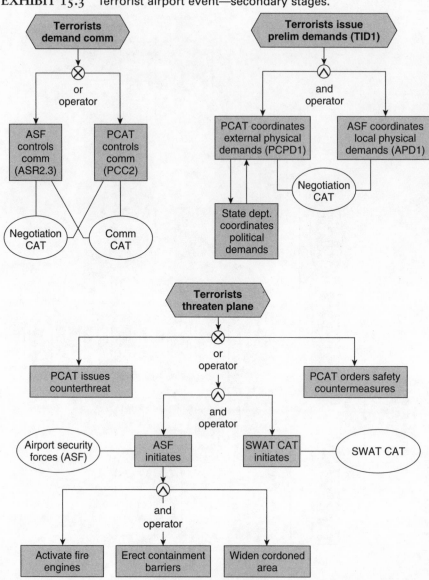

EXHIBIT 15.4 Government-sponsored terrorist event—secondary stages.

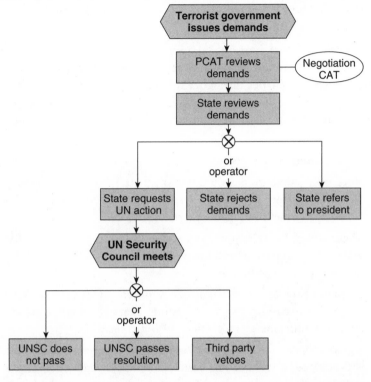

be premature but, for full effectiveness, it is certainly beyond the resources of almost any single state or local government.

Future Development and Applications

Obviously there are many questions, which arise in connection with the EMOC concept:

- What level of process detail is required at what EM response levels from the federal down to the local and FRU levels?
- How can the hierarchical levels access their processes in a timely fashion and at the appropriate level of detail (e.g., will the process data be "pushed" or "pulled")?
- What AI tools would improve concept performance?
- Since state and local levels of response units, at least, are proliferated across the country, should there be some review authority which

examines processes submitted for inclusion in the library in order to eliminate apparent duplication and identifiable inferior or substandard processes?

Many of these questions can be addressed, and should be, before a full-scale EMOC is attempted. Many can be solved with coordination and integration of interested parties through a simulated EMOC that starts to build a library, possibly virtual in nature, and allows the interested parties to interact with the library. In this case, the simulated EMOC could be quite simple for a number of reasons:

- There would be no need for real-time interactions or data retrieval.

- Since only simulations would be run, there would be no possibility of an EMOC failure providing false information and compounding rather than ameliorating an emergency.

- There would be no requirement to establish strict guidelines for organizational participation or verification and validation (V&V) of process software submitted.

- Scoping of the order of magnitude requirements for data storage, data processing capability, AI tools, communications capabilities, and other factors would emerge as participation increases.

- As experience in the roles and responsibilities of the simulated EMOC is developed, it will become easier to identify what organization(s), at what response level(s), should assume those roles if and when a real EMOC may be feasible.

Plans are already underway to integrate information from other FRUs within the United States such as the Washington, D.C. NMRT. Widening use of these methodologies will increase their utility. As explained earlier, other FRUs with particular experience in specific EM situations will provide unique data, subprocesses, and training and exercise information to the database being created.

In summary, the ultimate goal is clear—information integration and sharing of functional and event-driven process models. However, the path to the goal has not, and cannot, be laid without careful preliminary planning and the coordination of organizations at many levels in the EM community all along the way. Such endeavors are easy on paper until you hit the real-world minefield. Then you have to look toward your goal frequently—but you have to take each step very, very carefully.

SECTION IV

MODELS AND TOOLS FOR ADDRESSING NONTRADITIONAL WARFARE

Military modeling has received a great deal of attention over the last few decades. Unfortunately, despite this attention and serious effort, the results derived in terms of accurate forecasts and prediction models have fallen short of desired outcomes. The simulations and models available for planning have frequently lacked accuracy and realism, and most of the models have been cumbersome and difficult to employ or understand. To add to the challenges involved, these models have generally dealt with conventional warfare involving deployed, structured combat forces and with weapons systems that are comparatively well understood.

Further adding to the difficulty of the situation, each service and many individual commands and branches within individual services have developed and employ their own models and approaches to testing and evaluation. The resulting gamut of approaches and attitudes toward models, simulations, and tests and evaluations has created an unwieldy mass of such activities and efforts. The opportunity exists to bring a degree of uniformity to the modeling and testing-evaluation communities. A similar opportunity is unlikely to arise again, and it would be a disservice to both modelers and the employers of evaluations and models to miss this chance for real reform.

Modeling and simulating nontraditional warfare (NTW) presents additional problems and challenges. Not least among these challenges is the growing importance of accuracy and reliability in the needed models and simulations. The U.S. defense community, both civilian and military elements, cannot afford to employ poorly developed, inaccurate, and clumsy modeling tools. It is true that models and simulations may be used to take the place of actual live experience. In such circumstances, even a poorly derived and inaccurate computer simulation may still serve a valuable role, especially if most of its shortcomings are widely recognized.

Clearly, though, it is necessary for the models, simulations, and testing and evaluation techniques to be accurate and applicable to the situation being considered. With these admirable goals in mind, a sound and widespread understanding of the basic techniques employed in these activities is essential. The greater the degree of coherence and uniformity, the easier it will be to secure and maintain consistent goals and outlooks, standardizing both inputs and results.

The range of issues and concerns associated with modeling and simulation represent only a part of the whole picture of planning and preparing for NTW scenarios. Rigorous, uniform, and effective testing of new equipment, organizations, and methods of operation will also be essential. Indeed, those "soft" techniques may be of greater importance for national security preparedness than will new and improved models and simulations.

This section deals with a range of issues, including testing and evaluation techniques, approaches to modeling and simulating NTW, and effectiveness methods for dealing with NTW threats.

16

TESTING AND EVALUATION OF EMERGING SYSTEMS IN NONTRADITIONAL WARFARE

James F. O'Bryon

For many years, conventional wisdom has espoused the popular and accepted notion of always testing and evaluating (T&E) before acquiring new or improved systems. This axiom sounds simple enough; however, in practice many impediments rise up to challenge or thwart T&E efforts. Nevertheless, congress has mandated that T&E be conducted to ensure military systems will meet performance requirements prior to acceptance.

The threats to the United States and our allies are shifting from the Cold War conditions to situations dealing with a new array of threats, technologies, and concepts. This new problem set is designed to create asymmetries in U.S. defense capabilities through the application of chemical and biological weapons, electronic warfare, urban and guerrilla operations, and terrorist attacks.

All of these nontraditional warfare (NTW) situations generate major perturbations to the conventional T&E program. In addition, new weapons effects manuals will need to be constructed and expanded to address the methodologies and database requirements necessary to deal with those problems that evolve outside the boundaries of conventional weapons. These emerging conditions will cause changes in technologies, system vulnerabilities, and employment strategies for U.S. land, air, and sea weapons. As a means to adapt to the emerging NTW threats, the T&E program will also need to expand to accommodate the push to conserve resources and pursue cost-effective solutions by revising and improving already existing highly sophisticated, expensive equipment and devices.

Full-scale mockup of M-1 Abrams main battle tank.

Emerging Nontraditional T&E Concerns

These emerging new threats or technologies can be categorized as management information and communications support systems, directed energy systems, precision strike systems, nonlethal weapons, robotic combat systems, and counterterrorist weapons. Each of these categories create unique problems for the T&E program from the standpoint of how to test, what to measure, and what criteria to apply. Major new initiatives must begin to address these concerns now.

Exhibit 16.1 provides an overview of the T&E objectives and critical issues for each of the concerns listed earlier. Without a sound master plan and investment strategy for addressing these T&E requirements, U.S. and allied systems will fail to be ready to counter NTW threats and protect our valuable military resources, personnel, and infrastructure.

Management information and communications support systems form the backbone of our information technology and include computers, radios, sensors, wired and wireless networks, and data collection systems. Directed energy weapons (DEW) as depicted by lasers, RF weapons, and EMP are emerging as threats to battlefield systems and civilian infrastructure and

EXHIBIT 16.1 Testing and evaluating nontraditional warfighting equipment and systems.

Emerging nontraditional warfighting T&E concerns	T&E objectives	T&E issues/requirements
Management information and communications support systems	• Determine vulnerability of U.S. systems in electronic warfare (EW) conditions	• Determine critical nodes in information transfer process • Define EW threats and engagement concepts • Establish equipment performance threshold criteria • Identify means to intercept information transfer and processing
	• Evaluate means to enhance survivability of U.S. C⁴I systems by adapting design changes and process improvements • Develop test data for V&V of modeling and simulation	• Show impact of design changes/hardening on survivability improvements • Create knowledge base on phenomenology associated with coupling of electronic effects to C⁴I equipment • Determine sensitivity to countermeasures and engagement constraints
Directed energy weapons (DEW) systems	• Determine susceptibility of U.S. combat systems to damage from DEW systems • Develop data to support methodology for predicting DEW effects using M&S and test data	• Investigate compatibility of EMP hardening for other DEW systems including RF and lasers • Expand knowledge base on coupling effects of DEW on combat systems • Determine sensitivity to countermeasures and engagement constraints
	• Establish bounds on lethality of DEW against foreign combat systems	• Develop insights into utility of focused non-nuclear EMP, RF weapons, and lasers against foreign combat systems • Identify means to enhance performance of DEW against foreign systems
Precision strike systems	• Investigate lethality of precision gun-launched projectiles against high value military targets	• Show trades between employing velocity and guidance-combinations versus mass to achieve target kills • Clarify promise of electromechanical-chemical technology to reduce cost and weight factors
	• Develop data to support methodology for projectile lethality based on velocity rather than mass for target kills	• Develop concepts for testing precision guided sensor weapon combinations • Evaluate consequences of hitting "sweet spot" or tight hit patterns rather than general vulnerability areas to predict damage • Assess the validity of current models for JLF/LFT shot planning in precision strike tests

(continued)

EXHIBIT 16.1 Testing and evaluating nontraditional warfighting equipment and systems *(continued)*.

Emerging nontraditional warfighting T&E concerns	T&E objectives	T&E issues/requirements
Nonlethal weapons	• Determine vulnerability of U.S. and foreign systems to nondestructive weapons concepts to include nonnuclear EMP, electrical energy dispensing personnel debilitation, and mechanical energy material debilitation	• Develop performance objectives/criteria for nonlethal weapon requirements against personnel and material • Determine battle damage assessment methods and processes
	• Support methodologies for predicting nonlethal target damage	• Evaluate personnel and material damage levels necessary to accomplish mission degradation
Robotic combat systems	• Determine vulnerability of emerging combat systems to antiarmor robotic systems	• Evaluate implications of target size, mobility, and stealth capability to achieve target kills
	• Assess lethality of U.S. weapons against threat robotic systems	• Investigate options and techniques for defeating robotic threat systems with lethal and DEW systems
Counterterrorist weapons	• Determine capability of U.S. armored systems to withstand chemical/biological attacks from mortars and artillery rounds	• Translate threat scenarios into framework for test planning including simulations, burst locations from targets, and instrumentation • Determine vulnerability of combat vehicle occupants as a function of test conditions and engagement parameters
	• Determine capability of U.S. personnel in combat vehicles to withstand chemical/biological weapons by onboard rapid detection and protective measures	• Assess utility of current and planned measures to protect combat vehicle occupants with detection devices and inoculation, protective clothing, overpressure, etc.

depend on countermeasures or hardening to provide protection and ensure operation of electromechanical equipment. A new group of precision strike munitions are surfacing that rely on accuracy and velocity rather than mass to cause target damage and means are needed to define test procedures, criteria, and methodology for assessing threats and utility. New classes of nonlethal weapons are being developed to limit casualties and include modular crowd control, munitions and grenades, rigid and slippery foam, portable barriers, pulsed chemical lasers, odorous substances, microencapsulation, electromagnetic beam guns, and electrical land mines, to mention a few development items. For further discussions on these technologies, see Essay 27, Impact of Radio Frequency Weapons on National Security and National Infrastructure, Essay 28, Development of Smart Sensor Webs for Future Warfare Operations, and Essay 29, Impact of Electromagnetic Impulses on Future Warfare Operations.

Expendable and reusable robotic combat systems constitute part of the culture of the future. They are designed to reach and observe hostile areas and reduce casualties by using remote control devices, GPS, smart sensors, and wireless information transfer devices, so new T&E guidelines and methodologies are necessary to determine combat suitability and utility. Finally, new T&E initiatives involving systems for countering terrorist operations are necessary and include neutralizing chemical/biological agents, detecting locations of unexploded ordnance preventing weapon ignition, protecting personnel, and limiting collateral damage.

Exhibit 16.2 lists some factors and considerations that must be dealt with in performing the new T&E missions. These concerns include the availability of appropriate testing resources and instrumentation, the generation of testing standards and criteria, the capability of existing models and simulations (M&S) for predicting and evaluating effects, the implications of advanced concept technology demonstrations, and commercial off-the-shelf (COTS) systems, plus the treatment of collateral damage.

EXHIBIT 16.2 Factors affecting T&E requirements for nontraditional warfighting equipment and systems.

Emerging NTW systems	Key considerations and factors				
	Testing standards/ criteria	Testing resources	M&S availability	ACDTs	Collateral damage
Management information and communications support systems	!	!	!	!	#
DEW systems	!	!	!	∃	!
Precision strike systems	∃	#	∃	!	∃
Nonlethal weapons	!	!	!	∃	!
Robotic combat systems	!	#	!	∃	#
Counerterrorist weapons	!	!	!	#	!

\# Somewhat important
∃ Moderately important
! Extremely important

T&E Role in the Acquisition of New Systems

The acquisition of military systems is a complex series of activities that take place during the engineering design, implementation, manufacturing, and acceptance process. Milestones are set up to guide progress and make system changes according to test results and performance specifications. Exhibit 16.3 provides a correlation between the activities involved in each phase of the acquisition and the functions that are performed prior to the next milestone or signpost. While this acquisition process for emerging systems will still likely be followed, less information and greater uncertainties in the threat scenarios will make performance specifications and testing criteria more difficult to ascertain or project.

Exhibit 16.3 lays out some of the key aspects associated with the acquisition process and describes the testing events applied to measure performance acceptance. The level and type of testing and evaluation is tied to the stage of the acquisition process. Subsequent sections of this essay describe how the nature and characteristics of T&E must be revised or expanded to meet the NTW threats and responses.

The testing activities to support research, development, engineering, production, and acceptance testing take place in distinct but overlapping phases. These four phases are commonly referred to as developmental, live fire, joint live fire, and operational testing. Each of these aspects of testing is undertaken to ensure that the total working system composed of integrated subsystems, equipment, infrastructure, and personnel will perform as specified to meet military requirements, mission objectives, and training/combat conditions.

Developmental testing takes place to support concept exploration and definition, subsystem and component design, prototype configuration, and system technical performance. Live fire testing is congressionally mandated for developmental systems and involves the firing of live munitions at combat targets prior to final production decisions to ascertain lethality or vulnerability status. Joint live fire testing is applied to fielded systems when significant changes to the initially tested items are introduced that might affect the lethality or vulnerability state. Operational testing and evaluation begins during the low rate initial production cycle and is undertaken to assess the compatibility of the human-system operation interfaces and the capability of the system to accommodate or merge with other supporting systems and infrastructure in an operating environment. All of these categories of testing will need to be implemented in new ways to meet the challenges of the NTW problems.

EXHIBIT 16.3 System life-cycle acquisition activities.

Acquisition activities	Acquisition process				
	Concept exploration and definition	Demonstration and validation	Engineering and manufacturing development	Production deployment	Operation and support
Decision points	Milestone A	Milestone B	Milestone C (LRIP)	Milestone D IOC	Milestone E
Systems engineering	System level RQMT and functional analysis/synthesis/trade-off/description — SEMP	C1 level functional analysis/synthesis/trade-off/description	Component detailed design	Mod prelim/detailed design/integration	Mod prelim/detailed design/integration
Specification	System ———— Type A	———— Development ——— Type B	——— Product ——— Type C, D, E		
Test and evaluation	DT&E	TEMP	DT&E	IOT&E — TEMP — FOT&E	DT&E — TEMP — Joint LFTE
			LFTE		
Manufacturing	Production strategy	Mfg plan — Prototype	LRIP	Full-rate production	
Years	(0–2)	(2–3)	(3–5)	(3–5) (1–2)	(10–30)

SEMP = system engineering master plan
IOC = initial operational capability
DT&E = developmental testing and evaluation
IOT&E = initial operational testing and evaluation

OT&E = operational testing and evaluation
TEMP = test and evaluation master plan
LFTE = live fire test and evaluation
JLF = joint live fire

167

Model and Simulation Applications

Since the inception of joint live fire (JLF) and live fire testing (LFT), a debate has been growing over the relative roles of modeling and simulation (M&S) and test and evaluation (T&E). M&S has played an integral and vital part in T&E.

Pre-shot predictions mandate that the best M&S tools be exercised in test planning. Further, these predictions assist in making decisions regarding the placement and use of test instrumentation (e.g., gauges, cameras, thermocouples, fire suppression equipment). The models, coupled with prior test insights, provide the best sources of information about what to anticipate during the test. Furthermore, model predictions that indicate the extent of expected damage can be used for sequence testing and to make maximum use of limited test resources. Pre-shot predictions also provide a baseline for the evaluation of current M&S capabilities. Following every shot, a comparison must be made to reconcile differences between model expectations and test outcome. This process is sometimes painful for the M&S community because it often reveals inadequacies in predictive capabilities. The experience gained in the testing exercise is essential to improving modeling capability.

Many types of M&S exist to examine the behavior or characteristics of technologies, systems, processes, and operations. Exhibit 16.4 provides a brief introduction to test and evaluation models (TEM) for addressing new NTW conditions and problems. Characteristics and features of these models are shown in the exhibit. NTW conditions emphasize operations against unstructured or small units rather than the highly organized or large deployed forces that existed in the earlier times of the Cold War. For further technical discussion on the characteristics of M&S to support NTW needs, refer to Essay 17, Models and Simulations for Evaluating Emerging Threats.

JMEMs Process and Applications

Current joint munitions effectiveness manuals (JMEMs) develop effectiveness estimates for all conventional nonnuclear munitions. These tools are used by the Services for training and tactics development, operational targeting, weapons selection, aircraft loadouts, planning for ammunition procurement, survivability assessments, and development of improved munitions. The JMEMs are the standardized references and methodologies used to measure or predict the combat effectiveness of a weapon system. JMEM information includes damage/kill probabilities for specific weapon/target combinations, physical and functional characteristics of munitions and weapon systems, target vulnerability, and analytical techniques and procedures for assessing muni-

EXHIBIT 16.4 M&S for test and evaluation of nontraditional threats and responses.

Model purpose	Model operation	Limitations
To test and evaluate the capability of systems to perform as required to counter or operate in NTW conditions. To use models to assist in predicting performance. Also to support test planning and simulation of NTW environments and conditions.	TEM consists of a varied number and type of processes, automation, and analytical formulations to reflect performance of systems or technologies under a given set of conditions, specifications, and requirements. Models can be physics-based (showing effects based upon physical laws) or empirical-based (attempting to duplicate expected results) or formulations (representing concepts and processes). Models and test results form the basis for graphs and tables used to compare systems and evaluate new concepts, designs, or technologies. More details on TEM are presented in Essay 17.	• Models and simulations rarely predict results consistent with actual tests • Many NTW scenarios necessitate employment of surrogates, simulations, and new test ranges • Existing database for emerging NTW threats lacking • New test plans and models necessary for emerging threats from NTW problems

tions effectiveness. A pressing need exists to begin the process of designing formats and organizing effects data for NTW systems. These new initiatives will provide a basis for laying out the testing processes and defining testing parameters and concepts.

SURVIAC Support Program

The purpose of the Survivability/Vulnerability Information Analysis Center (SURVIAC) is to increase the knowledge and productivity of scientists, engineers and analysts engaged in nonnuclear survivability/vulnerability and lethality programs for the Office of the Secretary of Defense (OSD). SURVIAC's specific mission is to maintain a technology base, provide authoritative responses to user inquiries, provide technical assistance and support, produce authoritative technical reference works (i.e., handbooks, data books, state-of-the-art reports) and perform special tasks and studies. The SURVIAC's technical area is nonnuclear survivability/vulnerability and lethality as they relate to U.S. and foreign aeronautical and surface targets.

The nonnuclear threats included within SURVIAC's scope are (1) conventional weapons [i.e., small arms/automatic weapons, antiaircraft artillery, surface-to-air missiles (SAMs), air-to-air guns, air-to-air missiles, field artillery and direct fire weapons (i.e., tanks, tube-launched, optically tracked, wire-guided missiles (TOWs))]; (2) directed energy weapons including laser, millimeter wave, and particle beams; and (3) chemical and biological weapons. Data requirements in the threat area include, as applicable, acquisition, detection, tracking, fuzing characteristics, countermeasures, and terminal effects.

A new initiative should be undertaken to start the planning, collection, and compilation of relevant information on the aspects of NTW threats and responses. A master plan for producing and maintaining this critical information should begin immediately.

Future T&E Thrusts and Initiatives

Most of the current T&E efforts relate to previous threats and situations, while new problems and concerns are quickly surfacing on chemical/biological weapons, electronic warfare, urban and guerrilla operations, and counterterrorist incidents. Now, many government agencies are involved (Federal Emergency Management Agency, Defense Threat Reduction Agency, Department of Justice, and others), but none have a specific charter to develop commonly accepted test plans and methodologies to quantify the effectiveness of potential threats and responses.

Over the past three decades, a concerted effort has been underway to build a successful T&E program, consisting of top-of-the-line organizations, facilities, supporting systems, and trained personnel to address the demands caused by the Cold War threats. However, the program dimensions and understanding necessary to address our new problems are lacking. For example, the primary thrusts have necessarily been focused on the scientific understanding of technical issues and systems engineering associated with operations to deliver personnel and material to support conventional warfare; to find targets; to enhance battlefield command, control, communications, computers, and intelligence (C^4I); to increase lethality against opposing threats; to provide ballistic protection from enemy weapons, and so on. While some of these activities match requirements for future T&E efforts, many other aspects need to be dealt with including (1) ranges to test new technologies or threats from weapons of mass destruction, electronic warfare, and operations in less organized battlefield conditions; (2) environmental constraints on available test facilities; (3) instrumentation to measure the performance parameters; and (4) the availability of standardized new weapon effects data plus the models and simulations to support the evaluation process. Assessments are needed to define the shortfalls in current capabilities to meet these new and critical T&E requirements.

Unless well-conceived T&E plans surface or begin prior to the onset of new system acquisition to deal with emerging threats, the Defense community will not be ready to respond quickly in emergency conditions or to support the rapid buildup of suitable countermeasures. Likewise, appropriate Defense policy, test facilities and instrumentation, mission responsibilities, models and simulations, and weapon effects data must be prepared and available to support the revision in military concepts, thrusts, and systems that are currently under consideration. These initiatives are necessary to support new Defense strategies and movements that are expected to be implemented during the next decade and beyond.

In summary, intensive efforts will be needed to deal with this expanded view of the T&E program. Steps must be taken to define the master plan, to determine the funding requirements and other elements affecting the acquisition process, as well as to communicate these new requirements to DOD and government leaders of the nation.

Mr. James F. O'Bryon's work contributed to this essay. Mr. O'Bryon formerly served as Assistant Deputy Undersecretary of Defense and also served within the Office of the Secretary of Defense as Deputy Director, Test and Evaluation; as Director, Live Fire Testing; as Director, Weapon Systems Assessment; and as Deputy Director, Operational Test and Evaluation/Live Fire Testing.

17

MODELS AND SIMULATIONS FOR EVALUATING EMERGING THREATS

William R. Schilling

Both models and simulations (M&S) can represent the characteristics or behavior of a process, concept, or operation by portraying related physical laws, mathematical principles, technologies, or systems, often through the utilization of a computer program. Models rely on preprogrammed or stored data for program execution. Simulations tend to be dynamic, time-stepped, event-driven processes affecting the behavior or characteristics of the representation during program execution. M&S are important tools for assisting in the generation of knowledge and insights into complex problems involving combinations of people, processes, systems, and materiel. Obviously, they have limitations in fully duplicating or representing the actual problem. But M&S can still provide valuable leads and methods for reducing development, engineering, testing, planning, and training costs as well as substituting for unfeasible exercises or practices.

This essay is directed toward M&S problems, issues, and limitations that need to be addressed in order to deal with some of the emerging nontraditional warfare (NTW) threats. In addition, the presented exhibits offer a framework for instigating new M&S development initiatives to meet the NTW challenges. While the focus is on models to provide insights on force concepts, other relevant models bearing on the development and testing of technologies and systems to counter NTW threats are also introduced.

The M&S Dilemma

For the past 50 years, the U.S. national security policy has centered on the Cold War problems and the accompanying M&S necessary to support this mission. The need for new thrusts in M&S endeavors has been apparent for several years. However, the ingrained institutional processes and interests; the perceived needs to improve current forces and systems; the unavailability of approved scenarios and requirements; and the lack of new directions, authority, and resources cause great resistance to M&S developments for addressing emerging threats.

Currently, the analysts, programmers, and planners are faced with applying old models, war games, and training methods generated many years ago, using weapons data, technologies, performance/effectiveness measures, and engagement scenarios and concepts of operation that do not portray either today's or future problems. To overcome these shortfalls, the M&S generators have had to devise "work-around" solutions using submodels, surrogates, and subjective analyses to reflect the new world threats.

Force Models

Traditionally, force models have been used to devise force structure and tables of organization and equipment to meet mission and threat requirements. In addition, the models, usually highly aggregated in the form of war games, can support concepts of operation and training development.

Exhibit 17.1 portrays some attributes and limitations of three types of force models: (1) traditional, high-intensity warfighting; (2) nontraditional, low-intensity task operations; and (3) nontraditional, high-intensity task actions. The traditional force models are usually designed to reflect penetration by nationalized forces organized in the Cold War days with emphasis on armor and support fires to maximize casualties and achieve victory. The measures of effectiveness center on the forward edge of battle area (FEBA) movement and the rate/amount of attrition of opposing forces. These measures do not emphasize the need to be capable of operating against chemical or biological threats or the need to counter terrorist and guerilla operations.

For the new threats involving in-country operations (represented by civil unrest, insurrections, and terrorist campaigns), models based on measures of effectiveness such as FEBA movements and attrition rates are not appropriate indicators of national security or force requirements.

In these new situations, perpetrators are more interested in creating incidents to achieve political objectives without regard to boundaries or losses of

EXHIBIT 17.1 Overview of typical warfare model characteristics.

	Types of models		
	Traditional high-intensity warfighting force models (penetration models)	**Nontraditional low-intensity warfare task force models (area models)**	**Nontraditional high-intensity warfare task force models (perimeter security models)**
Model objectives	Determine battle outcomes involving opposing conventional forces deployed with full array of combined services and support systems. Battle usually involves penetration of national boundaries.	Determine task force capability to control area and subarea incidents from safe haven positions to restrict enemy's operations and access. Engagements usually evolve from inside country.	Determine task force capability to control incidents using perimeters of area or subarea positions to protect critical or vital regions/resources. Engagements usually evolve from inside country.
Applications	• Battlefield predictions and losses • Tables of organization and equipment • Combat support requirements • Training program guidelines • Battle plan evaluation	• Task force composition • Area/subarea deployment strategy • Survivability, mobility, and sustainability requirements • Information and intelligence needs • Task force plan evaluations	• Task force composition • Perimeter deployment strategy • Combat systems performance requirements • Early warning sensor needs • Task force plan evaluation
Model structure/input	• Large force arrays • Movement profiles • Force attrition rules • Target acquisition/allocation rules to maximize enemy casualties • Deterministic low resolution models drawn from combat samples representing time phased engagements	• Threat response rules • Area control factors • Target acquisition/allocation rules to minimize casualties • Accessibility/movement rules • Value optimization schemes and schedules • Expected value, high resolution, differential combat models using attrition rate methodology	• Alerting/detecting triggers • Perimeter control factors • Opposing perimeter force sizes • Target acquisition/allocation rules to minimize friendly casualties • Task force mission rules • Optimization schemes to increase saved target values • Expected value, high resolution, differential combat models using attrition rate methodology
Model products	• Opposing forces damage types and rates • Forward battle area changes • Munitions/resources expenditures • Battlefield time phased positions	• Incident outcomes • Resource accounting • Enemy area denial levels/fractions • Enemy incident capture and casualty levels • Sub-area force optimization to match available resources	• Incident outcomes • Resource expenditures • Response time—force trades • Perimeter leakage levels • Perimeter force optimization to match available resources • Target value savings
Limitations	• Directed primarily toward structured battle contexts • Inadequate for reflecting new technologies and threats • Databases developed from historical conventional warfighting experiences • MOEs not appropriate for nuclear, biological, and chemical attacks • Reliance on submodels to treat nonstandard problems	• Scenario/incident dependent results • Large variability in historical events and databases • Philosophical differences in opposing forces/national objectives • Uncertainty in force ratios to gain area control • Variability in area accessibility and road network protection requirements	• Perimeter positions vulnerable to overmatching forces • Scenario/incident dependent results • Dependence on intelligence and early warning • High-intensity conflicts may translate into structured warfare • Inability to cover all sections of perimeter due to national barriers • Lack of experiences and databases for perimeter defenses

personnel. Of course, these internal enemy activities still concentrate upon an attempt to control key transportation networks, hold critical economic facilities, capture political symbols of power, and destabilize and topple government organizations. For these cases, some form of area/subarea control or perimeter defense might be an appropriate concept where important regions, sectors, facilities, and infrastructures are protected. In area control, safe haven positions are employed to respond to enemy incidents so areas and subareas are selected to minimize casualties and required resources. As the number of incidents and the density of enemy personnel increase, perimeter defense along the area/subarea boundaries becomes necessary to avoid excessive requirements for personnel and resources. Then, leakage along the perimeters begins to become the significant problem and leads to the need to counter with more and more deployments of personnel/resources along the perimeter.

Both area and perimeter models may be better suited for operations that do not involve highly organized, structured, or deployed forces. Exhibit 17.2 shows a conceptual area model where many of the elements are still similar to the ingredients of a perimeter security model. These models require further study to develop the necessary calculus to design task forces capable of responding to enemy incidents that at least minimize friendly casualties.

Of course these models are not useful for chemical/biological engagements either, except to place emphasis on unit survivability rather than firepower.

EXHIBIT 17.2. Area force model concept.

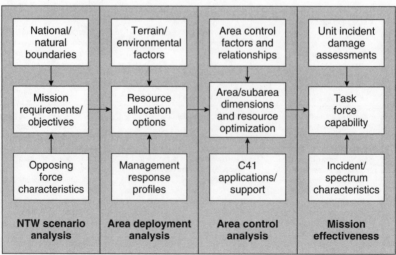

Before area or perimeter models can be utilized, representative scenarios must be available to develop insights on task force composition and system requirements. Fortunately, the U.S. Army and other services have ongoing workshops and programs to consider these needs to design task forces capable of responding to enemy incidents that at least minimize friendly casualties.

Most of these ongoing efforts involve Delphi techniques and subject matter experts to solicit qualitative judgments on the scenario spectrum. Quality function deployment (QFD) is an improved method and alternative for standardizing, exploring, and weighting the expert knowledge. Further analysis is warranted to develop relationships between opposing unit sizes, task response and mobility needs, area and perimeter coverage factors, early warning and intelligence assets, measures of effectiveness, and so on. Nevertheless, notional scenarios can be substituted now to develop the factors, relationships, and databases to support the new M&S needed to deal with some of the NTW problems.

As in-country enemy activities intensify and expand, area/perimeter defenses and models become unsatisfactory representations of the situation and the engagements begin to resemble guerrilla and urban warfare operations. Some details on these higher-level engagements are discussed in Essay 8, Guerrilla Operations in Nontraditional Warfare, and Essay 18, Factors and Considerations for Addressing Guerrilla and Counterinsurgency Warfare.

Other Relevant Models

Many types of models and simulations exist to examine the behavior or characteristics of technologies, systems, processes, and operations. For the purpose of this essay, with the concentration on NTW problems, Exhibit 17.3 provides a brief introduction into four types of models: (1) unit damage models for conventional and WMD attacks; (2) collateral damage models for nuclear, biological, and chemical (NBC) attacks; (3) emergency response and analysis models for defending against terrorist incidents; and (4) testing and evaluation models for addressing the new NTW data and problems. Characteristics and features of each of these models are shown in the exhibit.

The unit damage model is important for determining casualties to battlefield targets based on weapon systems characteristics and target vulnerability. Conversely, the collateral damage models treat the NBC damage caused by area coverage to nonmilitary targets. The unit damage models provide tools for use in the incident damage assessments shown in Exhibit 17.2 for area and perimeter models.

EXHIBIT 17.3   Other relevant model characteristics.

Type of Models	Model purpose	Model operation	Limitations
Battle unit damage models (UDM)	To determine units incapable of continuing to perform mission following attacks by conventional weapons and WMD. Also, to assess value of new technologies and shielding to improve survivability.	UDM calculates fraction of attacked unit covered by effects from WMD and aggregates damage from conventional attack. Based on total size of attack (number of weapons and type), acquired targets, delivery accuracy, and target vulnerability and size, number of targets damaged to specified levels are defined for various laydowns/allocations.	• Results driven by number of weapons and acquired targets in attack • Protection factors for targets in combat vehicles and facilities based on limited test data • Degree of awareness on pending type of attack and countermeasures affects amount of damage
Collateral damage models (CDM)	To determine area coverage to certain dosage levels from nuclear, biological, and chemical (NBC) attacks against noncombat targets.	HPAC model calculates area coverage from NBC warheads in terms of probability of lethal dosage and environmental conditions (wind direction, meteorological events) for exposed personnel based upon predictions of dosage dispersion and amounts necessary to cause casualties. Other models calculate similar effects for nuclear radiation/fallout.	• HPAC model predicts casualties for exposed personnel—effects of protection not treated or uncertain • Biological and nuclear warhead casualties from missile attacks are highly dependent on wind, meteorological conditions, and burst altitudes • Sensitivity to number and type of weapons plus defense measures to intercept/counter attack
Emergency response and analysis models (ERAM)	To translate terrorist threat response requirements into options for limiting damage and applying assets capable of meeting schedules, governing constraints, and engagement parameters. Serves as decision support tool for selecting and executing best response options to save lives and reduce cost.	ERAM consists of three parts: (1) an allocation concept to define options for meeting response requirements within time and cost constraints; (2) correlate response options to savings in lives, damage, and risk; and (3) automatic calculation process to portray top line options with cost benefits and limitations.	• National organized command structure for response and database on terrorist operations/history currently lacking • Governing constraints for emergency response to terrorists not yet approved • Current information and coordination process involves many departments, agencies, and levels of government • Terrorist response models for planning, training, managing, and execution awaiting funding
Testing and evaluation models (TEM)	To test and evaluate the capability of systems to perform as required to counter or operate in NTW conditions. To use models to assist in predicting performance. Also to support test planning and simulation of NTW environments and conditions.	TEM consists of a varied number and type of processes, automation, and analytical formulations to reflect performance of systems or technologies under a given set of conditions, specifications, and requirements. Models can be physics-based (showing effects based upon physical laws) or empirical-based (attempting to duplicate expected results) or formulations (representing concepts and processes). Models and test results form the basis for graphs and tables used to compare systems and evaluate new concepts, designs, or technologies.	• Models and simulations rarely predict results consistent with actual tests • Many NTW scenarios necessitate employment of surrogates, simulations, and new test ranges • Existing database for emerging NTW threats lacking • New test plans and models necessary for emerging threats from NTW problems

Quality Function Deployment

Quality function deployment has been used with some success by the U.S. Air Force and aerospace community to assist in defining system requirements. In addition, QFD has also been applied by other organizations to support technology forecasting decisions. Delphi techniques using expert knowledge require less planning and organization to make projections on requirements and needs, but rationale for choices are not as easily preserved or systematized as in the QFD process.

QFD is a disciplined approach for subject matter experts to evaluate ways to satisfy multiple requirements. As a matter of clarity, some of the characteristics of the QFD process are listed next for consideration by the planners who face major burdens in generating a sufficient but finite number of scenarios to represent the wide variety of conditions and threats affecting force composition and national security.

- Define the objectives to be accomplished (the "What")
- Establish the relative priorities among the "What"
- Define the potential means of accomplishing the objectives (the "How")
- Complete the relationship matrix
- Assess the importance and feasibility of the "How"
- Complete the correlation matrix

Summary

Serious shortfalls exist in the capability of current M&S to address many of the aspects of the NTW problems. Existing M&S do not adequately treat in-country force problems. Other models like area and perimeter can assist but further research is needed to define a representative group of scenarios to provide a baseline for defining potential incidents and developing model input factors. This design and automation of new models and simulations is urgently needed to expedite analysis, planning, and training exercises. QFD is a technique that can be applied to standardize, refine, and prioritize scenarios and concepts of operation using subject matter experts.

Historical data must be relied on to build baseline information for planning and analysis of the spectrum of in-country incidents. Validity of M&S results is limited by the large variability in the incident spectrum and the consequences of unforeseen conflict situations.

In general, high-intensity penetration models strive to maximize enemy casualties, area models tend to minimize overall casualties, and perimeter models attempt to minimize friendly casualties.

Now is the time to meet this new challenge from NTW threats, backed by designated responsibility and funds. New initiatives are required to build the M&S capability to support force planning, RDT&E, and training that will efficiently and effectively counter these threats.

18

FACTORS AND CONSIDERATIONS FOR ADDRESSING GUERRILLA AND COUNTERINSURGENCY WARFARE

David L. Bongard

The decreasing likelihood of major conventional warfare in the post-Cold War period has, in part, served to increase awareness of the potential for guerrilla or insurgency conflicts. Characteristics of guerrilla warfare operations are described in Essay 8, Guerrilla Operations in Nontraditional Warfare, to include historical summaries of conflict situations, tactics, assessments, and possible remedies. The civil strife in Somalia in the mid-1990s, and the civil wars in Liberia (1989–1996) and Sierra Leone (1999–2000) serve as other examples of these sorts of conflicts.

In many cases, the basic internal nature of such conflicts will serve to limit any potential for major power or United Nations involvement. However, as the civil wars in both the Republic of Congo and their larger neighboring Democratic Republic of Congo (DRC—formerly Zaire) have shown, international involvement can indeed follow. In fact, the once-revolutionary government of Laurent Kabila in the DRC, formerly a guerrilla movement based in the western part of the country, is now supported largely by troops from Namibia, Zimbabwe, and other states. The insurgents fighting against the Kabila regime are supported by Rwanda (itself the home of an ex-guerrilla regime, the Tutsi-dominated national liberation front that expelled the former government and ended the bloody pogroms visited on the minority Tutsis by the majority Hutus). As complex as the interrelationships may be in such situations, there is a real need for accurate and realistic modeling of guerrilla conflicts and insurgencies.

Such modeling would need to address two objectives. First, it must provide a means for studying and analyzing the conflict to uncover valuable insights, not only into the strengths and weaknesses of each side, but also into the dynamics and nature of guerrilla warfare. Second, it should develop a basis for decisions prior to major power intervention by offering a systematic and coherent method for determining the forces required. Current military models do not really deal well with insurgent and guerrilla situations. This is due both to the peculiar dynamics of guerrilla operations and campaigns, and to the political dimension of guerrilla campaigns, which generally dominates any military decisions.

Current Considerations and Capabilities

Basically, modern combat simulations are sometimes capable of modeling aspects of guerrilla conflicts, but are only partially successful. Several current models, for example, are relatively good at performing simulations of individual combat actions. In general, such models deal best with large-scale engagements, at the brigade level or higher. (See Essay 17, Models and Simulations for Evaluating Emerging Threats, for approaches and concepts for modeling NTW operations.) Existing models are useful, but less than satisfactory since most engagements in a guerrilla campaign will involve battalions, companies, and platoons, and a good deal of action will involve even small units (parts of platoons, patrols, and squads). One available model has demonstrated capability to handle battalion-level engagements, and has a more limited capability for handling company-level actions. A major problem in modeling small actions is that a single chance event (say a mortar round landing at the feet of the commander) may have a great effect on the outcome, but such events are difficult to predict, and may only happen rarely in comparable situations.

Clearly, this poses difficulties. One concept would be not to try and model each small-scale action, but instead to model the cumulative effect of many such actions, over the course of days or weeks. The intermittent and haphazard nature of combat in guerrilla and insurgent environments has led to their classification as *low-intensity* conflicts. As any veteran of such conflicts can testify, though, the "low intensity" element is applicable only in the larger, overall picture. Any line soldier or officer who served in such a conflict will remember several instances of fierce combat (however short-lived), high casualties, and sheer terror.

Another approach would be to try and model each clash, but rely on such modeling only to produce an overall effect, rather than striving for accuracy in individual actions. This would be a more complex and complicated idea, but would provide a clearer picture of what was going on. On the other hand, the first method, while less accurate in the sense of individual actions and engagements, would achieve substantially the same result, and at considerably less effort. The accuracy of the first method would depend on successfully modeling the correct "environment," in terms of tempo and scale of individual insurgent and counterinsurgent operations. Doctrine choices, sensitivity to civilian casualties, and economic dislocation from operational causes, and other related factors would certainly affect outcomes and modeling utility.

Modeling and Simulation Dimensions

From the foregoing informal critical survey, it is evident that a number of major holes or gaps exist in the current capability to model guerrilla conflicts or insurgencies. Leaving aside, at least for the moment, the political dimension, especially in terms of public relations, popularity, popular support, and so forth, there are four major areas for analysis, development, and innovation.

First, there is the problem of handling a representative sample of the spectrum of guerrilla conflict, ranging from terrorism and assassination through full-fledged major conventional battles. Guerrilla conflict will not include all of these methods of conflict, but at least some of them will always be present. Many of their effects, moreover, are not primarily military, but are more specifically directed at political, social, and economic ends. In the interest of keeping the modeling task within reasonable bounds, it may be desirable to handle this noncombat conflict abstractly, leaving it as part of the conditions or environment within which military operations take place.

Second, attention must be paid to the force sizes of combat operations occurring as part of guerrilla campaigns. Clearly, it will be necessary to treat individual large-scale actions (involving one or more battalion-equivalents on each side) as distinct modeling episodes. Company-level actions are something of a toss-up in this respect, but anything smaller than about 100 combat personnel per side will have to be abstracted in some fashion, similar to one of the two methods outlined earlier, due to the consequences of chance on outcomes.

Third, there is the issue of intelligence gathering, in terms not only of electronic and sensor networks and effectiveness, but also (and perhaps more importantly) of human intelligence (HUMINT), the networks of agents, informers, observers, and messengers employed by both sides. The effectiveness of HUMINT resources by either side would depend on the control they exercise over a given area, coupled with the capabilities of their forces on the ground. As a historical example, the U.S. long-range reconnaissance patrols (LRRPs) during the Vietnam war were extremely valuable and out of proportion to their numbers. This was in substantial measure because of the availability of helicopter resupply, casualty extraction, and air insertion, coupled with extensive and highly mobile radio communications. In contrast, the effectiveness of Maj. Gen. Orde Wingate's famous WW II-era "Chindit" forces in Burma was hampered by poor ground mobility, coupled with sporadic intelligence resources.

Fourth, and perhaps most importantly, these three main aspects of a guerilla conflict will have to be integrated to produce an overall picture. The guerrilla forces' capability to recruit new soldiers, the effectiveness and extent of their noncombat network of supporters, their capability to harass ordinary governmental and administrative activities in areas putatively controlled by the government are factors to be dealt with. Change among these general conditions will all be major ingredients in presenting an overall picture of success for each side. Special events, such as the capture of senior leadership cadre, would have to be modeled as well, at least in terms of their effect if not in terms of the activities themselves.

Initial Course of Action

Not all of this modeling can be accomplished at once, because of the special ties between combat and noncombat factors and actions particularly associated with guerrilla campaigns. Development and refinement of the four major elements will have to be coordinated and accounted for in model planning and construction.

Historical Analysis as a Base

A sensible first step would be to conduct a detailed analysis of twentieth- and twenty-first century guerrilla campaigns. Fortunately, much data and analysis has been collected by groups and organizations within DOD and other sources. Such an overreaching analysis should pay attention to the conditions (environmental, social, political, military) that prevailed. Pure guerrilla campaigns like the French and Second Indochina Wars would compose a major portion of such analysis. It would also be important to consider guerrilla campaigns that were part of larger conflicts, such as the Senussi rebellion in Libya and Egypt during World War I, the larger and more famous contemporary Arab Revolt in the Hejaz and southern Levant, and the operations of the British Chindits and Merrill's Marauders of the United States in the opening stages of the Allied liberation of Burma in spring and summer 1944.

An additional area of investigation should be the characterization of warfare in Africa (outside of the Western Desert and Torch campaigns during

World War II, and the recent Eritrean-Ethiopian War) as essentially guerrilla in terms of tactical and operational characteristics. The South African Army has sensibly paid particular attention to this issue and has developed a doctrine referred to as "bush combat" or "bush operations," emphasizing the dominance of small-unit activities, coupled with the demands imposed by difficult terrain and limited resources. The relative triumph of the South African approach may be demonstrated through a close analysis of operations in southern Angola in the early and mid-1980s, operations undertaken substantially in support of UNITA guerrillas against forces of the Marxist oriented government, with Cuban, East European, and Soviet support. Other instances of such "bush warfare" might include the official and unofficial Western intervention in the Belgian Congo in the early 1960s, largely related to the Katangese secession crises and the role of the mercenary "Commando" units, as well as more recent conflicts in Liberia, Sierra Leone, Rwanda, Democratic Republic of Congo/Zaire, Republic of Congo, Mozambique, and southern Sudan.

Model-Simulation Development

This historical analysis would serve as a basis for evaluating conditions of guerrilla campaigns and operations, and also as a reference point for the evolving guerrilla campaign model. In particular, this historical analysis will provide a benchmark for developing notional scenarios to provide model testing and the generation of engagement factors. As long as the guerrilla campaign model provides results for historical situations that reasonably reflect the historical outcome, the model-simulation developers would be relatively certain that they are on the right track. Such an approach does contain some potential pitfalls, not least the possibility of over-emphasizing certain aspects of particular conflicts, such as the role of TV influencing public opinion in the United States during the Second Indochina War.

Still, this approach provides a sensible alternative to actually conducting a series of guerrilla campaigns, collecting data from them, and using that data to construct a model. That approach, however desirable in a theoretical sense, is scarcely either realistic or affordable. So, we have to employ the next best thing: close historical analysis of past experience. Including guerrilla conflicts from before 1900 is certainly possible and may even prove instructive. However, the widespread import of guerrillas in the last 100-odd years, coupled with the near-overpowering influences of some modern technology innovations (such as radio and other telecommunications, aircraft and helicopters, man-portable mortars and antitank weapons), collectively serve to emphasize

EXHIBIT 18.1 Features of existing combat models for guerrilla operations.

Model name	Resolution scale	Graphic display	Manual/ computer	Combat resolution	Weather and terrain effects
ModSAF	Single vehicle up to battalion	Very high quality	Computer	Uncertain; individual weapon effects	Terrain present, weather and lighting abstracted
SOTACA	Counterinsurgency campaign	Map-board, abstracted transportation net and nexuses	Manual	Unknown, but likely abstracted	Abstract terrain, weather effects simplified
ATLAS	Large-scale conventional campaign	Corps to army group level	Computer-moderated	Converged weapon lethalities	Present in some detail, but not wholly verified
TNDM	Battalion to corps	None at present	Computer	Validated lethality scores	Extensive, historically validated scores

the importance of the guerrilla in the twentieth and twenty-first centuries. In addition, chemical and biological weapons could be adapted and included in this type of warfare.

Characteristics of models and simulations for use in nontraditional warfare including guerrilla operations are outlined in Essay 17, Models and Simulations for Evaluating Emerging Threats. As suggested in that essay, some variation of an area or perimeter defense model can provide the features and attributes for dealing with low-intensity conflicts like guerrilla warfare.

Before proceeding into the development of new models to address guerrilla and counterinsurgency warfare, some reflection on the capability of existing models is in order. Exhibit 18.1 provides a brief introduction into the characteristics of combat models that are available to address certain aspects of the guerrilla and counterinsurgency warfare problems. For the most part, all of these models deal with a structured combat situation where the opposing units are arranged in traditional formations and scenarios. Elements of these models can be used as input and points of departure for a model designed primarily to address the aspects and nature of guerrilla and counterinsurgency warfare.

The Goal

The intended end result of all this effort, both the historical research and analysis, and the subsequent model and simulation development, is the creation of a reliable, verifiable, and valid model for guerrilla conflict. Such a model would need to cover not only pure-guerrilla conflicts, but also the guerrilla campaign elements of wider conventional conflicts.

EXHIBIT 18.2 Utility of current combat models for guerrilla operations.

Category	Current situation	Future development objectives
Spectrum of conflict	Understanding of concept, but sketchy capacity (at best) to handle full gamut of conflict	• Development of clear, intimate, and integrated comprehension of spectrum of conflict • Creation of mechanisms to assess impact of political action, terrorism, and sabotage • Development of understanding and capacity to model cohesive picture of small-level military actions (company-size or less)
Range of military actions: squad patrols to brigade-plus engagements	General capability only to handle division-plus actions; TNDM can deal reliably with battalion level	• Large-scale actions least common in insurgencies • Overwhelming need for accurate modeling of battalion and brigade level engagements • Importance of effect of culmination of many small actions, especially for perceived security of population and for effective guerrilla and government control of country
Intelligence, especially humint	Understanding of mechanisms, in terms of sensors, but only information and sketchy modeling of HUMINT	• Capability needed to model overall effect • Desirability of modeling individual intelligence operations not necessary, although may be desirable for special efforts (like capture of insurgent leadership)
Fusion of components	Essentially nonexistent; this constitutes the largest failing in existing capability to model guerrilla and insurgency struggles	• Integrating these disparate elements is a major challenge • Focus on combined, overall effect rather than on primacy of any particular element
Other Issues	Political and social change left to civilian sociologists, usually poorly grasped by military and national security communities	• Role of strong nongovernmental institutions (civic and social organizations, organized religious groups, etc.) in limiting effect of insurgent actions on public opinion and attitudes • Effect of guerrilla actions directed against government actions and policies

In terms of outputs, the model or simulation should provide not only the traditional military categories of casualties and materiel losses, but also civilian casualties, infrastructure damages and changes in nongovernmental institutions.

Based on the features of the existing combat models, a critique of what exists, and what needs to be done, for effectively modeling guerrilla and insurgency conflicts is shown in Exhibit 18.2 (p. 187). This critique can assist in the structuring of a model designed specifically for guerrilla/counterinsurgency conflicts. The waxing and waning of influence from political parties, religious and humanitarian groups, and others will influence the modeling dimensions and utility.

These intermediate results will need to be integrated to provide an overall picture of the success or failure of the insurgency, in both relative and absolute terms. In Colombia, for instance, active guerrilla forces have been operating within the country for most of the post-1960 period. However, for much of that time the effect on national life was comparatively small, and has really risen only in concert with increased U.S. aid aimed primarily at drug interdiction efforts in the cocaine-producing regions. The de facto alliances between the cocaine cartels and magnates on one hand, with the guerrillas and assorted right-wing paramilitary militias and thug gangs on the other have transformed the nature of the warfare and the approaches to counter these activities. The contemporary emergence in Colombia of a popular, nonpolitical movement to limit violence against nonparticipant civilians may be notably instructive, given the waning influence of other civilian and religious institutions.

The ultimate goal is a valid, user-friendly, and short-term model of guerrilla campaigns and insurgencies. This short-term model or simulation should provide results quickly and permit comparison of different "runs" involving changes in environmental, engagement, and control factors. This would constitute a valuable planning tool, and also serve to increase our understanding of the nature and conditions of guerrilla and insurgency conflicts.

19

EFFECTIVENESS METHODS FOR ADDRESSING NONTRADITIONAL WARFARE THREATS

William R. Schilling

Methodologies for assessing effectiveness of options to counter nontraditional warfare (NTW) threats depend upon the formulation of appropriate military scenarios or conflict situations. This data and understanding provides a framework for examining possible damage to opposing elements caused by the employment of various classes of new weapons. For NTW problems, the classes of weapon effects may be divided into five categories. These are weapons of mass destruction or WMD (nuclear, biological, or chemical), electronic warfare or EW (information exploitation and countermeasures), directed energy weapons or DEW (lasers, microwaves, electromagnetic pulses), precision strike weapons (guided or ultra high velocity projectiles), and nonlethal weapons (activity incapacitation or restriction).

As with traditional warfare activities involving conventional weapons, relationships must be generated between the nontraditional mechanisms that cause damage, and the response operations that are utilized to counter the opposing side. Then, the consequences of responses, concepts, and systems may be ascertained. These relationships generally take the form of a series of events that proceed through a process using (1) functional analysis to define requirements, (2) performance analysis to understand system and technology capability, and (3) effectiveness analysis to assess the outcome of the damage producing mechanisms on mission operations.

For the classes of damage producing mechanisms, this essay addresses associated indicators of performance and effectiveness. It also describes the process and ingredients for relating the characteristics of each sequence in the methodology to the assessment of mission implications and goals.

The primary difference between nontraditional and traditional warfare approaches for developing and assessing effectiveness stems from the indicators used to measure performance and effectiveness rather than the general process or sequence of analysis. These indicators are dissimilar because the damage producing mechanisms and the context for applying threat responses for NTW are distinctly different from traditional warfare conflicts. This is due to the types of warhead effects and organizational changes necessary to overcome or exploit those possibilities.

Effectiveness Methods Process

Generally, the development and application of effectiveness methods center on three components or activities that relate conflict situations to mission accomplishment. The outcome of these relationships varies according to the characteristics of the threat, operational constraints, response options, capability of systems and technology, and engagement factors. The three components in this overarching relationship begin with a functional analysis to define response requirements, then move to a performance analysis to determine response capability, and conclude with an effectiveness analysis to assess mission implications.

Exhibit 19.1 presents a schematic of the process for determining the effectiveness of NTW responses. Under certain situations and conditions, variations in the management of assets plus the interface of contributing functions cause changes to this process. Nevertheless, this exhibit serves as a representation of many of the critical elements or components involved in the application of effectiveness methods.

Functional Analysis

In this part of the effectiveness process, military scenarios or conflict situations are postulated to provide a basis for defining what tasks must be undertaken to counter the employment of enemy weapon classes or damage producing systems. Each of the weapon classes of interest for the NTW threats is analyzed to define the task options appropriate for matching and countering the threat to targets. Such targets include military units, equipment, and support elements, as well as military and civilian infrastructure.

The layouts of opposing forces and targets within the terrain are depicted along with information on location, movement, environment, safety regulations, and other considerations. Tasks are described according to the allowable

EXHIBIT 19.1 Process for determining effectiveness of NTW response.

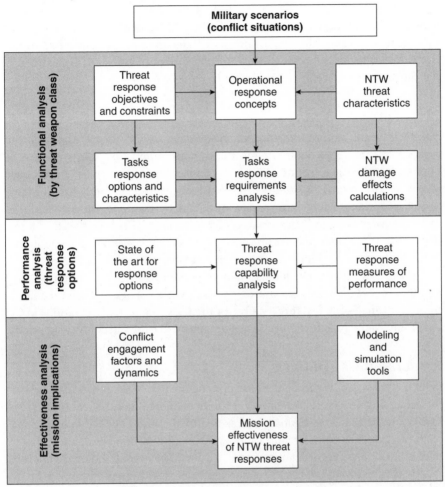

response time; the damage and damage limiting objectives; available resources and assets; and the existing logistics, intelligence, and communications network.

Based on the characteristics of the NTW threat, calculations can be undertaken to define the damage potential from allocations by each weapon class against military or civilian targets in representative conflict situations. In this damage analysis, the effects caused by the application of WMD, electronic warfare, DEW, precision strike weapons, or nonlethal weapons depend on the characteristics of the damage producing mechanism and the target vulnerabilities. Investigation and testing is necessary to provide a baseline for this damage analysis. See Essay 16, Testing and Evaluation of Emerging Systems in Nontraditional Warfare, and Essay 17, Models and Simulations for Evaluating Emerging Threats, for further details on testing and models, respectively. Other facets affecting the task response requirements are discussed further in the process section of this essay.

Performance Analysis

The focal point of the performance analysis deals with the capability of the systems, technologies, unit organizations, and supporting infrastructure to operate together as a means to limit or counter damage potential in response to the NTW threats. Measures of performance are generated for available response options, using information provided by the functional analysis on task requirements and potential target damage. These response options depend on the state of the art or knowledge base on systems and technologies along with an understanding of the response objectives and constraints.

Since systems and technologies may be combined with force elements, task bundling may be undertaken in order to deal with a series of integrated needs to meet a range of NTW threats. One of the keys to effective operations in the NTW environment is flexibility and adaptability to evolving conflict situations.

Effectiveness Analysis

With the information and understanding generated from the functional and performance analyses, sufficient input becomes available to conduct an effectiveness analysis. This investigation is designed to show the implications of threat response teams or force organizations, systems and technologies, and countermeasures on mission capabilities to deal with enemy potential damage effects.

By combining the conflict situation ingredients with the performance analysis, engagement dynamics, models and simulations, and other factors, the mission capability can be surmised. Representative models and simulations for supporting the performance and effectiveness analyses are presented in Essay 17, Models and Simulations for Evaluating Emerging Threats, and Essay 18, Factors and Considerations for Addressing Guerrilla and Counterinsurgency Warfare.

Performance and Effectiveness Indicators

Descriptions or indicators of performance and effectiveness are usually related to the capability to damage targets or affect mission accomplishment. Both traditional and nontraditional warfare situations employ the damage producing mechanisms as a prime indicator of systems, technology, and organizational capability to counter threats and support mission objectives.

In traditional warfare, damage producing mechanisms utilize some form of high explosive or kinetic energy to defeat targets. In such cases, the amount of damage depends on the accuracy of delivery, size of the warhead, and target vulnerability. However, in the case of nontraditional warfare, the damage producing mechanisms depend on other forms of energy applications and target structure or organization. Under NTW conditions, the parametric measures necessary to reflect performance vary according to weapon class. Generally, these weapons have the capability to damage several to many materiel or personnel targets per warhead or shot expended except in the case of precision strike systems.

Exhibit 19.2 illustrates the damage effects parameters, engagement variables, and measures of effectiveness for the five classes of weapons treated in this essay. While other facets of systems or organizational capabilities are important as indicators of performance and effectiveness, models and simulations usually consider some form of attrition bookkeeping to indicate or represent capability and mission outcome. Many other measures are available to reflect logistics burdens, intelligence accuracy and timeliness, protection and survivability, and mobility to mention a few. However, all of these other measures can be related to damage production rates.

Weapon Effects Parameters

A partial listing of suitable measures of damage production capability against military targets and nontargets (civilian personnel/infrastructure) are displayed in Exhibit 19.2. For each weapon class, representative descriptions are presented to indicate damage characteristics along with an associated physical term to reflect quantitative measures of effects on targets. These types of terms and values provide a basis for determining threat magnitudes and system or technology capability for use in the functional and performance analyses shown in Exhibit 19.1.

For the most part, the weapon effects tend to be area effects caused by (1) explosions or dispersions from nuclear, chemical, or biological warheads; (2) generated energy coupled to interfere with distant electromechanical equipment; or (3) projected kinetic energy designed to dispel, disable, or incapacitate personnel and materiel targets. Of course, the precision strike weapons depend upon the same damage mechanisms as conventional (traditional) explosives.

Engagement Effectiveness Parameters

In order to show the impact of weapon effects on groups of personnel, materiel, and support systems organized to defeat or counter a NTW threat,

EXHIBIT 19.2   Performance and effectiveness indicators.

Threat weapon classes	Exemplary weapon effects parameters	Conflict engagement variables	Measures of effectiveness
Weapons of mass destruction (WMD) • Nuclear • Chemical • Biological	Effects radio (m) Overpressure (kg/m²) Thermal (degrees) Radiation (rads) EMP (watts/cm²) Effects radiation (m) Dosage rate (E/sec) Warhead weight (kg) Warhead yield (KT)	Target vulnerability Delivery accuracy Burst altitude Target damage criteria Number of delivered warheads Countermeasures (vaccination, shielding, etc.) Disposition of military/civilian elements	Targets damaged Targets surviving Collateral damage Replacement/recovery time (units) Preserved target functions Destroyed targets per warhead Casualties per warhead
Electronic warfare (EW)	Produced energy (joules) Overpressure (kg/m²) Energy rate (joules/sec) Beam angle (degrees) Produced power (watts) System weight (kg) Frequency (cycles/sec) Bandwidth (frequency spread) Areas of effects (m²)	Target size Target altitude Target vulnerability Target range from energy source Countermeasures (shielding, resistance, etc.) Environment Mission information demand requirements Mission information waiting times	Mission downtime/degradation Mission information processing time Equipment replacement/recovery time Targets destroyed/damaged
Directed energy weapons (DEW)	Produced energy (joules) Overpressure (kg/m²) Energy rate (joules/sec) Beam angle (degrees) Produced power (watts) System weight (kg) Frequency (cycles/sec) Bandwidth (frequency spread) Area of effects (m²)	Target vulnerability Target range from energy source Target damage criteria Target energy coupling capability Countermeasures (shielding, absorption) Environment Equipment utilization requirements	Mission downtime/degradation Equipment replacement/recovery time Targets destroyed/damaged Preserved target functions
Precision strike weapons	Velocity-time history (m/sec) Projectile mass (kg) Maximum effective range (km) Accuracy (mills or CEP) Area of effects (m²)	Target vulnerability Target damage criteria End game countermeasures Number of warheads launched Target size	Targets damaged Expended warheads Number of shots Preserved target functions
Nonlethal weapons	Maximum effective range (kg) Area coverage (m²) Rate of fire (no./min) Accuracy (mills or CEP)	Target vulnerability Target incapacitation criteria Environment Target size	Targets incapacitation rate Targets downtime Preserved target functions

conflict engagement variables need to be known or surmised in order to provide a baseline for analyzing possible conflict outcomes. These conflict outcomes may be defined to reflect mission effectiveness. Exhibit 19.2 provides a representative list of engagement variables and effectiveness measures that can be used to describe conflict outcomes according to the component and factors shown earlier in Exhibit 19.1.

The engagement variables are based on characteristics of the opposing sides plus the damage producing mechanisms and limiting factors involved in the conflict. The measures of effectiveness are designed to show the impact of the conflict on capability of the opposing sides or facets to survive and accomplish mission objectives. Accordingly, the listed engagement items relate to personnel and materiel deployment as well as target vulnerability and survivability. The mission measures define the organizational status or capability at the conclusion of the skirmish or conflict.

Effectiveness Methods Utility

Effectiveness methods provide a framework for developing appropriate responses to NTW threats. The methodology is similar to approaches applied to traditional warfare problems. However, many facets are different. These include information on new target damage effects; valid models and simulations to reflect changes in conflict organization structure; restructuring command, control, communications, computers, and intelligence (C^4I) to manage and control the intelligence information and resources involved in counterstrikes; and new countermeasures to thwart enemy objectives.

Examples of possible applications for effectiveness methods are listed next:

1. To discern the value of various organizations postulated to counter the NTW threats
2. To evaluate the impact of advanced technologies on mission effectiveness
3. To assist in the development of system performance objectives and designs for dealing with NTW initiatives
4. To prioritize RDT&E plans as a means to conserve resources and select best options
5. To identify guidelines for data collection and HUMINT activities
6. To guide the generation and understanding of requirements and operational concepts for meeting the new challenges

In short, a need exists to utilize the effectiveness methods to assist in the development of appropriate responses to the challenges from the existing and formidable NTW threats. The current approaches are simply not adequate to treat the different conditions, measures of effectiveness, and engagement concepts expected under these new threat situations.

SECTION V

INSTITUTIONAL RESPONSES TO NONTRADITIONAL WARFARE

The realization in the U.S. national security establishment that future armed conflicts will substantially be characterized by so-called "asymmetric" dynamics points to an increased importance for dealing with the threats and risks posed by weapons of mass destruction (WMD). In addition to traditional nuclear weapons, WMDs also include chemical and biological agents, the latter embracing both active organisms such as viruses and bacteria, as well as biologically derived toxins such as *botulinus*.

Dealing with the risks posed by hostile WMDs requires not only the development of effective physical counteragents and countermeasures, but perhaps most importantly, the creation of resilient and effective institutional structures to handle responses to WMD attacks. These institutional developments are not threatening to other powers, and may more importantly be useful even in the case of natural emergencies or other nonmilitary crises.

The bulk of this section concerns responses to issues associated with the employment of, and policies relating to, WMD. Associated with that range of issues are additional issues of ballistic missile defense (BMD) and general approaches to NTW threat responses.

The issue of BMD has acquired particular importance within the United States, and consequently worldwide as well. There has long been a significant element of public opinion within the United States that has regarded the doctrine of deterrence, precluding the hostile use of WMD by the guarantee of a lethal and proportionate response, as too "touchy-feely" and uncertain a basis on which to build a major pillar of national security. The growing technical capabilities of U.S. forces and technologies to resolve some of the obstacles to effective BMD has served to make many foreign powers uneasy, and has placed the U.S. government in the position of possibly violating a treaty it is pledged to uphold, prohibiting the large-scale deployment of an antiballistic missile (ABM) system.

That particular aspect of national policy is properly a matter of political debate, and thus falls beyond the scope of this work. It is worthwhile, though, to provide a thorough understanding of the issues involved in such a debate, so that the parties involved are at least working from the same script, and discussing the same assumptions, facts, and risks.

The policy questions associated with ABM, WMD, and terrorist issues feed into a wider range of more general questions dealing with responses to NTW threats. One of the most important tasks facing the United States over the next few decades will be developing and implementing effective methods for identifying and responding to emergent NTW threats.

This section presents discussions on elements of the NTW threat responses and some R&D planning guidelines for overcoming these threats. In addition, some comments are offered on the role of BMD, living with nuclear weapons, and possible treaty initiatives for mitigating these threats from a diplomatic or national point of view.

20

NONTRADITIONAL WARFARE THREAT RESPONSES

William R. Schilling

Development of Response Options

To prepare for the nontraditional warfare (NTW) threats in the new millennium, the United States must begin to formulate universal approaches, concepts, and systems that can mitigate and defeat these enemies of the nation or our allies. By unifying and integrating responses, the number of solutions can be reduced to a plausible number of activities with a high probability of success. This effort eliminates many ad hoc approaches generated by individual government organizations to counter particular types of threats.

For each of the NTW threat categories, response objectives must be formulated and agreement must be reached among the participating stakeholders. Unless agreement is reached on program objectives, threat responses will continue to be ad hoc and resources will not be efficiently managed. Of course lead agencies for each type of NTW threat must take the initiative for generating the necessary responses. But coordination and integration will assist in technology transfer and consolidation of overall program objectives.

Program initiatives and options for meeting the required NTW response objectives can be derived by considering the current deficiencies, the threat criticality, and the feasibility of proposed solutions. In addition, prime emphasis must be given to the opportunities for joint efforts among participating users and the prioritization of NTW threats. Key aspects of this generation of NTW responses must be based upon threat potential damage, the availability of validated threat scenarios, and the likelihood of threat incident.

EXHIBIT 20.1   NTW threat response characteristics.

NTW threats	Response objectives	Program initiatives/options
Weapons of mass destruction	• Missile intercept to limit damage • Overwhelming response capability to provide deterrence • Preemptive strikes to destroy nuclear/chemical/ biological production and storage centers	• Threat agent neutralization • Dual warhead intercept capability • Directed energy applications for C/B kills • Reliable HUMINT resources to discern threat intentions/timing • Protective suits and equipment for operating in C/B environments • Weapons for attacking surface/ underground hardened targets • Early warning to limit casualties and other damage
Electronic warfare	• Protect and shield critical equipment items • Counter threat ECM devices • Filter directed energy illuminations/shots • Utilize multiple methods/devices for C⁴I	• Harden purchased COTS equipment for military/government users • Built-in broadband/multiple frequency capability • Eliminate close-in access for directed energy device applications • Replace/augment single source devices for C⁴I
Demining and countermine warfare	• Reduce civilian casualties and return land to peaceful uses from leftover mines • Counter C/B mine threats	• Detect underground/underwater mines • Develop means to explode mines in place • Develop technologies/methods to counter C/B mines • Employ joint signature fusion methods and devices to overcome false target problem
Economic and industrial warfare	• Security measures to protect information, trade secrets, and technologies • Financial controls to limit international bribery, laundering, dumping, unlawful competition	• Diplomatic agreements to foster lawful world trade • Information systems to monitor foreign trade and trading compliance • Application of severe penalty systems for trade violations
Urban and guerilla warfare	• Target acquisition of threat units and equipment • Pinpointing of terrorist positions • Protection of friendly forces/equipment • Control of collateral damage	• Sensors for acquiring concealed threats • Lethal weapons with controlled area coverage • Nonlethal weapons for limiting collateral damage • Fast, lightly armored vehicles for combat operations support • Light armored suits for personal protection
Terrorist operations	• Capture and avoidance of damage from small unit actions • Deterrence and damage limitation from large unit operations and rogue nations	• Track movement of threat units • Manage information on known terrorists • Coordinate and integrate organizations involved in countering terrorist activities • Identify terrorists at U.S. entry points

Representative response objectives and program initiatives are portrayed in Exhibit 20.1. Other objectives and responses will be generated by detailed analyses of requirements, capability to meet performance objectives, and cost-benefit considerations. Appropriate response options involve U.S. policy decisions, international agreements, new force configurations, advanced technology applications, and systems development and testing.

Evaluation of Response Options

In order to rank and evaluate NTW response options, databases on target damage potential, statistical methods, and tools in the form of models and simulations must be developed. Then, civilian law enforcement or military units, systems, and technologies can be formulated and prioritized to meet the NTW problems. These evaluations can be in the form of savings in money, people, equipment, and infrastructure based on possible options for military forces, civilian response units, systems, and concepts.

New models and simulations are needed to reflect and treat the shifts from previous interest on large combat operations involving forward edge of battle (FEBA) movements and force attrition to other measures of effectiveness (MOEs) such as mission capability, recovery/replacement time, protection factors, and capture of perpetrators. Emphasis on better usage of statistical methods (i.e., quality function deployment, Bayesian analysis, and Dempster-Shafer theory) are necessary to reduce dependencies on costly testing as well as simplify the decision process about false targets and for selection of options and responses. Another tool for consideration is the application of penalty functions to show trade-offs in benefits and shortcomings in concepts, technologies, and systems.

The nomination of response options can be derived from functional and performance analyses used to measure costs and benefits. Key NTW response functions can be described as actions to detect, classify, negate, and counter the threats.

By exploring the various NTW threats in terms of the functions involved in the applications of countermeasures and resources, systematic and efficient processes and solutions can be matched against requirements. In order to satisfy response objectives, system components and associated performance requirements necessary to satisfy each functional area can be defined and evaluated. Aspects of the functional areas of concern include the following:

1. Detection of the threat (using HUMINT, satellites, and aerial platforms)
2. Classification of threat (using collected/judgmental information on size, location, timing, and potential damage)

3. Negation of threat (damage prevention by preemptive actions)

4. Countering the threat application (by interception, protecting targets, and countermeasures)

Threat Damage Potential and Limitation Factors

Even before NTW threats are defined and prioritized, major initiatives should begin immediately to develop estimates of the potential damage and means to limit consequences of threat actions. This information will provide a sound basis for selecting appropriate cost-effective responses that save the most lives and protect the national infrastructure. Obviously, no affordable mix of plans, people, and materials will likely preclude all NTW episodes from occurring.

The damage potential is a key measure in ranking or prioritizing NTW threats. Other important measures include (1) the likelihood of a particular type of incident, (2) the possibility of detecting/identifying the perpetrators (threat groups or rogue nations), and (3) the cost to deter or defeat a potential threat action.

The capability to develop estimates of potential threat damage depends on the availability of standardized, representative attack scenarios. These scenarios can be employed to identify the size and type of threat, the attacker delivery system, the amount of agent or munition employed in the attack, the objectives of the attack, and the sophistication of the delivery and damage producing systems. In addition, the length of engagement time for the threat episode must be estimated. The total personnel casualty and infrastructure systems vulnerability can be calculated by using all the forementioned factors/parameters. These determinations should be made for each of the possible NTW threat applications. Plausible variations in parameters can be utilized to show sensitivity of key variables (unknowns) in the attack.

Damage limitation measures must be undertaken to reduce casualties and losses of facilities/equipment from NTW threat episodes. These factors will include early warning and intelligence on pending attacks, available protective actions, partial defeat of attacking threat systems, and execution of preemptive strikes.

The amount of potential damage from NTW threats is directly related to the representative scenarios. Large variations in actual damage occur from conditions at the point or area of attack. For example, some nonideal explosives used by individuals or small groups of terrorists against U.S. targets produced the results shown in Exhibit 20.2.

EXHIBIT 20.2 Examples of terrorist attacks in the United States.

Target	Date	Explosive		
		Type	Amount	Deaths
IRS Building, California	1990	ANFO*	2,000	0
World Trade Center, New York	1993	C4	1,200	6
Murrah Building, Oklahoma	1995	ANFO	1,200	168
Centennial Olympic Park, Georgia	1996	Powder	40	1
World Trade Center/Pentagoan	2001	Aviation fuel	>100,000	3,000

*ANFO—ammunition nitrate and fuel oil mixture

In short, wide variations in damage from small terrorist groups or activities are possible due to conditions at the time of the explosion. As the size and sophistication of the NTW threat increases, the potential damage or results become more predictable.

Now is the time to begin to estimate damage for the classes of NTW operations so suitable choices will be available to meet and respond to the most critical threats. The penalty for delaying or failing to integrate relevant plans and initiatives will result in major losses of lives and infrastructure. Likewise, civilian and military units will not be organized or sized properly to deter threats and limit damage.

21

RESEARCH AND DEVELOPMENT PLANNING GUIDE FOR COUNTERING NONTRADITIONAL WARFARE THREATS

William R. Schilling

Almost every country in the world is confronted with threats from nontraditional warfare (NTW) operations. The United States is a central target or focus for many of these potential threats due to the desire of many groups, organizations, and rogue nations to gain notoriety and leverage from attacks against a powerful nation. These NTW actions may be executed through the utilization of weapons of mass destruction, electronic warfare, demining and countermine operations, urban and guerilla activities, or terrorist incidents.

Earlier NTW essays discuss characteristics and responses to NTW threats. This essay provides a brief research and development (R&D) planning guide for improving capability to meet these NTW threats against our national infrastructure, our people, and our way of life.

Once the NTW threats are characterized and possible responses to the threats are nominated, then R&D plans can be prepared and implemented. These R&D plans may start in the form of guidelines derived from the NTW threat response requirements and the existing deficiencies to meet these threats. In short, based on the requirements (what we want to do) and the deficiencies (what we can't do), science and technology initiatives/investigations can be generated to indicate what R&D should be done to satisfy unfulfilled needs.

Artist's conception of DDG-47, later redesignated CG-47 class-guided missile cruiser.

Weapons of Mass Destruction

In the nontraditional warfare (NTW) problem areas, the most pressing and challenging requirements are found in the threats from weapons of mass destruction. From a strategic point of view, these weapons are delivered by missiles and other sophisticated employment techniques. Using nuclear, chemical, or biological warheads, these operations have the potential to inflict devastating levels of damage from square miles (by chemical warheads) to hundreds of square miles (from biological warheads) and thousands of square miles (from nuclear warheads). In short, weapons of mass destruction are considered as a threat involving nations against nations. Other NTW actions can also cause alarming levels of damage and usually involve small organizations or groups of terrorists.

Deterrence is still the main key to countering the nuclear and perhaps biological threats. For this approach to be credible, the threatened nation must have overwhelming capability to punish the user of weapons of mass destruction. Strategic solutions will have risks due to system imperfections (e.g., leakage) so the United States and its allies still must rely on international agreements and counterstrikes.

EXHIBIT 21.1   R&D planning guide to counter weapons of mass destruction threats.

Requirements	Deficiencies	S&T initiatives/investigations
Threat agent neutralization • Select kill mechanism options • Verification of type of threat • Employment of best/appropriate kill mechanism • Engagement control to affect threat warhead • Kill efficiency	Agent/warhead kill in open space	Testing of methods and predictions
		Ship-based boost phase intercept
		High-temperature incendiary (HTI)/chemical clouds, seeding
	Canister protection	Break-up of canisters
	Aim point accuracies	Miss distance/control capabilities
	Electromechanical interference with agent release	Directed energy weapons (DEW) • Electromagnetic pulse applications (EMP) • High-powered microwave (HPM) applications
	Threat cloud simulation	Cloud dimensions (density; range vs. time)
		Cloud agent interactions with defeat mechanism
	Explosives vs. hit to kill options	Response control vs. miss distance
		Proximity fuse vs. miss distance
Dual warhead interceptor capability • Break interceptor • Kill agent • Minimize resources • Maximize defender area • Avoid compromise to nuclear threats	Break open attacker warhead/kill agents	Feasibility of using one warhead to open attacking missiles and one warhead to kill C/B agents
		Utility of interceptors with mix of warheads for simultaneous attacks
	Payload constraints	Selection of warheads to break open attacker and warhead for agent kill
		Testing of dual warhead capabilities
		Warhead defender family (NBC)
	Type of threat (CBN)	HUMINT reliability
		Distinguishing characteristics of attacking missile
Counterstrike weapons for surface/underground hardened targets (UHT) • Destroy production/storage units • Limit collateral damage • Use warhead to match type of threat • Achieve resource efficiency	Determine critical nodes at target	HUMINT
		Satellite
	Achieve kills in complex-multiple storage units	Area effects (HTI/seeding)
		Destroy ventilation—AC
		Destroy/bury target entrances
	Prevent quick restoration of damage	Contaminate computer/electrical systems
		DEW explosives (chemical driven)
	Destroy NBC materials in tanks and vaults	Multiple warheads (explosives and high temperature (seeded)
		Foundation destabilizing
		Fuel air explosive (high impulse)

Exhibit 21.1 presents an R&D planning guide for weapons of mass destruction threats. Primary emphasis is placed on chemical and biological (C/B) matters. The requirements to meet these threats are expressed in terms of needs to perform agent neutralization, achieve dual warhead capability, and counterstrike weapons of mass destruction. For each of these requirements, deficiencies in current capabilities are cited and science and technology initiatives/investigations are recommended.

Some of the major technology issues and focus for further R&D efforts are as follows:

• Finding means to break canisters/missiles and destroy agents while still limiting collateral damage—a complex combination of events

- Employing prestrikes against nuclear, chemical, and biological (NBC) threat assets (political and international approval)
- Avoiding reliance on marginal means to counter weapons of mass destruction threats
- Developing new approaches to meet the weapons of mass destruction threat
- Determining feasibility of evolutionary approaches currently being applied (i.e., hit to kill and reliance on warhead penetration or explosives) to kill attacking C/B missiles
- Concentrating on reducing damage effects (protection and warning with emphasis on biological threats)
- Limiting effort to defeat conventional ballistic missiles as not a significant threat from a cost-effective standpoint
- Achieving capability to defeat both chemical and biological missiles with a single type of warhead to reduce need to identify warhead type
- Sharing approaches to counter weapons of mass destruction threats with allies and maybe some old enemies to alleviate suspicions and achieve politically acceptable solutions
- Ensuring missile defense footprints are larger than C/B area of effects

Other concerns affecting R&D initiatives are the following:

- Attacker submunition/canister survivability at intercept
- Predeployment of C/B submunitions prior to intercept attempt
- Accuracy/response requirements for critical intercepts
- Prevention of enemy NBC facility usage
- Application of nonlethal means for NBC production/storage
- Reliance on deterrence not very satisfactory when large damage occurs to our nation or allies—perpetrators must be convincingly rebuked
- Reliability/availability of HUMINT is critical to track the weapons of mass destruction perpetrators (this is a key part of deterrence to rogue nations)
- Spreading of disease (small pox, etc.) using missiles and other delivery means
- Overcoming barriers to addressing aspects of weapons of mass destruction threats due to absence of formal or certified evidence (focus the science and technology program on the real needs—not on continuing initiatives as usual)

Electronic Warfare Operations

A new emerging NTW threat is being directed at our operations, communications, and information systems and infrastructures. The electronic warfare threat is poorly understood because the concepts of employment and the potential damage effects are uncertain. In the past, infrastructures, operations, and management were not so dependent on reliable, transference, quick, and accurate information. But heavy reliance on high technology communications and data storage systems become tempting targets for those seeking asymmetries and potential vulnerabilities.

The United States must continue to expect new advances in electronic applications and new means to interrupt their use. Alternatives to our dependence on electronic means are not easy to find so the measures to provide hardening and reduce damage become even more imperative. In fact, replacements for command, control, communications, and intelligence (C^3I) are going to be less efficient and provide less area coverage. A principal focus of new R&D to counter electronic warfare must be based on means to locate sources of emission before or rapidly after their use to limit damage and punish perpetrators.

Exhibit 21.2 portrays overarching R&D guidelines for electronic warfare operations. The proposed science and technology initiatives/investigations are directed toward reducing vulnerabilities, providing deterrence, and achieving damage limitations.

The technology focus of the R&D guidelines are listed next and presented in more detail in Exhibit 21.2:

- Achieving rapid location and neutralization of electronic warfare threats
- Determining vulnerability of civilian and military equipment to new threats
- Developing survivability and performance standards for electromechanical equipment and devices
- Finding alternatives to electronic dependence
- Understanding phenomenology by which energy couples with targets to disorient/damage
- Evaluating implications of current and advanced electronic countermeasures (ECM) on mission capability
- Determining utility of ECM against civilian and government operations
- Introducing modularization to expedite repair/recovery of equipment damaged by ECM

EXHIBIT 21.2   R&D planning guide to counter electronic warfare threats.

Requirements	Deficiencies	S&T initiatives/investigations
Reduction in vulnerability of critical items of civilian and military equipment • Performance requirements/ standards • Susceptibility to damage • Engagement scenarios • V&V of protection measures	Commercial equipment unprotected from high electromagnetic pulses (EMP)	Criteria and standards for critical commercial items
		Tests and evaluation of commercial equipment to show compliance/acceptance
	Military equipment vulnerability to new nonnuclear generated ECM threats	New tests to verify survivability of critical equipment from emerging DEW and non-nuclear EMP threats
		Elimination of ECM sources prior to ignition of effects
Deference to use of electronic warfare by foreign nations and terrorist organizations • Tracking and location of threats • Rogue nation electronic warfare signatures • Mechanisms/weapons to attack electronic warfare centers	Identification and location of electronic warfare threats to civilian and military equipment	Mobile and remote sensors to detect electronic warfare activity
	Means to destroy electronic warfare generating devices	Short-range autonomous homing weapon for tactical battles
		Antiballistic missile terminal homing weapon
	Tracking and disclosure of rogue nation support for deployment of electronic warfare equipment/devices	Employment of HUMINT, satellites, and telecommunications monitoring
		Pinpointing and controlling technology for use in electronic warfare activities
	Attacking enemy electronic warfare centers used to support attacks against U.S. and allied interests	Developing nonlethal standoff systems for attacking electronic warfare operations and centers
		Developing collateral damage limiting weapons for attacking electronic warfare sites
Limitations of electronic warfare damage effects • Recovery, replacement, repair and reconstitution of damaged elements • Hardening of equipment to DEW and other effects • Utilization of multiple sources for C⁴I to overcome area effects from electronic warfare threats	Rapid diagnosis of electronic warfare effects on equipment	Prescriptive measures for repairing damage
		Equipment self-diagnosis to describe damage
	Availability of replacement items	Utilization of modular components (plug in/plug out)
		Stockage of critical nodes/components
	Adaptation of alternative measures to operate equipment	Training of maintenance/on-site personnel
		Increase standoff range for electronic warfare threats
		Utilization of filters to spread/decrease deposits/energy
	Built-in Faraday cage to protect equipment	Testing to ensure no opening for electronic warfare penetration
	Knowledge of phenomenology/ coupling of electronic warfare energy to various types of targets	Testing to determine energy transfer from electronic warfare source to targets
		Determining sensitivity to countermeasures and engagement constraints
	Augmentation of single source devices for C⁴I	Adaptation of nonelectronic methods for communications and control
		Transfer of critical information prior to deployment/attack
	Built-in broadband/multiple frequency capability	Tunable frequency selection based on knowledge of electronic warfare source
		Randomization and management of frequency selections

- Utilizing simulations to explore vulnerabilities and countermeasures to electronic warfare threats (civilian/military)
- Cataloging existing electronic warfare threats to provide reality checks on possible vulnerabilities

In executing R&D guidelines to confront electronic warfare threats, the following concerns should be dealt with and addressed:

- Achieving assurance that ECM users will be detected and captured
- Making sure concepts of employment of ECCM devices are feasible
- Introducing electronic counter-countermeasures (ECCM) so produced effects will be limited or negligible
- Addressing the right problems—prioritize and understand the needs posed by ECM threats
- Utilizing testing to understand vulnerability and develop countermeasures to negate electronic warfare threats
- Classifying certain aspects of electronic warfare knowledge to prevent acquisition by rogue nations and terrorist groups
- Balancing concerns with understanding of the dimensions, feasibility of electronic warfare threats

Terrorist Operations

During the past decade, the number and daring of terrorist activities against the United States has caused grave concerns within the government and civilian populace. The associated casualties and material and infrastructure damage has increased with more than 3,000 deaths produced by terrorist incidents in the United States alone. Terrorist operations are becoming the option of choice for rogue nations and extreme elements to achieve goals against superior powers (organized for traditional warfare problems). These threat elements are seeking to capitalize on asymmetries using tactics, surprise, and cunning that limit exposure to strong response force organizations.

An R&D planning guide to counter terrorist operations is displayed in Exhibit 21.3. The general R&D requirements are grouped under the categories of detection and capture of terrorists, deterrence of rogue nation initiatives, and limitation of damage from massive destructive actions. Proposed science and technology actions to counter terrorist operations involve some reliance on information sharing, technology insertion, international cooperation, reliable HUMINT, and unified response management.

EXHIBIT 21.3 R&D planning guide to counter terrorist operations.

Requirements	Deficiencies	S&T initiatives/investigations
Detection and capture of terrorists • Database on known terrorist groups/ intentions • Identification/recognition of terrorists at critical entry points/installations • Detection of terrorist weapons, equipment explosives • Removal of safe havens or sanctuaries for operations	Integration of all source terrorist identification and database/profiles	Development and maintenance of all source data warehouse on known/suspected terrorists
		Generation of profiles and composition of terrorist groups/locations/intentions
	Automated recognition of terrorists at critical entry points/installations	Application of stored data for comparison/identification of terrorists using advanced sensors exploiting IR, thermal, photo, fingerprints, other distinguishing signatures
		Processing and recording of data on known terrorists to provide required information for comparison
	Detection of explosives, munitions, equipment, and chemicals for supporting terrorist activities	Utilization of bees and dogs to locate presence of chemicals and explosives in remote areas
		Applications of lasers, sniffers, and other DEW devices
		Seeding and tracking explosives and support equipment
		Standoff weapons for penetrating and destroying caves and underground operations centers
Deference of rogue nation-sponsored terrorist incidents • Tracking and location of terrorist signatures from rogue nations • International penalty functions/agreements • Mechanisms/weapons to attack perpetrators	Identification and validation of terrorist sponsors and signatures	Limitations and controls on rogue nations' access to C/B weapons and other high technology means for terrorist actions
		Utilization of HUMINT, satellites, and telecommunications to monitor foreign activities
	Development of international protocols and tracking to limit terrorist access to critical areas	Adaptation of systems to verify nations' compliance with biological weapons bans/agreements
		Implementation of means to detect fraudulent visas/passports
		Utilization of remote sensors to detect border crossings and aid capture
	Credible response to penalize attacker's infrastructure and military power while limiting collateral damage	Development of low collateral damage weapons and agents to destroy production and storage centers for explosives, chemicals, and biological threats
		Investigation of feasibility of chemical and DEW means to neutralize,destroy terrorist supplies and technology support base
		Implementation of means to make foreign production and storage centers uninhabitable for laborers/transporters
Limitation of damage from large terrorist unit actions • Early warning and quick response • Availability of appropriate assets/resources • Integration of plans and crises management • Damage prediction and control measures • Prevention of access to vehicles, aircraft,a nd boats and HAZMAT areas	Streamline methods and systems for managing C/B crises	Investigation and analysis of functions and methods to integrate resources and merge threat responses
		Automation of information resources, status, and locations of equipment and personnel to meet critical demands
	Medical facilities and trained personnel and equipment to deal with advanced bioengineered threats	Capacity to stockpile and develop antidotes, vaccines, and antibiotics rapidly
		Automation of records on trained personnel, expertise, location, and availability
	Overarching federal blueprint for response	Development of comprehensive plans and process for integrating and managing crisis response assets
		Involvement of stakeholders sin process and transmission of plans to increase public awareness and confidence
	Sharing of intelligence information on terrorist plans and intentions	Transmission of available and updated information on potential terrorist activities and plans to stakeholders
		Early warning systems for terrorist alerts to stakeholders
	Limitation of terrorist access to civilian personnel and facilities	Emplacement of barriers and remote sensors around facilities to reduce effects of explosives and C/B usage

The science and technology initiatives and investigations for the planning guide include the following issues and factors:

- Monitoring and discovering terrorist/rogue nation activities/intent
- Integration of all source database of suspects/incidents/characteristics
- Automation to detect terrorists using new sensor technology
- Detection of chemicals/explosives (tagging, sniffers, dogs, etc.)
- Controlling access to C/B and explosives technologies
- Increasing capacity to stockpile and develop vaccines/antidotes and antibiotics rapidly
- Matching response resources and assets to the threat
- Application of unmanned and remote sensors/weapons and disposal systems
- Elimination of sanctuaries for terrorist operations

Other concerns affecting R&D planning guidelines are listed next:

- Availability/reliability of HUMINT in defeating terrorist activities— preventing and capturing perpetrators
- Credibility and value of international agreements to thwart terrorist operations
- Trade-offs involving response vs. prevention of terrorist actions
- Viability of blueprints designed to manage and address terrorist actions
- Automated decision analysis to obtain the qualified personnel, required assets, and on-site management within required response times

Demining and Countermine Warfare

Recently, there has been increased public interest in reducing casualties caused by unexploded ordnance (UXO) in the form of land mines, artillery shells, aerial bombs, hand grenades, and small arms ammunition. This unexploded ordnance can be found in almost every country throughout the world as a result of munitions testing, civil uprisings, and wars between countries and factions. The increased public awareness has generated demining initiatives sponsored by the United States, United Nations, and prominent world leaders.

These initiatives deal with some of the complex issues involved in demining operations such as applications of human and animal resources in high-risk environments, utilization of technology for mine detection and identification, logistic support for heavy equipment, and many other concerns dealing with training, safety and security, medical response, and equipment left behind on foreign soil.

Essential differences exist in the humanitarian demining operations since the necessity for no casulaties, standoff detection, and low cost solutions become overriding considerations. From the standpoint of the demining technology developer, false target identification and low cost per neutralized mine represent the key challenges. In the countermine operations, the mine clearing may take place under combat conditions involving enemy covering fire to retard or penalize minefield clearing and breaching activities. Again, false targets are a key problem and must be resolved by the use of multiple detection sensors. Still, many similar functions exist in both demining and countermine warfare, so opportunities exist for sharing science and technology information and development.

Exhibit 21.4 shows a derived R&D planning guide for demining and countermine warfare. The guidelines center upon the requirements to detect conventional surface and buried mines and the development of countermeasures to chemical/biological mines.

Key areas of concern affecting R&D guidelines for demining and countermine actions are as follows:

- Detection is the biggest concern in conventional countermine warfare.
- Prevention of deployment is the biggest concern in C/B mines.
- New technology advances can overcome measures being considered for detection.
- False target detection is the big problem.
- Multi-sensors are required in an automated joint signature fusion approach to overcome the false target problem.
- Little information is being generated to define and specify false target tolerance and performance.
- Test data for countermine and demining sensors are poorly developed, stored, managed, or evaluated.
- Performance specifications must include both mine detection and false targets.
- Countermine work has been going on for decades, but much emphasis is on evolutionary research and the approaches are still based on Cold War scenarios.

EXHIBIT 21.4   R&D planning guide for demining and countermining operations.

Requirements	Deficiencies	S&T initiatives/investigations
Detection of conventional surface and subsurface mines • Locating, recording, and tracking minefields • Classification of mines • Boundaries of minefields • Automated record keeping	Distinguishing signatures for metallic and nonmetallic mines	Signature profiles by sensor types
		Probability density distribution fuctions by sensor
		Standaardizes testing and recording—test objectives
	Separation of real and false targets	Develop false target profiles by sensor type/background
		Probability density distributions
		Standard testing—required objectives
	Application of joint fusion devices (automated)	Statistical methods for automatic target recognition (Dempster-Shaefer)
	Recording of minefields and mines location/boundaries	Historical database on previous mine users and locations
		Centralized computer mapping center tied to overflight sensors plus automatic target recognition
		Utilization of bees and dogs for detremining presence of mines by type
Countering chemical and biological mines • Detect deployment • Classify/locate mine • Recover mine • Prevent C/B damage	Establishment of threat plausibility	Feasibility assessment of threat
		Concept for development and deployment of threat
	Tracking of mien deployment vessel	Protocol/process for monitoring movement of deployment equipment/systems
		Prevention of C/B mines dispatch
	Determinatiaon of type of mine deployed (i.e., C/B, conventional)	Standoff mine classification devices
		Remote control mine detection and calassification devices
	Capture and response to mines before initiation	Application of remote control net capturing devices to prevent mines from surfacing and to move mines to safe disposal area
		Early warning to potential ictims to limit casualties and take protective measures
		Development of protective gear and equipment to assist in mine caputre
	Prevention of C/B damage	Standoff devices to explode mines in safe location
		Utilization of directed energy/other methods to prevent pop-up initiation

- DOD is ignoring threat from C/B actions and avoiding problems which could be devastating.
- Equipment and personnel protection is needed to address the C/B mine problem area.

R&D Guideline Applications

While many federal and state governments as well as commercial organizations and other institutions have addressed components of the NTW threat problems, most R&D activities are sponsored by individual agencies or industries based on perceived ownership (mission) or authority to meet a part of the threat. This ad hoc approach tends to deplete resources and cause duplication of efforts. Nevertheless, the government, in connection with industry, has held planning and testing sessions to focus attentions and identify strategies for treating portions of the NTW threat.

This essay generates some viewpoints and observations into the characterization of the science and technology needs for countering the NTW threats and the opportunities to integrate and transfer some of the R&D efforts to meet multiple user requirements. The previous sections of this essay present nearly 50 current deficiencies along with about 100 R&D planning guidelines for addressing threats from weapons of mass destruction, electronic warfare, terrorists, and mines.

These first-order R&D guidelines are expected to advance future efforts in the following manner:

1. Provide a framework for detailed evaluations of science and technology options and initiatives.

2. Present a starting point for understanding the R&D requirements and processes to meet these potentially devastating threats.

3. Serve as a catalyst or primer for advancing integrated user actions.

4. Identify and determine science and technology responsibilities, sponsorships, and priorities.

5. Identify and adapt technology transfer opportunities to meet other potential user requirements.

22

APPLICATION OF BALLISTIC MISSILE DEFENSES IN NONTRADITIONAL WARFARE OPERATIONS

William R. Schilling

From a military sense, ballistic missile defense (BMD) has become one of the most controversial topics in the world. The controversy or unrest about the possible U.S. deployment of BMD systems to counter limited missile threats involving weapons of mass destruction (WMD) centers on two concerns. The first deals with the likelihood that the development and general deployment of a BMD system would be in violation of the current antiballistic missile (ABM) treaty. However, this concern could be alleviated if an agreement was executed between the United States and Russia to allow changes to the existing document. The second concern stems from the widespread belief that deploying a BMD system would lead to an arms race among the nuclear powers as a means to ensure or preserve nuclear deterrence capability.

Prior to the signing of the ABM treaty in 1972, the United States and the Soviet Union, led by Russia, expended substantial fortunes in attempts to develop BMD systems to defend against large nuclear missile attacks. All of these previous efforts concentrated on the use of terminal defenses around critical military assets, national infrastructures, and heavily populated cities. The large number of targets to be defended, the expected radioactive fallout from nuclear detonations, and the difficulties in warhead discrimination combined to cause the major nuclear powers to cease the pursuit of a vast and costly BMD program as well as to seek agreements to limit the number of allowable offensive nuclear missiles.

In recent years, a new threat has emerged from the efforts of a number of lesser powers to develop longer-range offensive missiles with WMD capability (nuclear, biological, and chemical warheads). For the most part, these new threats are considered limited from the standpoint of (1) probable number of missiles and launchers to be developed/deployed over the next 10 to 20 years, (2) the difficulties in obtaining or developing nuclear warheads, and (3) the complexity of the technological infrastructure necessary to produce reliable, accurate, long-range missile systems. Because these threats are limited, at least from the standpoint of numbers of long-range missiles, interest has surfaced on the possibility of developing an affordable and effective BMD system to negate this WMD capability.

The purpose of this essay is to provide an overview of the limited ballistic missile threat, to describe possible concepts for defending against these threats, and to summarize the prospects for success in countering those threats. Accordingly, this essay serves as a useful framework for understanding the issues and utility of BMD as a means for countering limited offensive missile threats.

Limited Offensive Missile Threat Characteristics

Nation-states that might be seeking to deploy long-range offensive missiles and acquire WMD capabilities could pose a critical threat to the security of the United States and its allies. A few of the critical factors that provide a basis for introducing and understanding the situation include the national motivation behind the buildup of the emerging missile threats, the capability to cause significant damage with the long-range missiles, and the time and resources required to produce a viable threat. These emerging missile threats can be characterized by the efforts underway in China, India, Iran, Iraq, North Korea, and Pakistan. These are the countries most likely to develop up to 20 intercontinental ballistic missiles (ICBMs) over the next two decades.

Acquisition Motivation

The national motivation for acquiring longer-range missile systems evolves from the following factors and speculations:

1. The perceived need to have the capability to launch communications and surveillance space satellites consistent with regional language and cultural interests

2. The desire for deterrence against other nations in the region that have or are in the process of acquiring WMD

3. The belief that possession of long-range missiles with WMD capability will enhance national recognition and prestige and increase world influence

4. The deliberate development of a capability to threaten other nations, including the United States, into acceptance of views or aggressive actions

Threat Development

Exhibit 22.1 provides an overview and projection of the offensive ballistic missile capabilities of the six countries cited earlier. The chart excludes efforts on missiles with ranges less than 600 km. For each of the six countries, information is presented on the system identity or origin, range, payload, and status along with a few comments on type of warheads, propulsion system, and accuracy. In some situations, the information is speculative or derived from scaling from previous developments. Of course, access to foreign experts, technology, and manufacturing processes can expedite both the time to reach operational status and the system performance. At this time, North Korea, Iran, and Iraq have not publicly demonstrated nuclear capability through either testing or demonstrating missile engineering capability.

Except for China, the other five countries do not have near-term capability to reach the lower 48 United States. However, North Korea has demonstrated a capability to launch a three-stage missile to a range of about 6,000 km which could reach Alaska and Japan. To reach the continental land mass of the United States, these six countries would need to have a missile range greater than 10,000 km. Multiple stages are required to achieve intercontinental ballistic missile (ICBM) ranges. The payloads for these projected threats are generally quite small—from about 500 to 1,000 kg—so nuclear warhead yields are likely to be between 250 and 750 KT.

Other than the Chinese, the accuracies associated with the longer-range missile systems are above 1,000 meters circular error probability (CEP). However, India is reported to have a highly accurate terminal homing system with a 40-meter CEP based on GPS applications, probably configured for high explosive and chemical warheads.

Developmental work is underway in India, Iran, and North Korea to improve range, accuracy, and payloads. Most of these developmental initiatives will not lead to producing highly capable systems before 2010 or 2015. However, North Korea could restart testing on the Taepodong 1 and 2 (TD-1/2) in 2003 which could lead to some operational capability by about 2005. The next 2 years could be used by North Korea to enhance TD-1/2 missile manufacturing and performance capability.

EXHIBIT 22.1 Threats from countries developing limited offensive ballistic missile capabilities.

Country	Ballistic missile system identity	Range (km)	Payload (kg)	Status	Ballistic missile characteristics and comments
China	DF-5	12,000	3,000	Operational	Warhead type: nuclear (3–4 MT) Propulsion: 2-stage solid propellant Accuracy: 800 m CEP
	DF-31	8,000	700	Tested	Warhead type: nuclear (250 KT) Propulsion: 3-stage solid propellant Operational by 2003 or 2004
	DF-41	12,000	800	Developmental	Warhead type: nuclear (250 KT) Propulsion: 3-stage solid propellant
India	Agni-1	1,500	800	Tested	Warhead type: chemical, HE, or nuclear (45 KT) Propulsion: 2-stage solid-liquid combination Accuracy: 40 m CEP (terminal guidance-HE)
	Agni-2	2,000–2,500	1,000	Tested	Warhead type: chemical, HE, or nuclear Propulsion: 2-stage solid-liquid combination
	ASLV	4,500	1,000	Developmental	Conversion of satellite-launched vehicle Key components available for conversion
Iran	Shahab-3	1,300–1,500	750	Tested	Warhead type: chemical or HE Propulsion: 1-stage liquid propellant Accuracy: 4,000 m CEP
	Shahab-X	ICBM range	500–1,000	Speculative (2010–2015)	Estimated to be space launch vehicle-based on scaled up SCUD technology (Taepodong)

Country	Missile			Status	Details
Iraq	Al Hussein	600	500	Operational	Warhead type: chemical, biological, or HE Propulsion: 1-stage liquid propellant Accuracy: 1,000 m CEP
	Unknown	ICBM Range	500–1,000	Speculative (beyond 2015)	Estimated IOC depends on foreign country support and existence of sanctions against development of weapons of mass destruction
North Korea	Nodong-1/2	1,300–1,500	770	Operational	Warhead type: chemical, HE, or nuclear (?) Propulsion: 1-stage liquid propellant Accuracy: 3,000–4,000 m CEP
	Taepodong-1/2	1,500–6,000	300	Speculative (possibly by 2005)	Warhead type: chemical, biological, or nuclear (?) Propulsion: 3-stage solid-liquid combination Accuracy: Very poor
Pakistan	Ghauri-1	1,300–1,500	700	Tested (Nodong derivative)	Warhead type: HE or nuclear (?) Propulsion: 1-stage liquid propellant Accuracy: 4,000 m CEP
	Ghauri-2/3	2,500–3,000	500–700	Developmental	Warhead type: HE or nuclear (?) Propulsion: 2-stage solid propellant Accuracy: unknown

Note: Information sources include Report #2000/09, Ballistic Missile Proliferation, Perspectives, Janes, 1999, and Carnegie Endowment for International Peace Proliferation News and Resources, 2001.

All of these countries will soon have chemical and biological warhead capabilities. But only China and India and perhaps Pakistan may have sufficient capability to engineer or develop nuclear warheads for long-range missiles in the next few years. Without substantial assistance from foreign experts or externally supplied warheads, the other countries will need major development programs involving manufacturing processes, tools, and experimentation.

Missile Damage Projections

Based upon the missile payloads projected in Exhibit 22.1 for the countries other than China, Exhibit 22.2 portrays area damage effects from WMD in the 250 and 750 kg payload range. Damage caused by nuclear blast and thermal effects is shown for comparison with biological and chemical warheads. With regard to the thermal effects, first degree burns are not very serious but the intent is to provide a gross indication of the area affected by nuclear detonations. On the other hand, second degree burns do produce casualties or incapacitation and the indicated areas in the chart will be reduced by about 10 to 20 percent, depending on warhead yield. This chart is designed to provide an indication of the level of damage effects that could be achieved by each offensive missile that penetrated in an attack under various BMD situations.

Interestingly, biological warheads are as much of a threat to exposed personnel as low-yield nuclear warheads. For example, with no BMD present, a 750 kg nuclear warhead will produce first degree burns over an area only

EXHIBIT 22.2 Potential damage from emerging ballistic missile threats.

Type of damage	Weight of Warhead (kg)	Area of effects per warhead launched (km²)		
		No missile defense (100% probability of penetration)	Good missile defense (10% probability of penetration)	Excellent missile defense (1% probability of penetration)
Nuclear-blast (5 psi overpressure)	250 (250 KT) 7705 (750 KT)	40 70	4 7	0.4 0.7
Nuclear-thermal (1st degree burns to exposed personnel)	250 (3 cal/cm²) 750 (6 cal/cm²)	510 1360	51 136	5.1 13.6
Biological (anthrax—50% lethality to exposed personnel)	250 (light rain) 750 (light rain)	320 1280	32 128	3.2 12.8
Chemical (VX—50% lethality to exposed personnel)	250 (opt. conditions) 750 (opt. conditions)	0.1 0.4	0.01 0.04	0.001 0.004

slightly larger than a biological warhead of the same weight (1,360 sq. km versus 1,280 sq. km). And, in the case of the biological warhead, the damage would be lethal against 50 percent of the exposed personnel.

Exhibit 22.2 indicates that chemical warheads are more of a tactical warhead and would not be considered as a strategic threat. In this situation, the area of chemical effects tends to be less than a square kilometer—hardly worth the bother, except for the terrorist-fear factor.

An attack from 10 missiles with 750 KT yields could destroy material targets over an area of about 700 sq. km (275 square miles) if no missile defense was present. A highly effective BMD system (i.e., 99 percent effective) could reduce this material damage to about 4 sq. km (less than 2 square miles). The area of damage to exposed personnel produced by the same size missile attack with biological agents would cover 12,800 sq. km (5,000 square miles) provided no missile defense is present. Of course material damage would be negligible. The presence of an excellent BMD system could reduce this personnel damage from 10 biological warheads to about 128 sq. km (50 square miles). Obviously, the number of actual personnel casualties will depend upon the target density (number of personnel per unit of area). For example, a highly populated center could approach 100,000 personnel in a 10 square mile area.

Ballistic Missile Defense System Options

Over the last four decades, an assortment of BMD options have been investigated and evaluated by the United States and Russia. While a large number of variants are possible for BMD, four concepts provide a reasonable basis for exploring defensive capabilities against limited offensive missile threats. These four concepts involve defensive missile launches against offensive missiles in the boost phase from earth surface and air platforms as well as launches from land surfaces against missiles in the mid-course and terminal phases.

For the last 5 years, the principal emphasis has been on mid-course missile intercept after booster separation. The primary benefit from this approach is the efficiency available from large area coverage using a few defensive missile sites to guard against attacks from launches either west or east of the United States. The primary drawback of this concept evolves from the difficulties associated with warhead discrimination of even simple decoys (like balloons, radar reflectors, and low signature observables). Also, the accuracy requirements to achieve warhead kill places stress on both the tracking radars and terminal homing interceptors. Nevertheless, several intercepts have been made against missiles during the last few years, albeit under less than realistic conditions.

Prototype of advanced medium-range air-to-air missile (AMRAAM).

Exhibit 22.3 introduces the characteristics of the basic concepts for intercepting offensive missiles with nonnuclear warheads. These concepts are described in terms of the defense plan, the rationale for selection, components of the system, and kill mechanisms. Details on the technical characteristics (like radar configurations and guidance and control technologies) for each defense concept are complex and beyond the scope of this essay. In every case, some combination of satellite/early warning radar is necessary to begin the sequence for missile intercept.

Provided means can be generated for achieving discrimination and warhead kill (through point or area kill), the mid-course intercept option is the simplest and least expensive approach. Augmentation by sensors from space or sea may aid the discrimination problems. Also, major efforts are continuing to focus on software processing improvements to isolate or separate warhead observables from decoys and booster fragments.

Of all the concepts under consideration, intercept during the booster phase may be the most preferable to other nuclear powers. The location of the weapon platforms would not impact on their offensive nuclear missile systems or reliance on deterrence for security purposes. Of course, the lesser nuclear powers will not be pleased with deployments near their countries' borders.

EXHIBIT 22.3 Concepts for limited ballistic missile defense (BMD) systems.

		BMD concept plan	Rationale for BMD plan	Components of BMD system	Kill mechanism
Offensive missile trajectory	Booster phase (atmospheric launch phase)	• Launch short-range ballistic missile from land or ship for intercept using conventional warheads	• Can achieve intercept prior to deployment of decoys or maneuvering reentry vehicle • Provides vulnerable target for ballistic missile intercept • Still intact booster simplifies missile tracking	• Satellite or early warning radar to alert land or ship BMD system of missile launch • Tracking radars to locate and guide interceptor to target • BMD interceptor to align with offensive missile trajectory prior to warhead separation and intercept	Hit to kill terminal homing or area kill with high explosives (HE)
		• Apply standoff airborne laser weapon against booster propellant section	• Can attack booster section with laser weapon from 40,000 feet altitude and 200 miles standoff • Provides uncluttered search area between 40 and 80 seconds after missile launch	• Satellite to notify aircraft with airborne laser weapon of missile launch • Airborne weapon system with 3 lasers to track missile, determine "sweet spot," and kill booster prior to warhead separation	Laser directed energy weapon (DEW)
	Mid-course phase (exoatmospheric flight profile)	• Launch long-range ballistic missile from land to defeat warhead using conventional warheads	• Can limit damage caused by warhead detonation in intercept area • Can protect land mass with limited number of ballistic missile launch sites as sufficient missile tracking time is available to permit intercepts or coverage over wide region of the exo-atmosphere.	• Satellite/early warning radar to alert BMD system of missile launch • Ground and ship-based radars to track missile cloud for warhead discrimination and to guide interceptor to warhead path • BMD interceptor to provide final discrimination, home on target and kill warhead	Hit to kill terminal homing or area kill with high explosives
	Terminal phase (atmospheric re-entry profile)	• Employ short-range ballistic missile at selected terminal points to defeat warhead in atmosphere near target area	• Can select critical targets for protection • Can simplify warhead discrimination problem by using atmosphere to strip some decoys and booster fragments plus identify warhead by ballistic missile coefficients and sensor observables	• Satellite/early warning radar to alert BMD systems of missile launch • Radars in terminal area to track incoming missile, perform discrimination, and guide defense missile to target • BMD interceptor to kill warhead above keep out zone	Hit to kill terminal homing or area kill with high explosives

BMD System Perspective

Many technical, political, and financial hurdles need to be overcome before an operational BMD system is likely to emerge. The easiest barrier to the implementation of a BMD system is technical. Some of the current ideas emphasize employing more than one option (i.e., layering of interceptor systems) to improve chances for technical success, including higher probabilities for missile intercept. However, this layered approach is likely to be the most costly and require the longest development time.

Exhibit 22.4 presents a perspective on the technical and developmental issues along with financial and political concerns for each BMD option. In general, the terminal defense concept is least likely to be implemented due to the cost involved in protecting so many targets and the concern about nuclear radiation fallout from high altitude explosions and other factors. In fact, the U.S. populace would likely abhor the presence of all those BMD sites throughout the United States. All of these proposed concepts would be in violation of the ABM treaty unless agreements are made between the United States and Russia along with acceptance by many of our allies.

Several tough technical problems arise in the booster intercept phase, but the problem of warhead discrimination is averted. These leading problems include the availability of sufficient time to maneuver (align) the defensive (interceptor) missile trajectory to make a near head-on intercept. Also, only a few minutes or less are available to achieve intercept prior to the offensive missile exiting into the exo-atmosphere so a new high performance booster for the defensive missile is required. Finally, both the accessibility and survivability considerations for airborne platforms using laser weapons could be insurmountable.

Except for the mid-course intercept, the other concepts would probably take at least 10 years to develop and deploy a sufficient number of systems to counter even a limited ballistic missile threat. This could change if major increases in BMD funding are approved and technological issues are quickly resolved.

With regard to interceptor launches from nearby ships or land sites against offensive missiles in the booster phase, an aggressive RDT&E program would be necessary to prove feasibility. Development of a high performance booster is necessary to meet the timing and guidance required to intercept the offensive missile prior to booster separation/fragmentation and deployment of decoys. But this concept might be more acceptable to other nuclear powers and our allies.

From a cost standpoint, terminal homing defenses really do not make sense for limited ballistic missile threats from 20 or so warheads. There are just too

EXHIBIT 22.4 Perspective on limited ballistic missile defense (BMD) system capabilities.

BMD concept	Technical and developmental issues	Financial and political concerns	Initial operational capability
Intercept during booster phase from land or ship launch	• High performance booster for interceptor • Sea launch of high performance booster • Availability of BMD land site near foreign missile launch • Radar tracking and guidance requirement for interception • Sufficient time to align interceptor with offensive missile flight trajectory	• Cost and time to develop BMD system will require major new commitments of resources for development, testing, and evaluation • World community might accept booster intercept plan as nonthreatening to major nuclear powers	Beyond 2010
Intercept during booster phase from airborne laser weapons system	• Accessibility to offensive missile flight trajectory from a few hundred miles standoff • Verification of booster vulnerability to laser weaponry • Survivability of airborne weapons platform or satellite to hostile actions	• Number of airborne laser weapon platforms could be excessive for covering potential world missile threats • Nations with nuclear weapons may be hostile to nearby airborne laser weapons systems • World community might accept booster intercept plan as nonthreatening to major nuclear powers	Beyond 2008
Intercept during mid-course phase from land-based intercept system	• Discrimination of balloon decoys and chaff from warhead • Development of highly reliable hit-to-kill interceptor • Employment of conventional area kill mechanisms with sufficient coverage to ensure warhead kill by high explosives or encounter of dispersed material	• Time to achieve operational capability with sufficient testing, warhead discrimination, and interception enhancements may exceed short-term deployment objectives • Deployment of BMD system violates ABM treaty unless U.S. and Russia agree to revisions/modifications • Deployment of BMD system may lead to arms race by major nuclear powers as a means to ensure sufficiency of offensive nuclear missile stockpile	2006-2008
Intercept during terminal phase from land-based system	• Upgrade and revision of pre-1990 RDT&E program to match limited missile threat conditions • Development of preferential defense packages to limit number of terminal defense launchers and guidance radars • Warheads with biological submunitions could achieve damage from deployment above missile keep out zone	• Cost and time to deploy sufficient terminal missile defense systems to protect all critical targets may be prohibitive • Deployment of terminal missile defense system will violate current ABM treaty and may lead to arms race by nuclear powers	Beyond 2012

many places to defend (hundreds of defense missile sites and radars would probably be required to protect that many targets).

The least costly approach and most likely to succeed is the current national missile defense system. However, warhead discrimination remains as the long pole in the tent. Perhaps sensor augmentation from accompanying missiles or additional tracking from ship-based radars or other observables collected by satellites can help solve this problem. Obviously, further efforts in data processing and investigations into differences (if any) in mid-course behavior for warheads and balloons may assist in this effort. Also, developing an accurate, reliable interceptor to kill the warhead will necessitate much more testing and perhaps different kill mechanisms.

Finally, the restraints posed by the ABM treaty as well as the use of space systems in a BMD role need to be resolved to provide a tolerant political environment for BMD development and implementation, even against limited offensive missile threats.

Mr. John W. Hindes contributed to some of the ideas and concepts presented in this essay through discussions and reviews with the author. Mr. Hindes is an internationally recognized expert in ballistic missile defense, analysis, and technology.

23

THE FUTURE
WITH NUCLEAR WEAPONS

Joseph D. Douglass, Jr.
William R. Schilling

Nuclear weapons, and other weapons of mass destruction, cannot be unin-vented. They demand that a new chapter in human social development be found and written. Once done, we will discover that existence of the weapons is no longer of great consequence.

Nations will decide whether or not to develop nuclear weapons based first on their own national interests, regardless of any international agreements they may have signed. If a nation believes it must have such weapons to ensure its survival, it will make a determined effort to get them. Such situations have historical precedents among emerging nations, those at the peak of their influence, and those in decline. It is now within the realm of possibility for many nations to assure their sovereignty at relatively low monetary cost. Thus, reforming political boundaries by military conquest has become far more difficult due to the possibility of nuclear response by an adversary.

This essay presents several viewpoints concerned with both the strategic and terrorist threat to the United States and the rest of the world from nuclear weapons. It also outlines the conditions likely to unfold in the future from these threat conditions.

The Nuclear Dilemma

The destructive power of nuclear weapons may appear to offer an attractive option to those nations having expansionist goals, and a nation that may have acquired the weapons originally for defensive purposes could change its objectives. The natural response by such a country's neighbors would be either to obtain perpetual security guarantees from a powerful friend, or to acquire nuclear weapons themselves. We might expect to see situations in the future that are analogous to the standoff between the United States and the Soviet Union during the Cold War; the eventual outcomes may also be similar.

Accordingly, relatively inexpensive nuclear weapons appear to point to a future in which geopolitical changes will be accomplished (at least in the industrialized parts of the world) less by the use of military force and more by other, undetermined, techniques. If more nations emerge from poverty, this situation will become more prevalent. Other means besides military action must be identified to deal with human conflicts. Terrorism, infiltration, and guerrilla attacks are certainly not the alternatives we seek.

The basic knowledge of how to manufacture nuclear weapons is nearly universal, although important design details are not well known. If nuclear weapons were to be totally eliminated from the world, their reappearance in the future would not be precluded. Knowledge is difficult, if not impossible, to eliminate. A regime of inspections and retributions to inhibit their introduction would have to continue in perpetuity, or until an equally devastating weapon was invented. Bureaucracy, corruption, and boredom would eventually so weaken such a regime that it could not be expected to remain effective forever. Forever is a long time.

Over the past 50 years an ultimate alternative—if all else fails, all-out warfare against one's enemy must be considered—was taken away. Nuclear weapons make all-out war unendurable—there can be no winners. So the task for statesmen, politicians, and, indeed all people, is to replace the age-old alternative for ultimate survival with another foundation upon which to rely when attempting to resolve human conflict. The same may be said of humans' ultimate technique for affecting change.

The elimination of all conflict between human beings is unrealistic, and may not even be desirable; however, the causes of conflict must be better understood. Emotional responses to real or imagined wrongdoing need to be dealt with before they lead to tangible acts that can escalate out of control. Old hatreds must be dealt with openly and with a new paradigm of tolerance. The luxury of harboring deep religious, racial, or ethnic hatreds, passing them on to each new generation, and allowing them to escalate to major conflicts is being lost, permanently.

The development of weapons that ensure that everyone loses in an unrestrained war, and even, potentially, that the existence of humankind can be at risk, demands a turning point in human social development and behavior. Changes may be needed in the definition of the nation-state and of sovereignty.

Little room would be available for despotism and ultra-nationalism. Attempts to legislate away the need for this turning point may be successful for a time, but cannot be expected to last forever. They may provide us some time to find true solutions for dealing with human conflict and producing change, but this time will be too short for the task—we must be careful not to waste it.

Nuclear Weapons Proliferation

As far as we know, fewer nations have acquired nuclear weapons than was expected 30 years ago. There have certainly been many reasons for this, but one is that nuclear weapons have not been necessary to ensure sovereignty or further national objectives.

Another important reason for the relatively slow proliferation of nuclear weapons is the difficulty in obtaining the heavy metal ingredients of such devices. Plutonium and one type (isotope) of uranium are the metals used in the nuclear weapons of the five declared nuclear weapon states. These metals are difficult to acquire. It is costly (and open to observation) to build a nuclear reactor and chemical separation plant to obtain plutonium. A large amount of equipment and money is needed to separate the isotopes of uranium to get the one needed to make a nuclear explosive. This expense and visibility have inhibited many nations from building nuclear weapons.

The physics principles needed to understand how a nuclear weapon works are well known throughout the world. While the engineering and manufacturing details may not be known, the knowledge that the problems of design and manufacturing can be solved will lead smart people to find solutions. In fact, it is generally believed that any reasonably advanced nation would have the knowledge base to build effective, albeit "clumsy" nuclear weapons—if they could obtain the necessary metals.

International inspections, seeking to uncover clandestine plutonium and uranium production, have had many successes; however, they have been unsuccessful in some instances. Their utility is dependent on a number of factors: continued vigilance; efficient, rapid, and cost-effective operations; the difficulty of obtaining the necessary metals. Given the importance of the activity, it is not prudent to trust that vigilance and interest (and funding) will persist into the indefinite future. It is also difficult to believe that bureaucratic inefficiency will not someday undermine inspection organizations. If it were not so difficult and expensive to obtain enriched uranium or plutonium, the task of ever-vigilant inspections would be nearly impossible.

A considerable amount of enriched uranium and of plutonium has been produced in the world. A number of attempts are now being made to inventory, secure, and dispose of this material so that it cannot fall into the hands of would-be nuclear weapon proliferators. These attempts underscore the importance of the metals. However, if a new technique were to be invented that could cheaply, rapidly, and in a modest amount of space separate the naturally occurring isotopes of uranium, safeguarding the already separated material would become almost moot. In that case, inspection would be nearly impossible and nothing would stand in the way of large-scale proliferation of nuclear weapons.

Whether such an invention can be made is not known. Since no such device has come along in 50 years, perhaps it cannot be done, but that seems a slim thread upon which to hang global security. Since natural uranium exists around the world, we appear to be one invention away from potentially wide-scale proliferation of nuclear weapons. We must live with the knowledge that nuclear weapons will either be present or potentially present in the world forever more. Something better than constant fear must be found to allow us to deal with that fact.

Future Nuclear Weapons Development

Some potential nuclear states contemplate how to gain access or acquire nuclear weapons capability. At the same time, current nuclear nations search for means to ensure deterrence and security, preserve international status, reduce operation and maintenance costs, and match nuclear weapons to damage and nondamage objectives.

Several compelling motives operate to expand this desire for new weapons development. Among these factors are the following:

1. The belief that nuclear stockpiles of the major powers (United States and Russia) can be reduced without affecting or degrading deterrence under arms control agreements

2. The desire for new designs as a means to limit the proliferation and costs from too many nuclear weapons and launch systems

3. The limited ability to guarantee required nuclear warhead performance without relying on nuclear testing or new expensive laboratory testing that may not be available to potential nuclear foes

4. The possibility of introducing new, low yield, simple warhead designs that could be combined with new terminal homing systems to reduce collateral damage, match warheads to target damage objectives, and improve confidence in performance

5. The incentives for lesser nuclear powers (China and India) to expand and improve nuclear stockpiles as a means to guard against the introduction of national missile defenses

A report entitled "Nuclear Weapons in the Twenty-First Century" was published in June 2000 by Stephen M. Younger, former Associate Laboratory Director for Nuclear Weapons, Los Alamos National Laboratory, and now the Director of the Defense Threat Reduction Agency. The report states:

At this time, Russia maintains very large strategic and tactical nuclear forces. China is actively modernizing its nuclear arsenal. India and Pakistan have dramatically demonstrated the ability of mid-level technology states to develop or acquire nuclear weapons. There are grave concerns about the future proliferation of nuclear weapons among such countries as North Korea, Iraq, and Iran. The nuclear age is far from over.

Some targets require the energy of a nuclear weapon for their destruction. However, precision targeting can greatly reduce the nuclear yield required to destroy such targets. Only a relatively few targets require high nuclear yields. Advantages of lower yields include reduced collateral damage, arms control advantages to the United States, and the possibility that such weapons could be maintained with higher confidence and at lower cost than our current nuclear arsenal.

An important consideration in thinking about lower-yield nuclear forces for most of the U.S. strategic nuclear requirements is that such weapons could be much simpler than our current highly optimized nuclear designs. Given sufficient throw-weight on our missiles, we could use gun-assembled or other simple, rugged designs that might be maintained with high confidence without nuclear testing. These low-yield weapons can be built with enriched uranium and the old, well-proven "gun assemble" design used for the Hiroshima bomb in 1945. At its heart is a block of enriched uranium that explodes when just the right amount of uranium to cause fission is shot into it by a chemical explosive trigger. Scientists are so confident of the design that the new weapons could be fielded without testing. Such designs would require a significantly smaller industrial plant for their maintenance than our current forces. Based on uranium weapons designs, a much smaller plutonium infrastructure would be required. Other technologies specific to high-yield nuclear weapons could be placed in a standby mode rather than a production mode. Finally, simpler weapons might be maintained with higher confidence for longer periods by a weapons staff that has little or no direct experience with nuclear testing. However, should the United States elect to follow such a path, it will still be necessary to retain expertise in more sophisticated nuclear designs as a hedge against changing conditions in the future.

There are additional, non-technical considerations that will influence future nuclear policy. Given current and projected scientific capabilities, it is difficult or impossible to confidently field a new, highly optimized, nuclear warhead design without nuclear testing. For this and other reasons, the United States intends to maintain its existing nuclear designs into the indefinite future. This is a fundamental change in how we maintain the U.S. arsenal. Recent concerns about espionage in the weapons programs raise questions about our ability to keep weapons designs secret over many decades. Some in the intelligence community contend that a fixed target, such as our nuclear designs, will be compromised by a determined adversary given sufficient time. Information about U.S. nuclear designs could provide important guidance to countries that wish to improve their own nuclear arsenals. Such information would also be advantageous to countries attempting to optimize some future ballistic missile defense system of their own for use against our systems. Finally, it could assist potential adversaries in deploying their strategic forces in a manner designed to make it difficult to assure their destruction.

The certification of substantially new nuclear weapons designs is difficult or impossible to do with high confidence without underground nuclear testing. However, the United States has a large archive of previously tested designs that might be fielded with reasonable confidence to meet low-yield military needs. In addition, the current stockpile has significant flexibility for modification for new requirements. Such flexibility was most recently evidenced by the modification of the B-61 bomb to provide earth-penetrating capability.

Reliance on Deterrence

For more than 50 years, the United States and other nuclear powers have relied on deterrence as the principal measure to guard against the first use of nuclear weapons by enemies. Except for the intermittent R&D exploration of ballistic missile defense initiatives by the United States, Russians, and others, deterrence has continued to be the national strategy for protection from nuclear attacks.

Today, the United States, Russia, China, India, Pakistan, France, and Israel still depend on deterrence to prevent the use of nuclear weapons. In short, deterrence works when opposing sides have overwhelming capability to destroy the other, regardless of who strikes first.

In fact, deterrence also works when a small country has a few nuclear weapons to guard against intrusion by a conventional attack force from a larger nearby or bordering country. In this type of situation, the stronger, larger power with conventional forces, and even nuclear weapons, would hesitate to attack when the defender could retaliate with nuclear weapons. Such a situation could be envisioned if Iraq or Iran threatened Israel, or Taiwan gained nuclear weapons to counter Chinese pressure.

The real concerns evolve in situations where one country with nuclear weapons threatens the national survival of another country without nuclear weapons. In this case, deterrence does not exist. Then, other means like diplomacy or changes in human social behavior may be the only options.

In addition, the world community must stand united in bringing some pressure on an aggressor country that is threatening to employ nuclear weapons against a nonnuclear state. Until other means become available, this pressure would have to take the form of complete social, political, medical, and economic isolation from the rest of the world. A less favorable action would be the use of nuclear fires from other countries against the aggressor country that dared to make a nuclear first strike.

Other situations exist where a country with a few nuclear weapons could threaten or blackmail a larger country with nuclear weapons. In this kind of situation, ballistic missile defense against nuclear weapons might be an acceptable response. Of course, failure to destroy the attacking nuclear missiles would likely lead to nuclear retaliation so deterrence and ballistic missile defense would have failed to prevent a nuclear exchange.

Nuclear Terrorism

The problem of nuclear terrorism is a practical reality. Even though no terrorist nukes have yet been exploded, it is still a very real problem. Most people are beginning to recognize its seriousness, yet some of the most obvious countermeasures have not been taken. United States intelligence must increase vigilance to reduce the likelihood of attacks similar to the terrorist attacks of September 11. More information is becoming available, but facts are few, and unsubstantiated rumors abound.

Existence of Terrorist Nuclear Weapons

There have been many claims or rumors that terrorists have acquired at least 3 and possibly more than 100 nuclear weapons. The source of these warheads is uniformly regarded as Russian—an unfortunate result of the confusion and economic strife following the breakup of the Soviet Union. No responsible official would deny this possibility. There is also a serious likelihood of theft by terrorist groups from national stockpiles in South Africa, Israel, China, India, Pakistan, France, Britain and, of course, the United States.

Moreover, there are others who could provide warheads to a terrorist group or camouflage their own operatives to mimic a suspect terrorist group.

Such countries might relish the opportunity to use a U.S. city as a test-bed for a newly developed warhead—countries such as Iraq or North Korea.

These weapons could range in weight from roughly 30 pounds to 150 pounds. Heavier, larger weapons exist, but are not as desirable from a terrorist's perspective. Warheads in this weight range could have yields as low as 50 tons (high explosive equivalent) to tens of kilotons, several times the size of the first nuclear weapons that were dropped on Hiroshima and Nagasaki. The most available warheads and easiest to manage would be in the 100 ton to 1 or 2 kiloton range. Insofar as size is concerned, an implosion nuclear warhead could be as small as a soccer ball and weigh less than 50 pounds. The "Davy Crockett" warhead was developed in the early 1950s as the warhead for an Army bazooka. It had yields in the tens to hundreds of tons and weighed only 40 pounds. A good warhead design team such as the Soviets undoubtedly had at their Arzamov-16 laboratory could probably pack 10 kilotons or more into an even smaller package.

Because of their very low weight and small size, terrorist delivery presents few problems. The warheads described previously could be carried in a backpack, canvas travel bag, or small wheeled carry-on suitcase. Because these are all common, none would be suspect. Who would think to question any individual carrying or wheeling such a container in a subway, in the middle of any city, or leaving a parked car in a garage. Because of the destructive nature of these warheads, they need not be placed in a targeted building, just anyplace in a city would thoroughly terrify the population. For the urban terrorist, one of these warheads could topple the Sears Tower if it were resting next to the building, and it would be more than adequate to take out San Francisco's Golden Gate bridge or New York's George Washington bridge.

From a military perspective, even the smallest of these warheads, say 50 to 100 tons, would be more than enough to disable an aircraft carrier just because of the radiation, if a terrorist in a fast "cigarette" boat such as those used by drug smugglers could get within a few hundred yards.

Countering Nuclear Terrorism

All of the problems described previously have been known for many years. One would hope that something had been done, but as in the case of biological and chemical terrorism, little more than nothing has been accomplished.

Currently, if one (or more) suitcase nuclear weapon were to go off in the middle of several major U.S. cities, it would be difficult to identify the perpetrator. Serious efforts should be initiated to collect data that would allow us to track nuclear materials and technologies and to identify nuclear capability of various nations and groups.

Several defensive actions could be undertaken. The most obvious action is to crack down hard on illegal immigrants and those with citizenship acquired over the past decade who provided false information on their citizenship papers. Estimates of terrorists and foreign-intelligence agents illegally in the United States exceed 10,000. It contributed to the tragedy we experienced on September 11, 2001, and continues to occupy the attention of internal security forces and resources.

There are also technical defensive options. The weapons described earlier are all rather old technology and all have radiation signatures that can be detected by appropriate sensors. These sensors have been available and used for finding lost nuclear weapon and for tracking nuclear weapons for more than 30 years. The U.S. government might position such sensors to detect warhead radiation in regions where attacks are deemed most likely to take place.

There is almost no limit to the ways in which such sensors could be used to help counter the suitcase nuclear weapon problem. These sensors should be installed at debarkation points such as international arrival ports and border crossings. If sensors were also part of the equipment on police cars and mail delivery vehicles, who knows what might be detected? The former Russian military intelligence officer, Col. Stanislav Lunev, wrote that, in his opinion, the Russian Spetsnaz forces already had suitcase nuclear warheads in the United States. If there are nuclear warheads already in the United States, there should be radiation signatures that are detectable.

The last set of items deserving some attention is the role played by our own policies. There are numerous long-standing U.S. policies that deserve critical examination: sending money and weapons technology to enemies and terrorist nations, as well as sweeping terrorist activities under the rug to avoid embarrassment.

Consequences of Nuclear Terrorism

The object of terrorism is not just to cause terror, but, more importantly, to cause the people to lose faith in their government and begin to believe that any government that can promise safety, peace, and security is more desirable than the one in place. Nuclear terrorist weapons might be used as the straw that breaks the camel's back and makes the country vulnerable to revolution, internal or external, or to invasion, or anarchy. We all hope this event will never come. But the best way to prevent it from happening is, first, to take the necessary precautions and countermeasures, such as those identified in this essay.

Coexistence with Nuclear Weapons

The foremost problem to be addressed by the community of nations, particularly the developed nations, is how to deal with human conflict without warfare. Since the invention of nuclear weapons, warfare between industrialized nations includes the eventual escalation to unendurable consequences. The proper question is not, "How do we avoid nuclear war?" but "How do we avoid war?"

An alternative approach would be to avoid conflict, which derives from human beings' different views of the world, and the demand to think and behave as they perceive to be proper. It would appear that to avoid conflict would require that all people think the same way and have the same economic status. Indeed, in a number of totalitarian regimes different degrees of "mind control" have been attempted. However, this has been accomplished with a commensurate loss of freedom for most citizens under authoritarian control. This loss of freedom of thought, expression, and action is so onerous to humans that it too leads eventually to conflict with the autocrats. This may result in civil rather than international warfare, but its toll in human suffering is immense. Attempts to make all citizens think in lock step, and thereby avoid conflict, detract too greatly from what it means to be human.

If we accept that forcing everyone to think alike and eliminate the causes of conflict is not a path we choose to pursue, then we must find ways to deal with the inevitable conflict of opinions and objectives that will arise from free expression. Once we allow this natural conflict to be expressed in the taking up of arms, we have failed. The United Nations provides a forum for "talking it out." Each nation is free to express its opinions and objectives, with the hope that negotiated settlements will avoid war. This does not appear to be enough. Having a meeting place to state one's point of view is very useful, but if the objectives of one nation contradict the existence of another, merely hearing that does not settle the conflict. Logic and persuasion can often be successful, as well as economic or political compromise. These are the basic tenants of diplomacy, and it has had many notable achievements. But we cannot always count on having the superb diplomat, with the winning argument, at the right place at the right time. In spite of having many experienced, capable diplomats we have seen many wars. Something more is needed.

We do not yet know what the solution to conflict is. We do not even know a solution exists, but hope demands that we believe it does. We also do not know from where the solutions will come, but we must be open to all attempts. Just as technology, and eventual products, derive from basic scientific research, so the sociological products we seek may derive from the thoughts of philosophers and poets. In fact we are seeking a new method or process for individuals and nations to deal with each other—a significant change from the methods of history. There will be many who feel threatened by such change.

Today's leaders may find their positions being defined away. The United States, in particular, being the leading nation of the world today, will be suspect simply because it acquired that position "by the old rules." It will not be easy, but the invention of nuclear weapons leaves us no alternative but to find an end to war.

The authors would like to acknowledge the major contributions by Stephen M. Younger for the use of his material on future nuclear weapons developments and to Dr. Damon Giovanielli for his contributions on sections of this essay dealing with coexistence with nuclear weapons, weapons proliferation, and the ideas associated with nuclear confrontation avoidance. Dr. Giovanielli was a senior member of the staff at Los Alamos National Laboratories for many years and led many of the nuclear weapons development programs. Also, Dr. Sam Cohen, a noted authority and participant in the early development of nuclear weapons, contributed to the section on nuclear terrorism.

24

INTERNATIONAL INITIATIVES FOR NONTRADITIONAL WARFARE AGREEMENTS

David L. Bongard
William R. Schilling

This essay presents a brief look at some of the possibilities for and aspects of international agreements to address the nontraditional warfare (NTW) problem areas. The emphasis is on surfacing areas for further review and diplomatic initiatives to modify or reduce these serious threats to the safety of the United States and the rest of the world.

NTW policy initiatives will demand a willingness among nations to sacrifice some elements of traditional national sovereignty in the interests of reducing vulnerability to attacks with nuclear weapons, toxic chemical agents, and bio-weapons. This will not be an easy task. International initiatives will also be required to significantly increase the effectiveness of law enforcement operations against international criminal and terrorist organizations, regulation of trade, sharing of electronic warfare assets and capabilities, as well as mining and demining efforts.

Weapons of Mass Destruction

The deliberate anthrax infestations within the United States has provided clear proof of the risks in the modern world from the employment of weapons of mass destruction (WMD) in terrorist operations, particularly against civilian targets. While there are some actions that national governments can do to reduce their vulnerability to such attacks, truly reducing these risks to lower levels will require major international initiatives. These initiatives will likely encompass not only new treaty arrangements between sovereign states, but also increased cooperation between intelligence and law enforcement agencies throughout the world.

The production of chemical weapons is relatively complex and requires considerable care to manufacture safely and effectively. The requirements for producing bio-weapons are even more stringent. The production situation for nuclear weapons, even simple fission devices, is difficult and demanding and requires sophisticated and exacting engineering processes.

Many of these weapons of mass destruction (WMD) have already been developed, tested, and used by several nations. The technology exists and can be acquired by other nations and even by terrorist groups. To prevent these WMD from falling into the hands of terrorist or outlaw groups will require a new approach to treaties and international agreements.

The greatest danger comes from nuclear and biological weapons, which can inflict more casualties and terror than chemical weapons. Chemical weapons, with their more localized effects, are easier to manufacture and the technology needed to produce them is now widespread. Since the production technology can also be employed for a range of nonlethal tasks such as making fertilizer, placing any meaningful and effective restrictions on the spread of chemical weapons technology is likely to be only marginally effective. Therefore, international and national policy efforts aimed at limiting the spread of nuclear and biological weapons production and technology are of more importance.

Creating and maintaining global restrictions on WMD may be separated into several areas. First, and most obvious, would be restricting or eliminating trade in finished products or required technologies. An effective international ban on testing such weapons would also provide a measure of security. A test ban on bio-weapons would be difficult to enforce, since detection of bio-weapon tests poses considerable technical challenges. In addition, international treaties already exist to prevent the development of biological weapons.

One area of improvement on the current international situation is in the field of control of imports and exports of components and component technologies. This poses some difficulties because of the challenges inherent in dual-use technologies. This challenge becomes still more complex when the long-term political stability of some nations is taken into account.

The safeguards established for nuclear weapons and nuclear testing is comparatively well established by international treaty. Beginning with the Limited Test Ban Treaty of July 1963, a succession of measures have been implemented to produce a degree of stability in the proliferation of nuclear weapons.

Effective proliferation controls for biological weapons are more complicated. Not only do more nations possess the capability to produce biological weapons than belong to the so-called "nuclear club," but the technologies involved are more difficult to track due to their dual-use nature. Fortunately, most nations do not publicly support programs for the development of biological weapons, and international public opinion is even less tolerant of bioweapons programs than it is of nuclear research.

To further complicate the situation, biological weapons programs are far less infrastructure dependent than nuclear programs, and require far smaller industrial bases to produce strategically significant quantities of weapons materials. The small-scale release of anthrax spores through the U.S. postal system in October 2001 provided an example of the panic and disruption of infrastructure that can result from even a minor contamination. The anthrax attack made it clear that the existing national bio-security systems are inadequate to such a threat.

The only real answer to the biological security demands of the twenty-first century is a new kind of international, multilateral structure to control international exchange of capabilities and facilitate international law enforcement efforts. It will take some time to design and implement such a structure, and such a global framework will moreover have to address not only the security needs and demands of states such as Great Britain, Russia, and the United States, but also the security concerns of nations such as Iraq, North Korea, and Bangladesh. These considerations mean that an effective international regime will require not only effective and objective international inspection of facilities and products, but also a format for international trade in biological products that permits trade of vaccines, antibiotics, drugs, and serums, but limits or prohibits exchange of raw or refined pathogens.

Exhibit 24.1 presents an overview of possible initiatives and considerations affecting international agreements for WMD. This brief look is expected to provide a framework for further investigations into the characteristics of future agreements for WMD.

Terrorist Operations and the Criminal Connection

The experience of the United States and its struggle with Ossama bin Laden's Al Qaeda group demonstrates that a considerable overlap exists between terrorist groups or operatives and international or global criminal organizations. Terrorist groups rely on illegal activities both for financial support and for movement of the raw materials for their operations, such as weapons and explosives. The FARC in Colombia, for example, has close ties with the

EXHIBIT 24.1   Considerations for international agreements on WMD.

NTW threats	International concerns and issues	Aspects and options for international agreements	Utility/value of agreements
Nuclear weapons	Surety of nuclear weapons and materials	• International protocol/procedures modeled after U.S.-USSR approaches • Enforcement of nuclear security measures • Record keeping and reporting	Strategic protocols for protecting against unauthorized use or loss of nuclear materials and weapons
	Ballistic missile defense development and testing (applications for low-threat situations)	• Modification of ABM Treaty of 1972 to allow testing rights • Reduction of offensive missiles as trade for defense deployment • Sharing missile defense technology with major nuclear powers	Promote research and tests to develop defense against threats from rogue nations with nuclear missile systems
	Nuclear weapons: proliferation and testing	• Ensure testing compliance with nonnuclear testing, especially underground by in-country monitoring • Prevention of transfer of missile technology to rogue nations • Enforcement of critical missile technology transfer and dual capability controls by international oversight	Reduce rate of spread of nuclear technology and weapons to other nations, and sharing satellite usage with other countries complying with nonnuclear development restrictions
Biological weapons	Surety of biological weapons and technology transfer including research and testing of materials and weapons	• Tracking and recording all biological technology materials used in defense research • Monitoring new biological technology threats such as sea mines	International on-site inspections and monitoring of compliance, in order to prevent illegal spread of biological technology materials and weapons
	Research into biological technology contamination and spreading phenomenology	• Sharing of biological defense measures and medicines	
	Warning of biological technology thefts, threats, and deployments	• Sharing intelligence data on biological threat agents • Swift transfer of defensive research, medicines, material aid	
Chemical weapons	Surety of chemical weapons and materials	• Tracking and recording of movement of chemical weapons and materials	International on-site inspection and monitoring to prevent development and stockpiling of chemical weapons plus interdiction of suspected movement of chemical materials and weapons
	Notification of chemical thefts and incidents	• Decontamination processes for people and physical materials • Detection devices and technologies for countering chemical releases	

Medillin and Cali cocaine cartels. The FARC provides security and muscle in exchange for access to the cartel's international trade avenues, considerable cash resources, and banking access. Other guerrilla organizations have utilized both kidnapping for ransom and bank robbery to provide financial support (see Essay 9, International Criminal Operations in Nontraditional Warfare).

Fortunately, there are some mechanisms already in place for limiting the effectiveness of such actions. Interpol, for instance, whose primary purpose is the limitation and eventual elimination of international criminal activity, currently serves as an information and tracking center for criminals and criminal organizations with international scope. Until recently, however, Interpol devoted relatively few resources to the problem of terrorism. One major challenge faced by any international law enforcement agency is national sovereignty. The prerogatives held by nations in enforcing their own standards of law and order do not readily permit activities by international law enforcement agents.

A truly international law enforcement mechanism must be immune to the demands of individual national policies, be accepted and allowed to operate in all nations, and be answerable to some sort of international body such as the United Nations or the International Court of Justice in The Hague. The loss of national sovereignty should be acceptable when posed in the context of providing greater security for all national citizens worldwide and for sharply limiting the activities and safe havens available to such outlaws. Only a set of mechanisms that provides such a global law enforcement authority with worldwide capabilities and resources will have any real chance of long-term success.

Exhibit 24.2 displays some key considerations bearing on some of the characteristics of international agreements to counter the terrorist threats. These include identifying, tracking, capturing, and punishing terrorists and involve a host of international interfaces and supports.

Electronic Warfare and Information Warfare

The increasing reliance on electronic devices for a wide range of human activities also increases their value as a target. Essay 4, Information Systems Survivability in Nontraditional Warfare Operations, deals more specifically with the vulnerabilities and safeguards of electronic systems.

Electronic warfare comprises two distinct elements. The first is protection of one's own electronic assets. The second element is the capacity to destroy or disrupt an opponent's electronic assets. International agreements would have little effect in protecting a nation's electronic assets during wartime unless those assets were jointly and severally crucial to the conflicting parties. The Internet might be such an asset that is perceived to be valuable to all parties and could be subject to an international agreement to be inviolate. International corporations' assets that are used by all parties might be subject to international agreements. Such assets might include the following:

- Telecommunications
- Broadcasting (radio and television)

EXHIBIT 24.2 Considerations for international agreements on terrorist operations.

International concerns and issues	Aspects and options for international agreements	Utility/value of agreements
Sanctuaries	• Right to pursuit by international consortiums into regions suspected of harboring terrorists • Implementation of international sanctions against nations supporting and protecting terrorists form capture • Right to implant sensor systems and utilize airborne surveillance to locate suspected terrorist positions/bases	Obtain international agreements to deter and hold protecting nations responsible for actions committed by terrorist groups/ leaders. This measure will help to limit number of hiding places for terrorist movements.
International enforcements and intelligence sharing	• Cooperative agreements to investigate terrorist plans and crimes against international and national laws • Cooperative agreements to share intelligence information on possible terrorist plans and membership	Reduce options and impose constraints on terrorist movements and support without their fear of prosecution or exposure to plans/interests.
Terrorist capture and punishment	• Terrorists treated as criminal or prisoners of war with commensurate civil rights under Geneva Rules convention • Captured terrorists to be tired in military courts or international tribunal in either the country where the crimes were committed or in an agreed court location • Terrorists punished according to international standards for crimes against innocent people in accordance with laws of nation where trial is held	Provide an approved method for capturing and punishing terrorists for crimes against peoples, nations, or groups of nations with limited rights for judicial review (i.e., make justice swift and certain).
Terrorist financial and technology transfer transactions	• Denial of terrorists rights to money and resources within institutions or nations • Monitor and track terrorists' assets, travel, and communications between regions or nations	Prevent terrorists access to funds and benefits from crimes and provide measures to aid in tracking and capturing terrorists.

- Financial institutions
- Space-based shared assets

However, terrorist and criminal organizations are not bound by international agreements and treaties. Therefore, these international agreements should include pledges of mutual defense. The global characteristics of both electronic warfare and information warfare demand that effective resolution of the issues posed will require an international effort. Exhibit 24.3 shows some factors bearing on the nature and features of international agreements for EW/IW.

Mine Warfare: Mining and Demining

One of the major international success stories of the past two decades has been the initiatives undertaken to clean up landmines that have been left as a legacy

EXHIBIT 24.3 Considerations for international agreements on EW/IW.

International concerns and issues	Aspects and options for international agreements	Utility/value of agreements
Technology accessibility	• Patents restricting use of electronics technology by out-of-country groups • Commercial off-the-shelf (COS) items for application by competing countries and threat groups	Limited level of risks posed by available electronic equipment as a means to safeguard and preserve military C^{4}I assets, procedures, and applications.
Controls on applications of electronic technology	• International restrictions on use of electronic technology to damage other countries' information systems and defenses	
Standards and administrative criteria	• Development of international standards for specifying electronics performance, definition, and theory	

of past military operations. While these efforts have been encouraging, the vast numbers of mines still remaining serve to demonstrate the dimensions of the problem. In addition, none of these efforts have been directed toward naval mines, which fortunately have not been a significant factor since the end of World War II.

Despite the relative success of recent international demining efforts, antipersonnel land mines remain a serious problem in a number of regions. Several factors increase the complexity of the task. First, land mines do not require much skill to be emplaced. Removing them may often only be accomplished through a painstaking, inch-by-inch probing and examination of suspected mine areas, followed by removal and defusing. All of those tasks require relatively skilled personnel. Current demining efforts have focused on areas of recent conflict, such as Cambodia, Afghanistan, Ethiopia-Eritrea, Somalia, and Liberia-Guinea in West Africa. Due to the intensity and nature of conflicts in those countries, many mines still remain. Effectively demining these areas will require extensive humanpower, considerable resources, and years of steady effort.

The international convention to ban the manufacture and employment of antipersonnel land mines has made some progress, but it is not yet universally embraced. The ease and low cost of manufacturing and emplacing mines makes them too useful for some to abandon as a weapon of war or terror.

Effective international control of trade in armaments and explosives would significantly assist in limiting or eliminating after-war risks posed by future employment of land mines. That sort of international framework will require a general agreement on its desirability, and a consensus on the methods to be employed to reach that desired end.

The issue of naval mines is potentially more serious. A number of navies, especially that of the United States, has drastically reduced the size of its minesweeping forces in the aftermath of World War II. Further, there are a number of navies, such as that of North Korea, holding extensive stockpiles of fairly sophisticated mines for use in the event of war. While the risk of outright traditional warfare may have declined over the last 10 to 15 years, the available arsenals have not diminished. The proliferation of well-funded terrorist organizations also poses a risk.

Deliberate employment of naval mines as a device for terrorist operations at sea poses a more serious and larger-scale risk. Larger numbers of adrift mines would mean a notably elevated chance of striking passing sea traffic. Fewer naval forces available for mine removal would make effective control of the problem more difficult. A few hundred, or perhaps even a few dozen, mines at or just below the surface at locations such as New York Harbor, the English Channel and the Thames Estuary, the Straits of Gibraltar and the Straits of Aden, and the Straits of Malacca would cause grave disruption to global sea traffic.

This risk makes it very clear that it is in the interests of many nations, and not just those that are heavily involved in ocean-going trade, to work together to reduce if not eliminate the opportunity for such an occurrence. Such a multilateral regime would require several components. The first and perhaps most important would be close export controls on naval mines, restricting their trade, and perhaps eventually eliminating their production and stockpiling. This would also have to apply to states that have not produced mines but merely maintain a supply for use in time of war. Coupled to this agreement, or set of agreements, would be a detailed global inventory of naval mines, so that it would be possible to track the origins of any mine recovered at sea, and to periodically conduct a sort of census to ensure that such mines are where they are supposed to be, and remain in responsible hands. Additional ancillary agreements might be useful to restrict production of mine components, provide multilateral supervision of the disposition and disposal of naval mines, and penalties for states that violate these agreements to ensure that the benefits steadily outweigh any potential "profits" from violation.

A brief look at considerations affecting future international agreements on mining and demining is presented in Exhibit 24.4. These considerations are described in terms of problem areas, options for resolution, and utility of possible international agreements.

EXHIBIT 24.4   Considerations for international agreements for mining and demining operations.

International concerns and issues	Aspects and options for international agreements	Utility/value of agreements
Control of proliferation of mines	• Component controls on end users • Mine stockpile controls and elimination • Compliance with international regulations regarding surface and buried mines	Limit employment of mines to prevent civilian casualties and expedite removal of existing minefields.
Detection and clearing of minefields	• Support for international testing and evaluating demining technologies for detecting, clearing, and detonating mines • Provide system and technologies for use by other countries to eradicate minefields	
Employment limitations for minefields	• Implementation of self or remote detonation of surface and buried mines • Restriction of mine emplacement near populated centers and transportation nodes • Conditions for employment of defensive minefields	

Conclusion

The risks from NTW activities to global security outlined in this essay threaten many nations simultaneously. They are not simply threats to the United States or to the emerging community of European nations. Reducing or eliminating these threats will require more than just creative and effective national policy choices on the part of the major powers. Resolution of parts of these challenges cannot be accomplished except through large-scale initiatives, involving most if not all the nations of the world. The major powers will have to accommodate the goals and preferences of smaller states, at least to some degree, simultaneously bringing them into the decision-making and negotiation process. Then major powers will also have to realize that they will not be able to expect adherence to such agreement frameworks by all states if those states do not have some sort of stake in both the formulation and the outcome or goals of the process. Ignoring any community member poses the real risk that the eventual solution will not work, and will be ignored even by some of its designers. Nevertheless, agreements have to be structured so that a few countries cannot thwart the will or security of the large community of nations.

SECTION VI

APPLYING NEW AND EMERGING TECHNOLOGIES TO NONTRADITIONAL WARFARE

Emerging technologies provide several avenues for the development of new types of weapons and military equipment. Some of these innovations build on long-existing technological advancements, while others are substantially the result of recent developments. Broadly speaking, several of these areas of technological innovation provide not only the opportunity for expanded capabilities for U.S. forces, but also pose the real potential for enhanced risks to U.S. forces and interests from hostile elements armed or equipped with such technologies.

One of the most important aspects of dealing with these advanced technologies is determining which ones will be useful for what objectives, and evaluating them in terms of the amount of effort and funds needed to bring workable, effective mechanisms employing these technologies to fruition. The goal of evaluating and assessing emerging technologies is one that has traditionally been handled in a rather ad hoc fashion, but that sort of sporadic and inefficient approach will not serve, particularly not when a considerable range of advanced technologies are simultaneously under development. The United States will have to exercise some care to ensure that it not only acquires valuable advanced technologies, but also that the technological developments it chooses to support result in workable and effective items with a comparative minimum of development and testing.

Among other issues discussed in this section are the general challenges of land force modernization, including the difficult task of maintaining or improving ordnance lethality while simultaneously reducing weight to improve strategic mobility. It is unlikely that, in the event of a future conflict, U.S. forces will have the luxuries of either (1) months of advance preparation or (2) major ordnance close to the region of conflict. Issues of force modernization are distinct from more general aspects of the development of advanced technology. Other considerations include the development of radio frequency weapons, which essentially direct high-powered microwaves at electronic and personnel targets, and the related development of (probably nonnuclear) electromagnetic pulse (EMP) devices, again primarily directed against unshielded electronics.

Another major aspect of the military impact of advanced technologies on military forces is the emergence of so-called smart sensorwebs (SSW), which serves to greatly increase the ability of small tactical units (companies and platoons) to absorb and process information from a variety of sources, and to act on that data swiftly and accurately. Parallel to the advent of SSWs is the increasing use and importance of robotics and RPVs. At the dawn of the twenty-first century, these systems are employed primarily for reconnaissance, but steady increases in capabilities make it very likely that the range of roles assigned to such unmanned systems will increase significantly over the next 10 to 20 years.

Of particular note is essay 26 dealing with the impact of advanced technology on future military operations where the reader and the R&D managers are urged to look at new ways of thinking to exploit the opportunities and changes offered by scientific knowledge. All of these emerging and developing technologies will exert considerable impact on warfare and military operations, and on the ways military organizations are structured to function, both on and off the battlefield. Although these essays devote only cursory examination to the effect of these developments on more traditional forms of warfare, especially those involving conventional armies in action with each other, those considerations cannot be ignored. Still, the growing importance of nontraditional warfare makes that arena particularly noteworthy, and should therefore draw special attention and analysis.

25

ENABLERS OF LAND FORCE MODERNIZATION FOR NTW OPERATIONS

Andrus Viilu

L and force modernization objectives can be described using a variety of terminologies and relationships. Fundamentally, all of the modernization concepts depend on shifting the burden of defeating the enemy by using fires from rear areas (indirect fires). This results in reducing the emphasis on delivering fires in direct view of the opposing side (direct fire systems) and the attendant risk of high casualties. The Defense Department lists information dominance, stealth, and precision or accurate strike as the key enablers for force modernization. Five pillars of modernization underpin this vision of the future tactical battlefield. These are discussed in this essay along with the progress to date in implementing the revolution in combat capabilities. In many cases, responsive operations are built around using brigade level forces (about 3 or more brigades with a total of about 2,500 personnel). Reshaping branch responsibilities for engineers, artillery, and combat support services is also required although progress to date has been uneven. A summary of the key challenges is provided at the end of this essay.

This discussion of land force modernization is focused on combat operations at the brigade level and below. There are broader, more encompassing, modernization goals such as focused logistics, full-spectrum force protection, and decisive maneuver. The modernization pillars to support those broader modernization goals are beyond the scope of this essay.

Many aspects of this modernization endeavor have utility for both traditional warfare and NTW. However, the traditional warfare operations are directed toward employing organized and deployed forces where many assets are available for acquiring and destroying enemy targets and for supporting fielded systems and personnel.

On the other hand, in NTW operations, the enemy target sizes shift to smaller units that use cover and concealment to (1) protect resources and material, (2) hide attack objectives, and (3) enhance surprise conditions. As a consequence of this shift, information dominance becomes the key enabler or factor for force modernization.

Five Pillars of Force Modernization
Available Digital Terrain Data

The first pillar is the use of digital terrain data to represent the world land mass and the global positioning system (GPS) to navigate within the terrain, down to the platform level. An achievable objective is 1-meter sensor resolution with 1-meter location accuracy. This level of precision would certainly be used by dismounted forces for line-of-sight calculations and for planning avenues of approach. However, a significant combat burden is introduced because 33 terabytes of data are required to record 1-meter resolution data for the world landmass. The National Imagery and Mapping Agency (NIMA) plans to provide 1-meter resolution data for specific land areas of military interest, but will only provide 30–meter resolution data for wide area coverage. It is not clear how rapidly NIMA can develop 1–meter resolution data, how the data will be disseminated, and whether it will be feasible to manipulate and display the high resolution data at the platform level. Currently, capability exists to display three-dimensional 30-meter resolution data for a tactical area of operations. The deployed land combat systems have the capability to display two-dimensional maps that are roughly equivalent to 1 to 50,000 scale tactical maps (30-meter resolution).

The ability to navigate using digital terrain is more accessible than the terrain information. Differential GPS can achieve the 1 meter accuracy goal. Widely available GPS receivers that cost a few hundred dollars are capable of navigation within the 30-meter resolution available from the digital terrain data.

The access to three-dimensional digital terrain data that is linked to GPS coordinates is in itself a major improvement over existing tactical maps that require corrections with respect to local data. The ability to display terrain and navigate in a common GPS reference base offers the potential of easing the friend-or-foe identification problem for ground forces, if the commonly displayed data can be updated at a sufficiently high rate. Updating the no-fire line for indirect fire systems appears feasible, but the problem of inhibiting direct fire against friendly units remains a concern especially if the targeted system is a fast moving aerial platform.

Accurate Target Location

The second pillar consists of accurate target location throughout the depth of the battlefield. The ability to use imagery to locate targets within 5 to 10 meters in GPS coordination is within reach. The land forces would need to invest in the technology that is available at the national level, to make the capability available within the combat zone. Unmanned aerial vehicles (UAV) with GPS and laser ranging have the potential of equivalent accurate target location. The inability to field a UAV that is accessible to combat units in the forward area remains a key land warfare shortfall. There are other sensors that can contribute to the task of accurate target location. Differential synthetic aperture radar coverage of an area in the high resolution mode is a capability that should be explored.

In addition to accurate target location capability, there is the need for surveillance assets to guide the employment of targeting sensors. Standoff, side-looking airborne radar that can track moving targets is an important component of the surveillance capability. To fill in gaps in radar coverage, a relatively short-range system, such as the Longbow radar on the Apache AH-64D helicopter, can be used to cue forward combat units.

Unmanned ground systems provide another tier of sensors that can be repositioned near enemy movements, or even inserted into areas of intelligence interest. The advantage of the unattended ground systems is the capability for 24 hours a day coverage along with accurate target location capability. While unmanned systems have the potential to reduce casualties, there is a need for concepts of employment that integrate unmanned systems information with manned units.

Efficient Delivery of Munitions

The third pillar concerns accurate delivery of effective munitions throughout the depth of the battlefield. GPS guided munitions, with an inertial measuring system as backup, are capable of delivering ordnance on target to within an accuracy of 20 meters (circular error probability). A number of guided carrier rounds are in development. The army tactical missile system (ATACMS) is the most mature and has demonstrated the capability to deliver guided submunitions to a range greater than 100 km. The guided multiple launch rocket system (MLRS) is in development and is capable of delivering a variety of ordnance to a range of 60 km. The tube artillery community is developing the Excaliber system jointly with the Navy guided ordnance program and both unitary and submunition payloads are envisioned. What is missing from each of these guided weapons programs is the correlation between priority targets, target defeat criteria, munitions terminal effects, and the design of a warhead or submunitions that utilizes the capability for accurate target location and accurate delivery of ordnance in the same coordinate system. The targets of interest extend from dismounted personnel and light materiel targets, to heavy armored vehicles. If guided rounds are to be effective on a future battlefield, then warheads and submunitions have to be designed to defeat specific classes of targets consistent with the greatly improved weapon delivery accuracy.

In short, warhead improvements are necessary to allow homing submunitions to hit 1-meter targets within the 20-meter delivery accuracy. Focused lethal effects based on explosive formed distributed fragment patterns as well as flechette warheads are potential candidate warhead designs for soft targets. To kill hard targets, sensor-aimed concepts with explosively formed penetrators may be an acceptable option.

Unmanned Combat Systems

The fourth pillar is the introduction of unmanned combat systems into the force as partners with manned systems. There has been sufficient progress over the last few years to build an affordable unmanned ground vehicle that can operate semiautonomously across terrain, at tactical speeds, both day and night. The Army and the Defense Advanced Research Projects Agency (DARPA) have joined to develop the Future Combat System, which will take advantage of unmanned ground vehicle technologies for casualty reduction, personnel savings, and for achieving the goal of a full, mission-capable force that can be airlifted by the C-130 aircraft fleet.

The organizational and operational concept for the Future Combat System has not been published. At this time, it is not clear how unmanned systems will be integrated into combat operations, but they will likely be part of the future light force concept.

Digital Battlefield

The fifth pillar has been designated as the employment of digital battlefield. The 4th Infantry Division (Mechanized) at Ft. Hood has been making steady progress in digitally linking the Army Battle Command System to platforms such as the M1A2 tank and the M2A3 Bradley infantry fighting vehicle. An initial set of variable message formats has been demonstrated with these platforms. Properly equipped and trained units have successfully executed rapid changes in orders and unit organization on a tactical battlefield. While somewhat limited by communications bandwidth, and the lack of participation of critical combat elements such as Army aviation, the experiments have demonstrated the ability to display the friendly situation, the location and activity of opposing forces, and the ability of command elements to respond rapidly to tactical opportunities. Programs are underway to improve the connectivity and interoperability of the combat arms team with the Joint Tactical Radio System. Also, the capabilities demonstrated by the 4th Division are being replicated in the Interim Armored Vehicle brigades at Ft. Lewis.

Shortfalls in fielding the digital battlefield concept have been demonstrated. Branch cooperation has not been enforced. The need for troop protection has not been met in a responsive matter at the tactical level (i.e., priority in counterbattery fires when infantry is exposed during attack) and the requirement for cover and deception at all combat echelons has not been emphasized. A broader understanding of the threat posed by commercially available imagery to the security of friendly military operations is needed. The role of active defense capability against precision guided munitions on the future battlefield and the utility of countermeasures against both targeting and terminal guidance sensors need further evaluation.

Enhancement Actions for Force Modernization

The future tactical battlefield offers a revolutionary improvement in combat capabilities, while substantially reducing casualties. As summarized in Exhibit 25.1, the pacing technologies to implement the five pillars of modernization are available and affordable. There are some programmatic shortfalls that need to be overcome. Actions necessary to achieve the tactical battlefield modernization goals of shifting the burden of defeating enemy forces to indirect fires and of reducing casualties on the future battlefield are listed in this exhibit.

The first pillar of modernization focuses on getting operators on the battlefield familiar with manipulating digital terrain data and laying out a path for achieving the goal of 1-meter resolution digital terrain. The second pillar addresses the capability to register satellite imagery at the lower force levels (e.g., brigade level) so the targeting function can be more responsive to the user. The third pillar requires additional investment in research and development but the benefits could be large in terms of both enhanced lethality and reduced collateral damage for traditional as well as nontraditional warfare operations. The fourth pillar builds on the 4th Infantry Division troop trials

EXHIBIT 25.1 Modernization of the tactical battlefield.

Modernization building blocks	Key capability	Pacing technology	Key shortfall	Proposed priority actions
1st pillar	High resolution digital terrain in GPS coordinates	Worldwide satellite imagery with precision registration	Dissemination and manipulation of high resolution imagery	Develop a phased implementation plan with NIMA and fund a competitively down-selected hardware approach with industry
2nd pillar	Accurate target location in depth	Integrated surveillance and targeting at tactical level	A funded fielding plan for the sensor suite	Develop a precision workstation capability for integrating sensors at lower level echelons
3rd pillar	Precision delivery of tailored lethal effects	Affordable precision carrier rounds with directed lethality	Lack of munitions design efforts consistent with accurate delivery system	Begin a terminal effects design effort that takes advantage of precision delivery capability
4th pillar	Expanded combat capability based on unmanned systems	Semiautonomous operations day/night at tactical speeds	Lack of operational and organizational concepts for integrating unmanned systems	Deploy first generation unmanned system with combat units and refine concepts of employment based on lessons learned at instrumented training sites
5th pillar	Digital integration and interoperability of tactical forces	Wide band communications links with variable message formats	Lack of communications systems interoperability between air and ground elements	Deploy multiband radios and develop operational concepts for integrating the combat arms team on the digital battlefield

that are envisioned for the unmanned scout vehicle and the unmanned aerial vehicle experiments using helicopters as the manned component. Support for the fifth pillar is already underway. Joint tactical radio system architecture has been developed to provide a common basis for fielding future communication systems. The lessons learned at the National Training Center and other instrument training sites will permit orderly progress in digitization of the Army light forces.

Technology Enablers for NTW Responses

Based upon the implementation of modernization enablers listed in Exhibit 25.1, small military units or special forces can operate more efficiently and safely in the terrain previously under the control of guerrilla or irregular or terrorist groups. New dimensions in force projection are possible with these advanced technology applications.

Possible enhancements or changes in capability for small unit operations in the terrain include the following:

- Units can know their locations, prevent isolation from support elements, and allow safe maneuver in the terrain.
- Units can know a lot more about enemy locations, find enemy targets, and track enemy movement patterns.
- Units can call for accurate fires, tailored to match lethal and nonlethal damage objectives.
- Units can communicate with supporting units, commanders, and intelligence sources.
- Units can rapidly deliver fires and limit collateral damage by accurately selecting aim points and weapon types.
- Units can employ robots to clear paths and operational areas from mines and unexploded ordnance.
- Units can utilize remote sensors and smart sensor webs to provide early warning, avoid ambushes, and detect targets.
- Units can operate more safely without heavy losses due to "friend or foe" dilemmas and friendly fires.
- Units can more accurately observe terrorist activities in terrain and infrastructures plus detect presence of munitions and chemical/biological threats.
- Units can maneuver more safely in environments of poor visibility and nighttime conditions.

In short, enhancements such as those listed will allow security forces, special operations, emergency response teams, and small military elements to (1) perform more safely in areas under control or threat from irregular forces, guerrillas, or terrorists; and (2) gain a force multiplier by effectively utilizing the available resources provided by command, control, communications, computers, and intelligence (C^4I), indirect fire support, logistics, and intelligence.

26

IMPACT OF ADVANCED TECHNOLOGY ON NONTRADITIONAL WARFARE

Clive G. Whittenbury

Previous essays in this series provide a point of departure for surfacing issues and developing answers to the challenges posed by nontraditional warfare. This essay sets aside ongoing efforts in near-term responses that are part of today's national security programs and looks at how advancing technology might play a significant role in the resolution of nontraditional conflict.

Warfare is foremost a sociological matter. Technology provides a means for conducting and resolving conflict. It has a long history in casualty production and in increasingly efficient methods for the destruction of material and social assets. Most programs for advancing technology in warfare focus on increasing such performance. This essay considers different goals for technology: the opportunity for dramatic reduction of casualties and damage in conflict resolution.

Society is at a watershed in warfare: a rapid move away from massive casualty and damage production as the sine qua non of warfare toward a more surgical application of force. There is no science of history to tell us whether models of this behavior are just temporarily credible or whether they point to a distinct trend. It does seem reasonable at the moment, however, that large-scale warfare between major societies will be gone for awhile. In its place we now find the feasible and possible threat of nontraditional warfare, wherein small groups of people employ a small number of very damaging weapons to terrorize or hold hostage other groups, societies, or countries for various purposes. Today's published responses to this threat are straightforward adaptations of existing and emerging technologies for countering these threats in real time.

This essay suggests that a different view of the threat and its neutralization might evolve in the next few years. It considers how we might think about this and how technology might help. To provide a contrast for this view this essay first reviews a simple construct of traditional warfare.

Background

Traditional warfare is defined through its use of traditional weapons: rifles, tanks, artillery, aircraft, ships, and the people that man them (Air Force and Navy) or who are equipped with them (Army and Marines). The purpose of traditional combat is to produce casualties, gain ground, and subdue the occupied ground and survivors. In support of this primary thrust, traditional weapons are used in parallel against the opposing support base of logistics, industry, and population.

In traditional warfare, a society mobilizes either to defend itself against an aggressor or to become an aggressor. The purpose of mobilization is to man weapons, or to equip personnel with weapons, and organize them to create casualties and damage material assets on a large enough scale to defeat an opponent. Traditional weapons create blast, thermal, or kinetic, damage and use information, delivery systems, and supporting logistics to find the targets, transport the weapons to their location, and feed the people who operate all these related functions. As the principal ground-gaining component of traditional warfare the Army is organized around the individual infantryperson, who is supported by direct fire, indirect fire (combat support), and by logistics functions (combat service support) that provide munitions, fuel, and food. This organizational structure is driven by the delivery of fire through force and without its actual use or threat of actual use is not functional for conflict resolution.

Most technology developments for traditional warfare focus upon the weapons and systems for carrying them as well as the information systems for finding and locating their targets. While the performance of specific techniques has improved dramatically over the centuries, their objectives have been similar: increase the explosive effects per pound of explosive used; increase the speed, accuracy, and range of delivery systems; and, meanwhile, constantly improve the economics of the logistics system that supports the weapons.

Planning technology developments for national security has continued in the forementioned context with little need to go back to basic principles and question its very purpose. The structure and organization for traditional combat has worked well for decades, while its basics have survived for centuries. While some will argue that traditional warfare will always have a role to play somewhere in the world, the major world powers will probably not engage in it except to punish, in a very one-sided way, lesser aggressors who make the mistake of adventuring out for limited objectives. Modest weapon inventories and force structures should serve that purpose. In the meantime, the adventures of major powers have been stalemated by the nuclear weapon, whose continuing "dry storage" should maintain that stalemate indefinitely, and allow it to tone down from a hair-trigger alert to a modest level of capability "just in case."

Conflict between societies has already taken a new turn: away from large-scale production of casualties and destroyed assets toward an exchange of words and the withholding of goods. In the middle of this change, the exploitation of the psychology of casualties and damage from specialized weapons has emerged as a personalized type of threat that attempts to influence societies from their inside. These threats are assimilated under the concept of a nontraditional warfare arena and described in other essays in this series. They represent a major shift away from the direct confrontation of armies found in traditional warfare and toward small hidden groups of aggressors with handfuls of powerful weapons that are to be used in clandestine rather than overt actions. The organizations that support these aggressors range from nation states to small dissident groups. Dealing with them through the use of advanced technology requires innovation in concepts and methods of operation, but innovation is not easy when confronted with the decades of modern traditional warfare and the centuries of experience that support it.

Technology's Role in Innovation

The role of technology in improving operational performance has been analyzed exhaustively over the last five decades through operations analysis (WWII), systems analysis (the missile era) and just plain analysis (everyone). Its role in national security is well defined, with DOD directives describing how its development should be planned and executed: generally by following requirements based on existing doctrine and operational concepts. Hence the problem of innovation.

New technology has had an evolutionary and sometimes revolutionary impact on well-established and operationally proven military functions, but its role in industry and commerce continues to be argued from different and important points of view. These arguments stem from how technology enables new commercial institutions and industries and how difficult it is to achieve innovation in those that are already established. It is particularly difficult to disrupt the organizations that control existing institutions if they are threatened with obsolescence by new technology. The theme of this essay is to draw a parallel to these arguments in exploring national security issues in nontraditional warfare. A key point is that these arguments are normal and to be expected and, as such, are not a deterrent to rethinking how to deal with these new threats.

New technology often appears as a threat to enterprises because the existing base of capital and entrenched organization serves as a simple deterrent to change. This is particularly true in day-to-day operations and within the context of the staff and management skills and experience embedded within them. Military organizations have to take extraordinary risks in battle, but they do not change organization and operational details without compelling reasons. Even the soldier who at one time held the horse's reins (so that it would not shy at the firing of the gun) was included in the organization until well after artillery was motorized.

The traditional organization for warfare is an organization for dispensing casualties and damage. It is overstaffed and underequipped for dealing with the numerical size and scope of limited threats in nontraditional warfare. In fact, the use of the word *warfare* might turn out to be a misnomer, as we shall see later in this essay.

Technology advances in traditional warfare have been assimilated into existing systems. Even the nuclear weapon fitted the bomb bay of the B-29 and continued a strategic blitz against urban and industrial areas already started through the wholesale use of incendiaries. The gas dynamic and materials technology of "tubes" dominated traditional weapons for centuries (the first nuclear weapon also contained an "artillery" tube). The technology of transporting tubes dominated the support organizations of traditional warfare for centuries. The dissected coastline of England, with short distances to anywhere inland, enabled the rapid economic development of that country and its subsequent domination of the high seas and coastlines of other countries: transporting weapon tubes to battle and achieving effective subjugation of lesser technology.

These brief comments show how general and useful a single simplification of technology in warfare can be. They also suggest how difficult it might be to innovate when confronted with the almost subliminally compelling military "tube logic." The discussion is intended to show the trap of seemingly effective innovation (e.g., improvements of tube technology) as against a possible need for *fundamental* innovation in conflict operations. The introduction of new or advanced technology into so-called nontraditional warfare should,

A-10A with wide array of ordnance.

therefore, be treated with care and with an expectation of surprise. Is nontraditional warfare simply a way of using existing weapon systems (like nuclear, biological, or chemical weapons) in a new operational context or might it lead to a new way of engaging in and resolving conflicts that are identified with those weapons?

Deliberate attempts to achieve innovation through new technology show an interesting history of failure in business and industry. One of the best explanations of this problem is found in Clayton M. Christensen's *The Innovator's Dilemma* (Harper Business, 2000) which describes the inhibiting influence of invested capital and the embedded knowledge and comfort of existing operations. Failure in business and in war is usually fatal, both literally and figuratively. Laws of "unintended consequences" are quoted often as a defense against unproven innovation. However, in warfare there have been many successful uses of disruptive technology that changed combat decisively: the long bow at Agincourt, the 117 stealth fighter over Baghdad, and the horse in Asia. But is that what we seek from advanced technology in the next generation of warfare? They all supported the functions of traditional combat: they did not deal with the stem causes and managers of the conflict.

The development of disruptive technology can *precede* concepts of institutional revolution or it can *follow,* and thereby enable, those concepts for revolution. In industry or business, invention usually leads to disruption by economically competitive displacement of obsolescing industries. This is achieved not through gradual improvement of existing businesses but their replacement by new businesses that are designed around new concepts and, often, new technology.

In national security, invention is solicited to meet compelling national needs. Usually it is asked to fit an existing organizational or operational context. Solicitation, however, goes through cycles, being high in times of emergency and low in times of security lull or complacency. We are wary of nontraditional warfare but the level of interest has not yet aroused innovation as much as it has evolved into "fitting" existing technology into a new role that still uses existing war-fighting institutions. This essay now takes a different line of enquiry or "solicitation."

A Revisited Look at Innovating through Advanced Technology: Systems Analysis

This essay cannot, in its few paragraphs, provide answers or even a scrubbed and acceptable logic for tying technology to nontraditional warfare. Its purpose is to stimulate an approach to a sound logic for needed technology developments and related innovation by discussing the future in a nontraditional or unorthodox way. Several following books on nontraditional warfare are planned. One is devoted to the impact of technology on RDT&E, military organizations, and operational concepts. In the last section of this essay, the staleness of thought represented by the previous discussion is replaced by an out-of-the-box approach to the nontraditional security threat. This approach should stimulate people to take the issue seriously, but practically, while perhaps irritating them into action in the national interest.

The old framework of systems analysis is always useful as an organizer of problem solving. What is the threat, why is it a threat, and what can we know about it? Methods for dealing with the threat came next and this is where the innovators were separated from the crowd: not always winning but surely able to create a stir and invite a "red-team" review. There is room only for a start on one approach in this essay. This is *it.*

The Threat and Countering the Threat

The threat is simple: small groups (not organized and mobilized by society and government as in the past) decide to strike against society (locally or at a distance) through the use of convenient and very destructive devices to promote their cause. The response to an actual attack, in many cases, will be too late. This includes the possible use of a nuclear device.

The counter to the type of small group actions mentioned earlier is not enabled through existing force structures (except for punishment of large and scattered groups that might back such actions—but then we are back to traditional warfare). The counter must be systemically effective well before any contemplated action gets underway: at the roots.

The roots of small group actions are generally understood today to lie in handfuls of individuals who maintain safe harbor in countries that cooperate or that are subjugated into cooperation. These individuals are protected either by their ruling of those countries or their finding sympathetic surroundings in them. In dealing with such threats, technology has two roles: acquiring information (who, what, and where) and then acting to terminate the root threat.

Conventional thinking would lead immediately to satellite surveillance of the most sophisticated (all weather/all condition) kind with the use of precision weapons—just like in the movies. Unconventional thinking would be Zen-like: let's think through this impossible problem and then develop technology concepts that fit the detailed circumstances and that take advantage of the basic weaknesses of these targets.

Their witting or unwitting hosts hide these targets. They are stable, at least for a while, and they can be expected to require some facilities that are co-located or connected in some manner to prepare their "munitions." They obviously have coming and goings. They interact with the community in some way, if only to use the sewer system. They also are attached in some way to a network of followers and supporters: why else would they be operating? If they have hosts at a national level, the target system then includes their hosts as well.

The Role of Technology

Technology has two standard roles in traditional warfare, and as starting points they are applicable in nontraditional warfare: acquiring *information* (who, what, and where) and then acting to *terminate* the root threat. In rethinking this problem, assume that no traditional force structure elements are available: What would you do if you were running a business and had limited budgets? Get clever and economical.

Many of the root threats, as target systems, are embedded in a commercial environment. That environment is teeming with information and "indicators" of what is going on in that environment. These indicators fall into different kinds with different classification structures. In the case of root threats these indicators will be masked deliberately or even falsified: a classic problem is extracting weak coherent signals from a noisy background. Revisit signal extraction methods, starting far away from military applications: radio astronomy (one of the great early achievements in signal detection and analysis) and, more recently, the search for extraterrestrial intelligence (SETI). Taking a lead from those examples, they required long time periods to collect and analyze data in order to extract weak signals. Nontraditional threat systems take a long time to organize and fester. They are not one snapshot events like those in traditional warfare (a history of individual snapshots).

The traditional logic of the surveillance and target acquisition sequence is still relevant but the nature of the root threat target system suggests using existing commercial systems as far as possible. The target systems are part of the social and commercial infrastructure and have to live off it. They will use the Internet—a great source of information from the surroundings of the targets—and so on. Direct information access to the targets may then be a matter of local use of systems that blend into the environment.

Countering the root threat target system in the present line of analysis then starts with an understanding of the target system as a root threat per se. Terminating its effectiveness or its very existence are the two extremes of a collection of possibilities. Innovation would be the combination of inventing a counter and invoking a technology concept to support it.

The role of technology in neutralizing root threat target systems starts with the target vulnerability in its conventional setting and the impact of any action on that setting. The spectrum of technology related actions could run the gamut from information system manipulation or intervention to physical actions that create isolation or more extreme measures. It might lead to technologies that blend into natural settings and that have minimal impact on those settings. Such thinking becomes the responsibility of national security organizations that execute and protect the appropriate programs.

The Different Approach and Its Consequences

The previously described line of enquiry illustrates a different mode of thinking from traditional military responses. It does not necessarily lead into a cul-de-sac of covert actions. In fact, the effectiveness of actions against nontraditional threats should be carefully publicized with messages of "no place to hide."

The discussion maintains that nontraditional warfare be thought about outside conventional force structures. The overview of these force structures in the introduction should serve as an invitation to innovative thinking but also a warning about how slow and difficult it is to change or replace these structures.

Technology has improved the performance of functions in the traditional structure of warfare. That structure is made up of the force structures that deliver casualties and damage to assets in order to achieve the primary objective of control of people and of their social and governing organizations. The by-product of the success of advanced technology in traditional warfare is increasingly toward "no casualties." This applies to combatants as well as noncombatants. The outcome of non-traditional warfare has been the opposite: cause casualties in both combatants and noncombatants. The answer is to employ advanced technologies to get perpetrators and supporters before they can act, because afterwards will be too late.

Setting aside the traditional means of warfare and focusing on the troublemakers who incite and organize society and institutions into open combat or mischief raises serious issues as it suggests revolutionary moves to maintain effective national security. Introducing new operational concepts is not just a question of inciting a move toward the disruptive technology that assists profound change in the commercial and industrial world. We are talking now about dealing with root causes instead of with the time-honored high casualty wars of history.

Past wars have had their figureheads and leaders, but society at large was fully involved. In recent years the focus has shifted from figureheads to instigators and personal organizers. Everyday communications have seen to it that opposing societies see each other's faces. What they see of each other is usually not too bad. As a result, individuals have moved into target sights rather than societies: "If only Hussein, Khadafi and Bin Laden would go away then things could be better."

In somewhat simple terms, past technology has increased the effectiveness (not necessarily the cost) of methods for producing casualties and damage of assets. Enough damage and casualties provide for capitulation or control of people and their societies and institutions that they own. But the value of casualties in conflict is passe, first in combat for the defender (the offender still pays the price) and for the noncombatants (who become refugees rather than casualties).

The previous two paragraphs lie at the core of how to deal with nontraditional warfare threats. Technology is the handmaiden that helps to deliver the solutions once these issues are resolved. The mission statement for nontraditional warfare might then include the following steps:

- No unnecessary killing, especially of innocents
- Identification of the instigators
- Break off all communications and contact between them and society
- Track down and eliminate the instigators

This statement is loaded because it is simple. It might even be an effective response to nontraditional warfare. But it needs leadership before technology can make it work.

Technology in Warfare

So what is the role of technology in warfare and where do we go from here? Technology provides the means through which scientific knowledge is applied to an artificial process—an engine of destruction and casualties. All technology in warfare either directly provides for or supports this objective function and its detailed development falls into a tried and true process that won two world wars. Engines of warfare fit the organization; needs for warfare and the state of the technical art determine the structure of that organization.

Explosives and tubes for propulsion of those explosives or kill mechanisms led to the design of the infantry squad (members close enough to shout to each other and carrying tubes called rifles), the tank (large protected tubes to damage defended positions to help the infantry seize them), artillery (unprotected tubes to hurl explosive shells indirectly from defilade into the defended positions or attacking infantry), the tubes of jet engines, the tube of missiles for defense and attack, and so on. The force structures required large numbers of people to operate in WWI and WWII and would have used only a fraction of these numbers for a WWIII nuclear exchange: dealing with the casualties from that exchange would have been a different story, involving much of the populations of western civilization.

The nature of warfare has already changed, but it is difficult to tell by looking at today's force structures, which are designed around tubes for a warfare we no longer expect to experience but whose memories we still fear and for which we are "prepared." Today's force structures use better and better tubes—they do not easily replace tubes nor can they easily retrain the tube holders or change the way that many people directly or indirectly support those who hold tubes.

Before technology of future conflict is best defined we therefore need to understand what its purpose might be and how difficult it might be to realize that purpose. The progress of innovation in industry provides a directly relevant model from which lessons can be learned and new ideas proposed. Existing institutions cannot easily innovate, even though they use technology. The reasons are cultural and economic—fear of change and the cost of change.

An underlying theme in this essay is to beware of traditional thinking in a nontraditional arena. The purpose of this theme has been to encourage the reader to think out of the box about nontraditional threats while being realistic about them. Doing so should provide invaluable service to the nation in a time of disturbing and growing challenges to its security.

27

IMPACT OF RADIO FREQUENCY WEAPONS ON NATIONAL SECURITY AND NATIONAL INFRASTRUCTURE

Howard J. Seguine

Radio frequency weapons (RFW) are systems or devices that produce sufficient electromagnetic energy, in the frequency domain from about 100 megahertz (MHz) to tens of gigahertz (GHz). These RFW systems are also often referred to as high power microwaves, nonnuclear electromagnetic pulse, and radio frequency munitions. These weapons are designed to upset or destroy electronic-based systems and components. Further, they can be used to harm biological-based systems and organisms. RFWs have been under development in the United States and former Soviet Union (FSU) since the 1960s. RFW technologies have proliferated to other nations, where they are under development. In some cases, claims have been made that they have been fielded. These countries intend to produce compact weapons capable of generating megawatts to gigawatts of power at ranges of tens of meters to hundreds of kilometers.

Although these weapons have been under development for military applications, none have been deployed to date. This is largely due to military commanders' unwillingness to rely on soft as opposed to hard kill. However, because of miniaturization of electronics and other strides in technology (see Exhibit 27.1), coupled with the growing reliance on electronics, RFWs are being looked at more seriously now than ever. This growing dependence on electronic and microelectronic technologies (in the critical infrastructure and the "digitized battlefield") is allowing these weapons to be an increasingly attractive option for terrorist groups to use in local conflicts, and for others

EXHIBIT 27.1   RFW focus and changes in the past 10 to 15 years.

	Past perspective	Current perspective
Participants	Superpowers (including U.S., Russia) and many other (i.e., Great Britain, France, Germany, Sweden, China, India, Israel)	Superpowers plus many other countries (i.e., Iran, Iraq, Korea, Taiwan, Japan, Brazil)
Security planning	• Destruction of target ("only") preferred way to kill target or mission • Superpower only real threat to homeland	• China/others: doctrine and procedures for unrestricted/asymmetric warfare • Due to widespread dependence on microelectronics, denial of electronics-based services can have devastating effects on U.S. national security and national infrastructure
U.S. interest level	Service HQ level	• Congressional, some OSD offices, CINCs, and some private industries
Technologies/threat conditions	• Information and research confined to classified programs (largely inaccessible to program managers, commodity managers and program sponsors) • Difficult to miniaturize power supplies, sources, etc. • Probable air breakdown at antenna (at today's energy levels) • U.S., USSR chief researchers	• Increased knowledge and understanding of vulnerabilities (far less energy needed to kill/upset microelectronics) • Delivery of very, very large amperage power sources in small packages • New antenna technologies prevent air breakdown (impulse radiated antenna (IRA)) • Information proliferating and in public forum • At least ten nations on four continents are known to have RFW programs; several proclaim intent to sell RFW technology • Technologies and capabilities to switch very large power sources (at tunable frequencies) • Concept provides opportunities for cheap, simple terrorist weapons
Status	U.S. led in some RFW source technologies	• "U.S. would fall behind other nations; no program to defend itself" (allied nation perception) • "U.S. could have stopped RFW proliferation, but said or did little" (allied nation perception)

desiring to wage strategic indirect warfare against U.S. targets. Such indirect warfare is defined as an adversary's attacking in such a manner that you may never know you are under attack until it is too late, and if you should detect the attack you may not be able to identify the perpetrator.

Potential RFW Target Sets

RFWs have been considered for use against numerous targets, just a few of which are listed here:

Military applications (to cause defense system degradation)

- Command and control centers
- Communications
- Data systems
- Defense suppression
- Tactical warning/attack assessment systems

Infrastructure elements (to cause denial of service or destruction)

- Banking and finance centers
- Telecommunications and civil aviation
- Electric power
- Industrial and business processes
- Transportation and fuel distribution

RFWs in the hands of criminals and terrorists could wreak great havoc on our society. Key criteria for these users would be weapons that could be easily constructed from commercial off-the-shelf components and not easily traced by conventional counterterrorist agencies.

The use of RFWs has the following advantages:

- Can be silent and easy to conceal
- Can emit short, repeated bursts
- Can be difficult to locate if they are not being observed
- Can be effective against unshielded electronics
- Can cause damage that cannot be readily detected
- Can offer possibility for remaining anonymous

RFW Characteristics

RFWs are a component of directed energy weapons (DEW), which also includes laser and particle beam weapons. They emphasize two advantages over conventional weapons: (1) RFWs rely on a power supply rather than a magazine of ammunition, and (2) RFWs attack at nearly the speed of light, thus making avoidance of the incoming bolt impossible, and negating the advantage of increasingly swift tactical missiles. RFWs have the added advantage of not requiring precise pointing and tracking such as lasers and particle beams.

RFWs may take many different forms, depending on the following conditions:

- Prime power source—explosive in the case of munitions and warheads, or nonexplosive (capacitive, inductive, or inertial) in the case of non-self-destructive systems

- Platform for deployment—fixed site, ground mobile, airborne, shipborne, or space-based

- Desired effects on target—upset or burnout

- Desired coupling mode—front door (where energy couples into the target through paths meant for the reception and transmission of energy, e.g., radar antenna and leads) and back door (where energy couples into the target through inadvertent points of entry, e.g., apertures and conductive paths)

- Mission scenario—overt or covert, military or terrorism

RFWs also may be classified according to other characteristics, including the following:

- RFW source
  - electron drive (Sources that convert energy from the power supply into kinetic energy of electrons inside a microwave tube, e.g., a magnetically insulated linear oscillator (MILO). This kinetic energy is then converted into microwaves, delivered to an antenna, and radiated. These are usually high-powered microwave (HPM) weapons.)
  - direct drive (Where the energy from the power source is delivered straight to the antenna and radiated. Direct drive sources can be very compact and lightweight. These are usually ultra wideband (UWB) weapons.)
- Repetition rate
  - single pulse
  - multiple pulses
- Radiated bandwidth
  - high power microwave
  - ultra wideband (UWB)
  - long-pulse noise

Each of these characteristics has its advantages and disadvantages, but mission and scenario are the chief factors as to what technologies and deployment modes are used.

High power microwave (HPM) weapons generate signals with a relatively narrow frequency band, but high spectral energy content. Conversely, UWB weapons generate a very broad frequency band, but lower spectral energy content (see Exhibit 27.2). Both have their pros and cons. For HPM weapons, prior knowledge of the target is required, since their narrow frequency band requires that the frequencies that will couple into the target must be known. However, if this frequency is known, sufficient energy at the proper frequency can be delivered to the target to cause upset or damage. UWB weapons do not require prior knowledge of the target, since energy in the band from 100 MHz to tens of GHz may be present and there will always be some frequencies that couple with the target. Their disadvantage is that the energy is spread over a broad frequency band and there is less energy to couple at specific frequencies and to cause damage.

RFW Target Effects

One advantage of RFW is that the actual attack would not necessarily be detected because the response would appear as either noise or some type of electrical surge or failure. Overall, the effects can be classified as:

- Temporary upset
- Permanent upset
- Burnout

Temporary upset occurs when the target functionally stops operating while it is being irradiated. The system will recover when the signal stops. Permanent upset occurs when some operating characteristic of the target changes and maintenance must be performed, for example, a computer's BIOS (basic input/output system) is changed and the operator must reset it. Burnout occurs when there is sufficient energy to cause various components, for example, leads and transistors, to be physically damaged either by melting or electrical breakdown.

According to Dr. A. B. Prischepenko, of Russia's High Mountain Geophysical Institute and designer of RFW sources, RFW effects should be classified in terms of the impact on the target mission. Temporary upset, he says, occurs when the operation of the target is upset for a few cycles of operation (computers, say in missile guidance systems, operate in a cyclical manner). A single pulse on a missile guidance system is not fatal to the mission since the

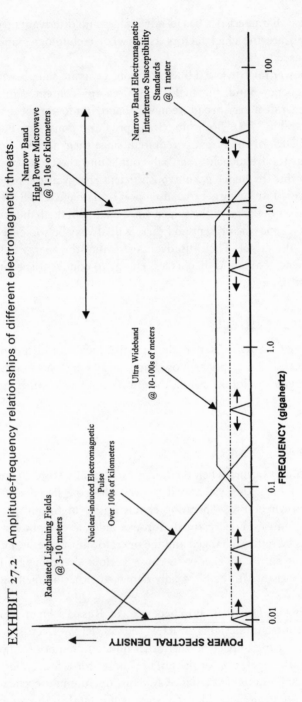

EXHIBIT 27.2 Amplitude-frequency relationships of different electromagnetic threats.

EXHIBIT 27.3   Biological effects and exposure levels from RFW.

Effect	Observation	Exposure level
Central nervous system	Transient function changes occur	10 mW/cm²
Behavioral effects	Effects on rodents occur	5–20 mW/cm²
Immune system	Initial stimulation of leukocyte production seen in rodents	10 mW/cm²
Auditory response	Audible clicks perceived under modulated illumination	1 mW/cm²
Ocular effects	Epithelial and stromal injuries to human eyes expected	10 mW/cm² at 35–107 GHz
Skin sensitivity	Warming sensation occurs	1 mW/m² at 35–107 GHz 27 mW/cm² at 2.45 GHz

missile can reacquire the target once it recovers. However, a train of short pulses could be fatal since it may prevent the reacquisition of the target.

Heating effects generally are observed when the target is exposed to either long pulses or continuous wave (CW) irradiation as a result of power absorption where the electromagnetic energy is absorbed and converted into heat. Electrical breakdown usually is caused when the target is irradiated with very short pulses (nanoseconds). The electrical fields in these short pulses are sufficiently high to cause materials to break down.

According to C. D. Taylor and D. V. Giri (*High Power Microwave Systems and Effects*, Washington, D.C., Taylor and Francis, 1994), "Biological effects from microwave radiation occur as a result of power absorption, the subsequent conversion to thermal energy, and the consequential increase in temperature." (See data presented in Exhibit 27.3.)

A real advantage of RFW applications occurs because the target may not be aware of the attack. It is also difficult to verify an RFW transmission even if an attack is expected. A positive way of detecting an attack is to have good intelligence that an attack is imminent and then to monitor for the expected waveforms. Several commercial firms have explored RFW detection sensors.

RFW Technology Proliferation

As RFW technologies continue to mature, be miniaturized, and proliferate, the threat to countries and commercial concerns dependent upon microelectronics dramatically increases. Today, at least 10 countries are developing RFWs, primarily with assistance from former Soviet Union scientists. Some of these countries have a demonstrated history of selling advanced weapon technologies to unfriendly and/or rogue states.

Dr. Ira Merritt, an Army physicist, testified before the Joint Economic Committee, 15 February 1998, that a study of open source literature clearly shows the worldwide interest in RFW technologies. Some of the study's key judgments are listed next:

- Construction of effective explosive-driven flux compression generators is entirely feasible for established military powers such as Russia, France, and Germany.

- No confirmed evidence exists in the open literature of employment of such devices to date.

- Most of the critical national infrastructure depends on modern metal oxide semiconductor technology and is extremely vulnerable to even low-power electromagnetic pulses, unless deliberately protected or hardened.

- The United States is disproportionately more vulnerable to RFW attack than less developed nations because of its civil and military reliance on sophisticated microelectronics.

Many of the technologies required to build RFWs have been described in open sources and have been sold to many countries. For example, Sweden announced, in 1997, that they had bought RFW technology from Russia, had reengineered it, and then used it to test effects on elements of their infrastructure. Dr. David Schriner, a former Navy engineer, testified before the Joint Economic Committee, 15 February 1998, that, ". . . such a weapon could be made by anyone with an engineering degree or even a bright technician with good hardware experience. The technical information required can be found in open sources, if not just from good common engineering sense. The required materials are not special and if the effort is made, advanced concepts can be made using everyday hardware such as automotive ignition systems."

Based on the author's recent discussion with former Soviet Union scientists, there is an RFW variant concept. If successfully weaponized, it will pose a significant threat to the United States, other modern countries, and selected commercial firms. The materials and technological approach for this variant concept may be the simplest and the cheapest option.

RFW Infrastructure Threats

Sweden has been particularly concerned about the potential for damaging or disrupting its infrastructure by means of RFWs. It has done considerable analyses and testing. France has the world's largest RFW test facility (called

Hyperion) which can be used to test large items of the national security and national infrastructure areas.

The author of *The Sunday Times* article, of 2 June 1996, claimed that since 1993 there have been more than 40 cases of financial institutions in London and New York subjected to extortion by "cyber-terrorists" threatening to disable important computer systems. The article states that these terrorists have been able to extort 400 million pounds from these activities. The methods used included electromagnetic pulses from "high emission radio frequency guns." Here in the United States, the emergency operations center (for local and federal first responders in disasters) for a large metropolitan area requested the federal government to test its communications suites in RFW environments.

RFW Trends

As RFW technologies continue to evolve and to proliferate, the following trends are expected:

- RFW sources with enhanced characteristics: higher peak powers (higher average powers, increased efficiencies, longer pulses, higher energy per pulse, and arrays of sources)
- Merging of HPM and conventional microwave tube technologies
- Miniaturization of RFW technologies (prime power, RFW sources, and antennas)
- Increased susceptibilities to RFW in modern countries due to increased miniaturization of solid-state electronics (less energy required to cause upset or damage) and increased reliance on electronics in critical functions
- Proliferation of specialists, technologies, and knowledge of U.S. vulnerabilities
- Wider recognition of the potential threat from RFWs

RFW technology is evolving rapidly and proliferating, and it can be expected that law enforcement and military units will encounter these weapons (or devices) in the relatively near future. History shows it does not take long for technologies to migrate from government to the private sector. For example, Los Angeles Police Department aircraft have been subjected to laser illumination, as have commercial aircraft landing in the Southern California area—in several cases, the pilots were temporarily blinded or dazzled.

Many planners and budgeters find it difficult to think outside the box when it comes to evolving threats today. The U.S. military and most elements of the federal government concerned with infrastructure protection (in areas other than cybersecurity) remain stuck in the past. U.S. strategy still is based on a Cold War-era view of the world, and U.S. technology is ill suited to many current missions. We must focus on the missions of the future rather than of the past. The alternative—more of the same—is too dangerous to even consider.

Underlining U.S. vulnerabilities are two significant books that should serve as wake-up calls to planners as to what the future may hold for us:

- *Unrestricted Warfare,* by Colonels Qiao Liang and Wang Xiangsu, Beijing, 1999. The authors advocate use of nontraditional methods and tactics for developing countries, notably China, to compensate for military inferiority vis-à-vis the United States in a conflict. They further advocate multiple military and nonmilitary means to strike at the United States.

- *War in the Gulf: Lessons Learned for the Third World,* by Brigadier V. K. Nair, New Delhi, 1991. He describes significant U.S. vulnerabilities, and emphasizes the meaning of USSR Admiral Sergei Gorshkov's adage, "The next war will be won by the side that best exploits the electromagnetic spectrum."

In other words, the time for proactive planning on how to protect critical elements is now, not after a "smoking gun" is found. The damage then may be so profound that it would be too late to mount an effective defense and/or offense.

28

DEVELOPMENT OF SMART SENSORWEBS FOR FUTURE WARFARE OPERATIONS

Jasper C. Lupo

There is an ongoing revolution in the world of sensors. It is now possible to proliferate sensors and mount them on any platform stationary or moving, from the individual soldier on up. We can literally buy sensors by the pound and toss them out into the environment as throwaways. It is possible to rapidly configure wireless networks of sensors that collect, relay, process, and archive the outputs of large arrays of heterogeneous sensor fields. For those of us who have spent our professional lives providing high-end sensors to the military, this realization comes as quite a shock for it changes the way we think about conducting military functions such as intelligence, surveillance, and targeting. This essay briefly explores the genesis of this capability and where it may lead for future military forces and operations.

Background

In 1997, Professor Burton Richter, Nobelist in Physics from Stanford University, was asked to convene a study on directions in sensing for the twenty-first century at the Arnold and Mabel Beckman Center of the National Academies of Sciences and Engineering. The study was called Advanced Research and Experiments in Sensing (ARES). This physics panel of the first ARES used an illustration entitled "The Sower" to represent their concept for a radical new direction in sensors. The physics panel said that the military does a great job of fielding high-end sensors that tend to be large, heavy, work well at long standoff ranges, and are too expensive to throw away. Their advice was to move to the other end of the spectrum and work on cheap, small, and low to modest performance sensors that could literally be sprinkled around the battlefield. They hypothesized that networking and clever processing of large sensor arrays could solve some of the more difficult problems facing the military. The word *sensorweb* was coined at ARES to connote the idea that these low-end sensors would be netted together to provide useful military information.

In 1998, the idea was endorsed by the Army Science Board in the context of providing situational awareness and organic sensing capabilities at the battalion and lower echelons. In 1999, the Smart Sensorweb (SSW) program was approved and funded as one of the five major thrusts of the Deputy Under Secretary of Defense for Science and Technology.

The Military Need

Exhibit 28.1 shows the unique capabilities that sensorwebs can provide. Current intelligence, surveillance, and reconnaissance (ISR) are roughly summarized on the right. Note that the sensors and platforms depicted are not viewed as throwaway systems. By being local and everywhere, the Smart Sensorweb can in principle see into urban canyons, buildings, windows, sewers, rough terrain, and deep forest canopy. Such capabilities are unlikely to accrue to

EXHIBIT 28.1 Smart Sensorweb augments standard ISR in difficult scenarios where geometry and physical barriers limit the power of conventional standoff sensors. "Being there" is the essential ingredient to rapid response and full awareness.

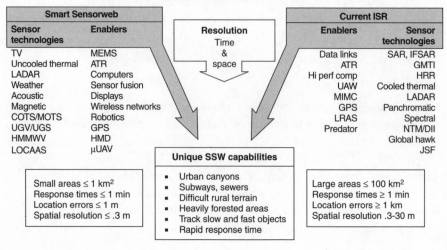

Smart Sensorweb					Current ISR	
Sensor technologies	**Enablers**	**Resolution** Time & space			**Enablers**	**Sensor technologies**
TV	MEMS				Data links	SAR, IFSAR
Uncooled thermal	ATR				ATR	GMTI
LADAR	Computers				Hi perf comp	HRR
Weather	Sensor fusion				UAW	Cooled thermal
Acoustic	Displays				MIMC	LADAR
Magnetic	Wireless networks				GPS	Panchromatic
COTS/MOTS	Robotics				LRAS	Spectral
UGV/UGS	GPS				Predator	NTM/DII
HMMWV	HMD					Global hawk
LOCAAS	µUAV					JSF

Unique SSW capabilities

Small areas ≤ 1 km²
Response times ≤ 1 min
Location errors ≤ 1 m
Spatial resolution ≤ .3 m

- Urban canyons
- Subways, sewers
- Difficult rural terrain
- Heavily forested areas
- Track slow and fast objects
- Rapid response time

Large areas ≤ 100 km²
Response times ≥ 1 min
Location errors ≥ 1 km
Spatial resolution .3-30 m

overhead sensors. Foliage penetration synthetic aperture radar (FOPEN SAR) is an example. Because of its long wavelength, the aircraft must fly a greater distance and create an aperture with adequate resolution to yield meaningful imagery of objects under trees. Geometry, terrain masking, motion compensation, and the specular nature of the target signatures pose physical limitations on the ultimate performance we may ever hope to derive from FOPEN SAR. Although we may expect to obtain useful cueing from it, albeit with a fairly significant false alarm rate, we will need to rely on other sensors for confirmation and identification. This problem can be addressed readily by the deployment of an intrusive sensor field surgically dropped in areas where cueing sensors indicate that a closer look is warranted. Taking this example a bit further, assume that FOPEN SAR has given us several alarms in a heavily forested area and that moving target techniques have confirmed that there has been recent vehicle traffic in the area. Using our new web technology, we can envision dropping disposable low light level cameras and even micro thermal imaging sensors into the area, perhaps mixed with acoustic and magnetic sensors to attempt to identify and pinpoint targets. We can then send weapons to points in the web, weapons that are not capable of sensing the targets on their own. To sum it up, the sensorweb provides resolution with more favorable geometries on the short time scales needed for weapons use.

The Technology

What makes the sensorweb possible? Extraordinary advances have occurred over the last decade in sensors, microelectronics, and communications—in both the military and commercial sectors. Imaging sensors include television cameras, low light level closed-circuit devices, cooled and uncooled thermal cameras, laser radar, multi-spectral imagers, and imaging radar. Nonimaging sensors include laser rangefinders, designators, weather sensors, chemical and biological agent sensors, physiological status sensors, seismic, acoustic, and magnetic sensors. In communications, we have the rapid growth of wireless and cellular networks. In navigation we have the global postioning system (GPS) and micro electromechanical systems (MEMS).

A notable example is the development of the MicroFLIR, sponsored by the U.S. Army Night Vision and Electronics Directorate (NVESD), Ft. Belvoir, Virginia. This device utilizes advances in uncooled thermal sensor technology and unique microelectronics to provide a system weighing only 70 grams, with a volume of approximately 12 cubic inches, and requiring only 540 milliwatts of power. The MicroFLIR provides real-time thermal imaging in video format for either direct viewing by the soldier or wireless transmission to a sensorweb.

EXHIBIT 28.2   Powered by advances in microelectronics and MEMS, military
and consumer markets will see the proliferation of low cost
and expendable sensors for use in wireless networks.

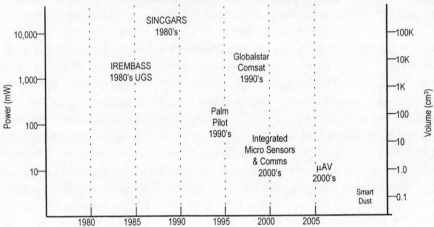

Numerous technology advances in the non-DOD commercial sector and
the rapid advances of the uses of the Internet are being leveraged in the pursuit of the SSW initiative. Exhibit 28.2 shows the trends in miniaturization for
communications and sensors. Thanks to major investments and advances in
MEMS, it is now possible to mount imaging devices on handheld micro air
vehicles. The Defense Advanced Research Projects Agency (DARPA) is working on a weather station in a 1 millmeter cube with communications; the nick-
name is Smart Dust.

The communications network of SSW will exploit advances in mobile,
wireless networks supporting cell phones, interactive pagers, and laptops with
communication cards. The miniaturization of powerful processors coupled
with novel user interface technologies (e.g., voice, touch screen, gesture recognition, heads-up displays) supports the development of personal data systems
that fit in the palm of a hand or on the back of a wrist, as well as hands-free
computers. These devices are significant for linking the individual combatant
to the power of the SSW.

Commercial wristwatches and other small, handheld devices now provide
global positioning system (GPS) information, weather information, and even
remote sensing (e.g., sensors that can determine the temperature of a remote
object). A remote connection through the Internet provides real-time control
of cameras (pan, tilt, and zoom), an important step toward the real-time, *virtual presence* that SSW will provide the warfighter.

To translate the vision of the SSW into reality, the Office of the Secretary of Defense (OSD) is sponsoring a test bed to demonstrate state-of-the-art hardware and software technologies, from ongoing DOD efforts and from the commercial sector, and to use experiments to assess technical and operational utility of these technologies. The other aspect of the test bed is to determine technical needs (power sources, bandwidth, etc.) and operational requirements (information needs, presentation capabilities, sensor employment, etc.).

OSD will utilize the Military Operations in Urban Terrain (MOUT) site at Fort Benning, Georgia, for test bed integration and demonstration. This site was selected particularly because local situation awareness is most difficult and most critical in built-up, urban areas. The MOUT site is fully instrumented for collecting experimental data that can leverage the site personnel knowledge gained from many joint and service exercises and technology demonstrations over the past several years.

To identify the major SSW components and provide a framework for this multidisciplinary effort, "sub-webs" were established. Initially, there were five sub-webs: image, weather, weapons, simulation, and information integration. Physio-med sub-web was recently added and additional sub-webs are being considered, as additional capabilities (e.g., chemical and biological sensing) are included in the experiments and demonstrations.

The SSW test bed activitiy is a joint, DOD-wide, effort, involving DARPA and all the Services, including the Air Force Research Laboratories (AFRL), the Army Research Laboratory (ARL), the Army Night Vision Electronics and Sensors Directorate (NVESD), the Office of Naval Research (ONR), and other service labs and research centers throughout the United States.

The First SSW Experiment

In late August of 2000, the first experiments with live troops were conducted at the Ft. Benning, Georgia, location of the McKenna MOUT site. Exhibit 28.3 shows the top level architecture. The results were encouraging and surprising. Troops using formative SSW products performed their missions much more efficiently. Furthermore, they felt that the potential for even greater advantage was very high and they provided numerous ideas on how to improve the next phase. The surprise was the fact that the oft-predicted cognitive overload associated with a glut of information did not manifest itself. The soldiers seemed ready and willing to adjust preferences and usage to siphon the information they felt they needed most.

EXHIBIT 28.3 The first SSW experiment blended a mix of simulation and real systems in a wireless network that was tied locally to a control center at the MOUT site.

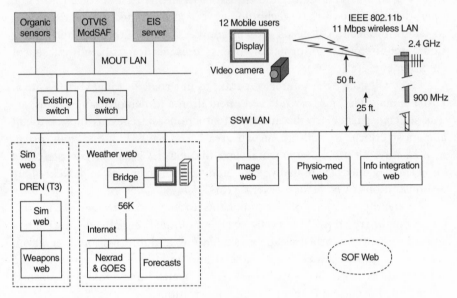

The Future

What can we expect as the concepts of Smart Sensorweb evolve and mature? We can answer this question by reviewing the ultimate vision behind SSW. The key ingredients are listed here:

- *Omnipresent local sensor fields.* These sensor fields will be deployed before, during, and after military operations by air, sea, and ground vehicles, and individual soldiers.

- *Layers of networks to move sensor data around the battlefield.* Information can be passed around local and global networks like that now emerging on the commercial Internet.

- *Visualization tools to provide virtual presence to the user.* Users at all echelons will be immersed in 3-D displays that provide pre-mission training, planning, and real-time operational capability. Our forces will have the ability to "be" and see nearly everything.

- *Distributed smart agents to refine the sensor data and infuse knowledge.* Users will be aided by invisible hoards of smart agents that perform automatic target detection, recognition, and identification; object and personnel tracking; planning advice; training scenarios; and weapons cueing, and delivery.

The path to Smart Sensorweb will be evolutionary. Not all the pieces will arrive at the same time. However, commercial and military technology will readily enable all of them in this decade. It will simply be a matter of using an acquisition strategy that allows this evolution to move smoothly and rapidly at reasonable cost. Since late 1997, the phenomenon of sensorwebs has exploded. Many Service and DARPA programs have appeared that work various aspects of the concept. Several preceded the actual ARES conference and were in place as the Smart Sensorweb effort in OSD began. There are too many relevant efforts to mention here. The key elements for future sensorwebs are now rapidly developing in excellent programs at DARPA and in the Services. The OSD program strategy has been to leverage these and fold them into the experiments. Finally, it is important to realize that a localized SSW concept can provide the framework for intelligence information, target acquisition/location, and weapons delivery in NTW operations involving counterterrorism, guerrilla and urban warfare, and drug interdiction.

Special thanks are due to Professor Burton Richter of Stanford who chaired the first ARES and Professor S. Koonin of CALTECH who chaired the physics panel, which developed the sensorweb concept. It is also important to acknowledge the enthusiastic support of MIT Lincoln Laboratory personnel Walt Morrow, Al McLaughlin, and Al Gschwendtner.

29

IMPACT OF ELECTROMAGNETIC PULSES ON FUTURE WARFARE OPERATIONS

Michael D. McDonnell

Even before the first nuclear device was detonated at the Trinity Site in White Sands, Enrico Fermi speculated that a by-product would be the emission of intense electromagnetic waves across the spectrum of all low to high frequencies. Of course, at the time, the interest in the more obvious effects of a nuclear weapon—the blast, thermal, and to a lesser extent, nuclear radiation—were of more concern. Nor was there any interest in such phenomena for the next 15 years. The high altitude nuclear test series over Johnston Island in Operation Dominic during 1962 included the event that confirmed an interest in what was then termed the electromagnetic pulse (EMP).

EMP is caused by the interaction of the gamma rays and highly energized plasma resulting from a nuclear explosion. These, in themselves, do not cause the EMP of concern but their interactions with the atoms in the atmosphere, through the phenomenon known as the Compton Effect, release other electrons that each generate electromagnetic waves, by themselves and through further interaction with other atoms. Thus, part of the energy of any nuclear device is translated into EMP.

Of special importance has been the case when a nuclear device is detonated above the atmosphere. In such a situation there basically is no surrounding media by which the resulting energy can couple. Essentially all of the resulting energy transforms the material of the device into a plasma that radiates out in all directions. By simple geometry, half of that plasma would enter the earth's atmosphere and, through the Compton Effect, create a significant EMP.

Nature of the EMP Threat

An electromagnetic pulse (EMP) was first observed as an effect associated with nuclear weapons in the 1960s during testing of nuclear weapons in the upper atmosphere. The effect is caused when there is little or no effective mass to the atmosphere around the nuclear weapon at the time of detonation. Under these conditions, the energy of the explosion cannot couple into the atmosphere by a shock wave and essentially all of the energy that would usually go into the blast wave associated with the weapon is locked into generating a high energy plasma of ionized nuclei and electrons. This high energy plasma radiates intense signals all across the electromagnetic spectrum but, for the cases of interest as a destructive weapons effect, especially in the microwave and radio frequencies.

These signals are picked up not only by radio antennas, microwave repeaters and receivers, and so on, but by any conductor such as telephone and electric transmission lines. Such lines act as very long radio antennas and can receive enormous amounts of electrical energy that is then channeled into telephones and electrical equipment connected to the lines.

Regardless of whether the ultimate recipient of the EMP is a radio, microwave receiver, telephone, or other electronic hardware, the results can range from temporary impairment of its operation to destruction. This is, however, especially true of electronic systems such as radio/microwave receivers that are designed to amplify the signals they receive.

While means have been developed to mitigate the EMP threat, these are expensive, especially if they have to be retrofitted onto the equipment rather than incorporated into the original design. Thus, aside from critical military equipment, few electronic devices are intentionally protected against the EMP threat.

HE Generated EMP

While EMP has the advantages of being essentially harmless to humans and other organisms as well as to simple real estate, it can be crippling to military and supporting civilian electronics. However, the use of nuclear weapons as EMP sources is often socially, politically, and even militarily counterproductive. Consequently, in recent years there have been attempts to generate significant EMP through the use of conventional high explosives (HE).

It is not the intention of this essay to describe the approaches being pursued in the development of HE driven EMP generators. Suffice it to say that the fundamental principles are based in well-established theories on magneto-

EXHIBIT 29.1 Highly simplified diagram of MHD generator.

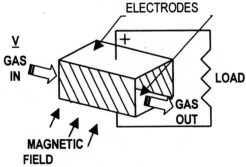

hydrodynamics (MHD). In brief, MHD has been studied as a way of generating electric power. The MHD generator is one in which an ionized gas is forced at high temperature, pressure, and velocity through a duct situated in a transverse magnetic field. An induced voltage appears in the third mutually perpendicular direction as a result of the Hall Effect, and this voltage may be tapped by electrodes (see Exhibit 29.1). An MHD generator can be used to create intense magnetic fields in lieu of electrical power. Theoretically, once an electromagnetic field is generated, it can be compressed by another explosion to create EMP effects similar to those resulting from nuclear weapons.

Providing Directionality to EMP Weapons
Disadvantages of EMP as a Weapon
Currently, one of the main disadvantages of EMP as a potential weapon is the indiscriminate nature of the effects. It is generated and propagated in essentially all directions. Friendly, as well as enemy, equipment becomes at risk. Providing some means of directing the EMP toward the target(s) of choice and away from friendly assets is therefore required if EMP is to be used as a weapon.

Focusing Nonnuclear EMP Effects
The possibility of providing directionality to EMP fields is based on the simple fact that EMP is merely a broadband electromagnetic effect. As such, it can be focused by metallic reflectors just as light is from silvered mirrors or radio waves are in radio telescopes. A parabolic metallic reflector with an EMP generator at its focal point, would reflect the EMP into any given direction just as the parabolic reflector in an automobile headlight reflects the light from the headlight into a concentrated beam.

EXHIBIT. 29.2   Parabolic EMP direction modification.

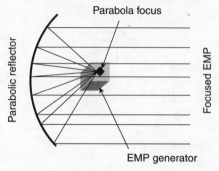

Simple EMP Director Design

Exhibit 29.2 portrays a crude drawing of the concept under consideration. The EMP generator is at the focal point of the parabolic curve. When the EMP field is generated, the EMP is directed by the reflector into the desired direction. The extent of focusing of the energy can be varied by proper construction of the parabolic reflector.

The first objection that would naturally be raised to such a simple concept would be that the HE explosion that creates the EMP would destroy the reflector. This, of course, is true. However, the EMP generated by the HE explosion travels at the speed of light and the shock wave produced by the HE travels, essentially, at the speed of sound. Thus, the EMP arrives at the reflector and is reflected before the shock wave arrives to destroy the reflector.

Simple Directed EMP Weapon Design

EMP Weapon Design Components

Exhibit 29.3 shows a concept for a simple directed EMP weapon. The EMP generator is component A. Component B is a gas generator (a simple CO_2 cartridge with a regulating valve would suffice). Surrounding these is a flexible, collapsible membrane (Component C) that is essentially transparent to most of the electromagnetic frequencies of interest as an EMP threat. Part of this membrane is coated with a sprayed on, bonded metallic reflector. There are strings/wires/filaments connecting this flexible membrane to the EMP generator.

Immediately prior to initiation of the device, the gas generator would inflate the flexible membrane. The strings/wires/filaments connected from the membrane to the EMP generator would cause the material to be inflated so that the EMP generator was fixed to the fully inflated membrane, which

EXHIBIT 29.3 Conceptual packaged EMP weapon.

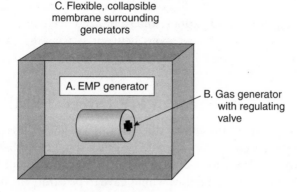

EXHIBIT 29.4 Concept when inflated.

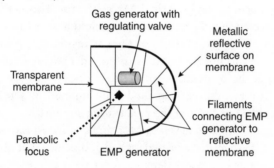

would form a parabolic shape around the generator with the EMP generator at the focus of the parabola.

Exhibit 29.4 shows the concept when inflated. Note that part of the inflated parabola is coated with a metallic reflector as suggested in Exhibit 29.2. The rest of the inflated membrane is transparent to the EMP. The exact areas of the parabola to be coated would depend on the extent of focusing desired and could be determined, to a first order, by simple optical analysis. Upon initiation of the EMP generator, the EMP would precede the shock wave to the reflector and be redirected and concentrated in the desired direction before the shock wave destroyed the membrane.

Secondary Benefit of HE Directed EMP

There is a secondary benefit of a simple directed EMP, aside from the protection offered to friendly equipment in the area. Since the EMP effects are highly concentrated and directed, the amount of HE required to produce the desired effect at target range would be significantly reduced (potentially by at least an order of magnitude.) This would result in an overall reduction in the size, weight, cost, logistics considerations, and so on, and make the simple directed EMP a possible candidate for weapons delivery systems that would be precluded by more massive, omnidirectional weapons.

Conceptual Employment of HE Directed EMP

As a battlefield weapon, the simple directed EMP might be prepackaged and capable of being positioned on a tripod or other support so that it could be aimed in the general direction of its target(s). The support would have to connect to the EMP generator and thus would have to penetrate the flexible membrane. This would require that the membrane be capable of first being inflated and then remaining inflated while the inflating gas leaks out around the support that penetrates it to support the EMP generator. This is not a significant problem. As stated earlier, the gas generator would have a valve to regulate the release of the gas. The first purpose of the gas regulation would be to insure that the membrane was not ruptured by too rapid a release of the inflating gas. The second would be to continue the release of gas until detonation of the device so that the membrane remained fully inflated and properly formed while the gas leaked out around the penetrating support.

Similar concepts could be developed for simple directed EMPs deliverable by missile or aircraft. Systems have been designed and fielded that use parachutes to stabilize submunitions or sensors deployed over the battlefield to attack targets out of range of ground-based sensors. Similar concepts could be used to provide stability and directionality to air-delivered simple directed EMPs.

The concept of an HE generated EMP weapon still requires further development. However, such a weapon, assuming its ultimate availability, will be of limited utility if its effects are omnidirectional and indiscriminate. Providing directionality to the effects produced through the use of the present concept will not only enhance the utility of any such weapon but offers the potential of reducing its size, weight, and cost and making it acceptable in a wider variety of roles.

Prognosis for the Future
Using EMP for Battlefield Situations

While effective EMP weapons would have obvious utility on the battlefield, there are two questions concerning the "effectiveness" of conventionally driven EMP weapons: the first deals with what electrical equipment of the opposing forces would be vulnerable to conventionally driven EMP weapons; the second is concerned with what electrical equipment of our forces would be vulnerable to our own conventionally driven EMP weapons.

There is no question that EMP can damage or destroy electrical equipment. The question is: which equipment is vulnerable to what EMP levels? Battlefield employment of EMP weapons might cause unacceptable damage to the sensitive electronic equipment that the United States relies more on than its expected foes at present. This is likely to become even more the case in the foreseeable future. It is conceivable that U.S. employment of an EMP battlefield weapon, even one delivered by air or artillery behind enemy lines, would provide only a short-term pyrrhic victory to battlefield U.S. forces unless the EMP could be directed toward the intended target.

Asymmetries of the EMP Threat

In the previous discussion on the use of EMP on the battlefield, the threat emphasized was the U.S. employment of such weapons causing possible fratricide of U.S. electrical systems. However, the possibility of an opponent taking advantage of the asymmetry presented by U.S. or allied forces' dependence on sophisticated, delicate electronics is too real to be ignored.

If fratricide is a problem, survival against a determined EMP attack, possibly preemptive, is even more serious. As earlier discussions indicate, conventionally driven EMP weapons are neither sophisticated nor expensive. Any opponent in a guerrilla war could produce numerous such devices, place them near U.S. forces or supporting technological infrastructures, and detonate them, thus seriously disrupting our ability to respond. The EMP threat environment in the guerrilla-style operation described here would be much more serious than that posed by the fratricide situation existing on the battlefield. In the first place, the devices could be detonated much closer to U.S. forces or critical infrastructure resources. Second, delivery systems used on the battlefield would be limited to the size of an artillery or air-delivered EMP weapon, whereas a much larger EMP device capable of generating a much stronger EMP field could be employed by mounting the system on a truck. Both of these factors would indicate the possibility of EMP environments that are orders of magnitude larger than in the battlefield fratricide case.

Vulnerability of Civilian Systems/Infrastructure

The discussion of the EMP threat to the United States has, so far in this essay, concentrated on battlefield systems (although the supporting technological infrastructure is mentioned). It is expected that some EMP protection will be provided to the battlefield supporting infrastructure although whether it would be sufficient to ameliorate a determined guerrilla or terrorist type of operation is problematical. However, there are civilian systems/infrastructures that, while not owned or operated by the military, are critical to supporting the modern U.S. battlefield forces. Production of logistics items such as ammunition, rations, and so forth, is basically outside of the military responsibility but is dependent on frequently sensitive electronic systems/infrastructures to monitor quality control, schedule the delivery of raw materials, and ship the finished items. Even the delivery of war ready materiel (WRM) would be vulnerable to severe disruption or even termination if subjected to successful EMP attacks.

The vulnerability of other civilian systems/infrastructures to EMP attacks (perhaps by terrorists) might not be considered a wartime threat. But disruption of electrical power lines or plants, interference with civilian air control radars, destruction of records in financial institutions, and so on, could wreak havoc with the U.S. society as well as threaten the lives and well-being of its citizens.

Living with the EMP Threat

As with any threat, there are defenses to EMP. What one invests in the defenses depends on the value of the asset being guarded and, to a certain extent, whether the defenses are built in or retrofitted. Proper design with built-in shielding, fail-safe fuses between communications antennae and delicate circuitry, hardened and/or redundant critical subsystems is generally considered to add less than 10 percent and frequently less than 5 percent to the total cost of a system. Retrofitting can, on the other hand, cost almost as much or even more.

In any case, simple, less sophisticated, slower electronic systems should be considered as potential backups for cases where successful EMP attacks could disable electronic systems for long periods of time. Planning and training for independent small unit operations should be considered for cases when units might lose the usual command, control, and communications assets.

Above all, the EMP threat must be studied and understood by all those who have responsibility for vulnerable systems/infrastructures. First, we need to develop a more realistic concept of the threat and what could and should be done about it. Second, we need to eliminate some of the fear that this relatively unknown threat can pose to anyone forced to consider it.

30

IMPACT OF ROBOTICS
ON NONTRADITIONAL WARFARE

David L. Bongard
Terry L. Sayers

Robotics has moved from the realm of science fiction to reality. Technology advances over the last two decades have created robotic platforms and sensors capable of operating in any environment (in the air, on land, on the water, under the water, and even under the ground). During the next 10 to 15 years, military analysts foresee the rapid adaptation of robotics technology into a variety of military applications.

Robotics technology can be divided into two main categories: remotely directed and self-directed. Remotely directed (or piloted) systems have a human operator located some distance away who controls the system through a data link. Self-directed (or programmed) systems are fully autonomous machines that require no human support, oversight, or control to perform their task.

The nature of robotics is ideally suited for a range of missions that pose significant risks to human life. Robotic systems can also provide a level of attention and dedication that is almost impossible for humans to sustain for any length of time. Another attribute of robotic systems is that they can be camouflaged, miniaturized, or screened to avoid detection.

At the dawn of the new century, several military robotic systems are in use, primarily employed for aerial or underwater reconnaissance. These are usually remotely operated craft with a human operator and a radio or television data link to control the system.

AGM-86A Tomahawk cruise missile.

Historical Developments and Trends

Although widespread practical applications of robotics technology in the civilian sector are comparatively recent, having occurred largely since 1970, military robotic systems are actually considerably older. Aerial target drones were used before World War II, although their control systems were purely mechanical and nonelectronic. The performance of this early example of a robotic system was not difficult to predict. During World War II, the Germans employed several types of remote explosive devices for use on land. These were organized into specially equipped tank companies (Panzerkompanien [Funklenk]), and employed to destroy obstacles, especially in built-up or fortified areas. The

Borgward Company produced a range of expendable remote-controlled, tracked, mine-clearing, and demolition vehicles. The B-I and B-II were small, powered by a 6-cylinder motor, had a range of only 1500 meters, and towed mine-detonation rollers. The tiny "Goliath" was powered by an electric motor and weighed only 370 kg, but could deliver a 60 kg charge over distances of 1500 meters. The larger, reusable B-IV was a 3.8- or 5.34-ton radio-controlled vehicle with a gas engine, and delivered a 500-kg charge. The Germans also used several types of wireless-controlled aerial "guided bombs" to attack heavily defended enemy targets.

The United States employed a similar weapon in a series of attacks against the Japanese air and naval base complex at Rabaul in early 1944, operating from Green Island. Employing an early form of television for data feedback and control, the attack units consisted of specially modified aircraft equipped with large cargoes of high explosives and were directed to their targets with some effect. Of about 80 or 90 craft launched in February of 1944, some 60 reached the target area, and about 40 struck their intended targets, either airfields or shipping facilities. The U.S. Navy, which had conducted the attack, regarded the operation's results as not worth the effort expended.

In a real sense, both the U.S. target drones (developed by Raytheon and Teledyne) and the German attack drones were really types of primitive guided missiles. For more than 20 years following 1945, most robotics development continued along those paths, developing a variety of guided missiles for aerial and antiaircraft combat, antitank warfare, and nuclear weapon delivery. Since these systems were intended for single use, and were destroyed on impact, they are not regarded as real robots. Exhibit 30.1 presents general features of robots and remotely piloted vehicles (RPVs) to provide a baseline for observing differences in applications and performance requirements.

Advances in computer technology and electronic data processing, together with more reliable and effective wireless video transmission, made development and employment of RPVs a reality in the 1970s, with early systems reaching deployment in the following decade.

The capabilities of such craft have increased steadily since their introduction, making full use of a wide range of electronic sensors; sophisticated and compact video cameras that can operate in the infrared and ultraviolet spectra as well as in the visible light; ground-scanning radar; and more reliable communications systems. In February 2001, the U.S. Air Force conducted a successful test of ordnance delivery, accurately striking the target (at a Nevada test range) with weapons delivered from an remotely piloted, jet-powered aircraft. The potential for robotic combat aircraft, which has hitherto been largely a fictional idea, has finally entered the real world.

EXHIBIT 30.1   Features of robots and remotely piloted vehicles (RPVs).

System type	Robots		RPVs	
	Capabilities	Limitations	Capabilities	Limitations
Land-based	Self-controlled with little or no human supervision	Complex control and navigation programs, sensor performance and reliance	Simple electronics, ready capacity for complex tasks	Human supervision, coupled with radio/ television signals or control cables (which limits range)
Water-based	Uniform environment makes navigation fairly easy	Water blocks data signals for reconnaissance	Need for human control balanced by lower costs	Problems with data links—sonar vs. lines vs. extremely low frequency
Airborne	Uniform environment but exacting standards for flight control	Mass, weight, energy supply, and endurance all notable design issues	Relatively inexpensive and simple	Requirement for skilled human operators ("pilots")

Applications in other mission areas are also moving forward. There is considerable interest among many nations in robotic mine-clearing systems. NASA and other institutions involved in the space program have developed several robotic (that is, fully self-directed) systems for unmanned exploration missions on distant planets. The most public of these was the successful employment of *Sojourner,* the robotic system deployed by the Mars Lander satellite in 2000. Undersea robotic systems have been developed and have seen wide use in the civilian sector. The famous undersea explorer, Robert Ballard, who discovered the wrecks of the *Titanic* and the German battleship *Bismarck,* employed tethered remote submersible robotic systems for both tasks. While such tethered systems have limited range and capabilities (above all they are unable to go farther than the length of their tether), they are much cheaper and easier to operate than a manned submarine.

Current Technology and Challenges

Current robotics technology is developing rapidly and advances are occurring not only in the United States and Japan (traditional robotics leaders), but also in Western Europe (Great Britain, Sweden, and Italy), Russia, and elsewhere. Robotic systems have been developed to perform in a wide range of missions, but there are still many possible mission areas with a great deal of work ahead before achieving reliable operational capability. For the time being, most military uses involve robotic systems used primarily in reconnaissance or security missions. The civilian use of robotics is also growing rapidly. There is now a great opportunity for technology transfer from the civilian sector to the military sector.

Robotic Technology Challenges on Land

To function effectively, a land-based robotic system has to achieve three basic tasks, beyond those associated with its military mission, for example, detecting mines or toxic chemical agents, or conducting reconnaissance activities. First, a robot must recognize and detect obstacles in sufficient time to alter its movement profile. Second, it must be able to distinguish real obstacles from other objects in the pathway. Third, the robot must determine and choose an effective path across the landscape surface while maintaining its primary orientation without mishap or accident.

These are not simple tasks. A human walking along a forest trail or down a city sidewalk littered with other passers-by, performs all of these tasks almost without thinking, except in the broadest sense of maintaining general direction of travel and orientation. Robots do not have the experience, subconscious thought processes, or artificial intelligence to traverse an obstacle-strewn surface. Robots must receive or utilize accurate and complete programming to allow them to perform those tasks. Land-based robots must evaluate and sift through a range of changing sensor data, determine what data is reliable and valuable, and then decide how to most effectively act on that data in accordance with the designated mission. The complexities can be quite daunting, especially when the limitations on physical data processing capabilities may be severe.

Despite their relative limitations, land-based robots may prove very useful in some applications. Reconnaissance activities in areas affected by chemical agents, radiation, or biotoxins are one such application. Related to those activities is the issue of explosive ordnance disposal (EOD). In any of these activities, minimizing risk to humans is one of the major criteria and employing RPVs, remotes, or robots would meet that requirement. Similar activities need to be performed for civilian, nonmilitary goals as well—chemical waste and hazardous waste cleanup actions pose similar challenges and risks to any humans undertaking those tasks.

Robotic and Remote Technology Challenges in the Air and under Water

The major drawback to remotes, RPVs, or robots operating without physical links stems from the possibility of control links being subjected to jamming and electronic interference. For robotic systems controlled through cables or other physical links, operations are severely limited in terms of range and flexibility. Underwater RPVs are typically restricted to a range of 2,000 to 3,000 meters (1 to 2 miles slant range) from the controlling ship, to include both descent distance and horizontal range.

Wireless control for underwater RPVs is essentially a nonstarter, because of the opacity presented by water to radio and television signals. Any wireless control signal will have to be transmitted either by an extremely low-frequency signal (presenting significant problems for transmission and reception antennae, although this technology has been successfully employed for communication with submerged nuclear submarines), or through some sort of sound signals transmitted directly through the water. This last method provides some capability for both control and data feedback.

Comparatively speaking, aerial RPVs present a much simpler technical challenge. Tethered aerial RPVs would have only limited utility, except perhaps for very local aerial reconnaissance. Power usage demands would require equipment to be tethered to a vehicle, in order to provide an adequate power supply. Wireless-controlled aerial RPVs have experienced widespread development and production efforts over the last 10 to 15 years, and have been deployed in the armed services of several nations. Still, the demands for detailed and finely directed remote control, coupled with increasing demands for data feedback, pose some significant challenges for the next iteration of aerial reconnaissance RPVs.

Upcoming and Emerging Technological Developments

The range of limitations imposed by existing technology on the effective use of robots and RPVs is certainly not a permanent set of restrictions. Rapid development in the related fields of materials, power plants, computers, and software virtually guarantees that current restrictions will only be temporary. In relatively broad terms, three main areas are available for likely development: (1) stationary land-based robots; (2) land-based robots operating in a severely restricted environment for a specific purpose; and (3) wide-capability land-based and submersible robots, which represent the expensive and upper-end future of such technology. Further, developments in materials and power plants especially promise increased capability for aerial and submersible RPVs (see Exhibit 30.2).

Stationary Robots

Technological developments in recent years have focused on moving, or mobile, robots. However, the United States employed a wide range of remote sensors to track Viet Cong and North Vietnam army troop movements and

EXHIBIT 30.2   Emerging robotic technologies and applications.

Vehicle type	Robotic technology	RPV technology
Land-based	• Static sentinels for security of installations • Mobile security units, with sensor suites and nonlethal weapons	• Mobile security patrol units, especially for temporary facilities in low- to moderate-risk operational environments • Antitank weapons and mine clearing devices
Water-based	• Reconnaissance units for both mobile operational use and patrol of secured water areas (harbors, drilling rigs, etc.) • Minesweeping units to find, identify, assess, and remove • Static, moored sentinel units for security of fixed locations	• Short-range mine detection and sweeping units, tethered to controlling vessels (submarine or surface ship) • Detecting and clearing/capturing underwater chemical and biological mines
Airborne	• High altitude (2,500 meters), solar-powered, long-duration communications relay and wide area surveillance • EW mission platforms for employment in areas with high density and high lethality air defense weapons	• Sophisticated strike aircraft with low-observable (stealth) technology, good payloads, and secure control-communications links • Employing ECM and RF weapons for selective targeting

activities, especially along the geographically remote regions of the so-called Ho Chi Minh Trail, during the Vietnam War. The size, and relatively easy-to-spot nature of those sensors made them easy to detect and befuddle. The U.S. forces soon realized that the intelligence gained from those sources was not reliable. Microcomputers, micro-circuitry, and modern video cameras had not yet appeared in the robotics arena.

Modern stationary sensor robots, made small and easily hidden, would be valuable for similar counterinsurgency operations, or for control of access across extensive land borders. In a more tactical scenario, scattering similar devices across the countryside during operations would increase the security of friendly forces, especially at night, and would provide valuable intelligence. Such devices would be closely related to Smart Sensorweb technology, discussed in detail in Essay 28, Development of Smart Sensorwebs for Future Warfare Operations, and could well be employed in tandem with Smart sensorwebs (SSWs).

The old U.S. Captor mine system, deployed during the 1970s, consisted of hundreds of units, each with a sonar sensor buoy and a torpedo-launch mechanism with a single torpedo. While outmoded by modern standards, the basic technology provides an example for another type of system. Once armed or activated, each Captor unit "listened" for the passage of a Soviet submarine, through its acoustic signature. When a mine heard the proper signature, a torpedo was fired at the sound source, and presumably destroyed one Red Fleet submarine. While comparatively unsophisticated, both of these types of technologies are useful and well within current U.S. production capabilities.

Robots in Restricted Environments

One of the major challenges facing land-based robots is the difficulty of navigating effectively across an unfamiliar landscape. One way to get around part of the challenge is to have the robots operate in an environment that is limited in scope and range of terrain, thereby making the twin tasks of navigation, and identification of hostile or interesting objects, persons, and machines, considerably simpler.

Clearly, such a limited-capability robot would not be useful in many situations. For security on a large military reservation or a sensitive facility with an extensive perimeter, such robots would be extremely valuable. Properly employed, they would reduce the need for human patrol personnel and sentries who would be deployed only when a robot encountered some unidentified situation.

Such a system would probably operate on a perimeter path, perhaps located between an inner and outer fence. The path would only need to be adequately surfaced, to enable the robots to traverse it in all weather and all light conditions. Faced with predictable and known terrain, the robots' navigation task could be accomplished. Of course, sufficient numbers of robots would be necessary to ensure adequate coverage of the perimeter at all times. The Mobile Detection Assessment Response System under development and use by the U.S. Army over the past 5 years is the forerunner of more sophisticated mobile security patrol systems that could be used to protect critical facilities and resources.

These security robots utilize sensors, including normal and low-light or infrared video, and a means for transmitting information to the control center. The human reaction team could be dispatched to a sighting location when one or more robots encounter something unusual. The savings in personnel costs, coupled with the fact that the robots do not get tired, bored, distracted, cold, or sick, provides a considerable advantage for a low- to medium-threat security situation.

Another opportunity for using land-based robots is in the arena of logistical support. Modern armies, especially those with lots of heavy mechanized equipment, devote a vast effort to maintaining that equipment in working order, and to moving supplies and replacement parts from place to place. Some of these tasks, such as routine surface transport of supplies, could be entrusted to robot vehicles. For such missions, speed is not essential, nor would the robots have to do more than follow a preprogrammed route, perhaps modified or updated at one or more checkpoints en route. Such logistical transport robots would have to be programmed to avoid obstacles on the route. Further, robots capable of performing this obstacle avoidance task are some years in the future, since this last requirement is beyond the capability of most land-based robot systems.

In a somewhat related direction, considerable development work has taken place recently on undersea robots, taking advantage of the uniform environment and relatively low speeds needed, to produce prototype vehicles for mine detection and removal, as well as for general reconnaissance. The undersea environment is, in many ways, more forgiving to the development of robotic systems. While there are few landmarks, there are also virtually no obstacles. Moreover, unlike aerial operations where RPVs are expected to move at 200 or more kph, a submersible robot only needs to move along at perhaps 50 kph, and may indeed be quite effective at one-third that speed. These conditions have impelled development of a range of prototype vehicles, not only in the United States, but also in Sweden and Great Britain.

High-End Robots

Recent advances in artificial intelligence, particularly in developing computer systems that can learn from their experiences, have provided considerable impetus to a new generation of nearly self-aware robots. Machines that are actually capable of creating new behavior and response patterns on the basis of experience do not have to receive complete instruction before they begin to function. This eliminates the detailed and exhaustive programming instructions needed by less sophisticated machines. Even with a significant savings in initial programming, such machines would require an even more extensive production lead time, since, like human beings, they would have to undergo a learning process before being able to venture into the field and perform effectively.

In any event, such machines will likely remain relatively uncommon, because of the expense involved in their production and development. Their considerable cost would argue against their employment in any but the most necessary situations, where only a robot would be able to perform the mission effectively. Probable missions would include chemical and bio-weapon reconnaissance in hostile or dangerous zones and other reconnaissance missions where human reconnaissance would either be too exposed or too vulnerable.

Advanced RPVs

RPVs, especially for aerial operations, are rapidly becoming more sophisticated and effective. Although reconnaissance will likely remain the primary role, the capability to attack targets will soon be added. The operational costs of RPVs are much less than using manned vehicles (especially aircraft). In addition, the lack of a human pilot enables commanders to place such robots at risk without the moral or emotional toll involved in launching manned missions.

Reconnaissance RPVs are ideally suited for loitering air missions such as spotting for artillery or guided missile strikes. Particularly in those situations where modern weapons systems can reach effectively and accurately to ranges of 150 km or more (and over 30 km for conventional artillery), the impact zone for warheads is far beyond the range of any ground-based sensors organic to the launching unit. Employing RPVs for such tasks makes the activity itself relatively inexpensive in terms of resources.

The successful test strike conducted with an RPV in February 2001, undertaken at a Nevada weapons test range, demonstrated the real feasibility of accurately and effectively delivering weapons by RPVs. Such missions have historically been extremely costly in both men and materiel, however great the benefits. With less need for ground strike aircraft, manned aircraft would be free to devote a greater portion of its resources to air superiority, both in terms of aircraft and mission goals.

Summary

The military potential for both RPVs and robots has as yet undergone only cursory examination, analysis, and development. This essay presents limited coverage of what promises to be a fertile area for exploration and development. Some of the technological initiatives and ideas presented in this essay are already underway and will lead the way toward better and cheaper approaches for dealing with both traditional and nontraditional warfare. Certainly, in the area of nontraditional warfare, a primary interest is directed toward saving lives and costly resources. Robotics technology provides an opportunity to achieve this goal.

At this stage, a range of appropriate mission profiles and needed capabilities for both RPVs and robots is apparent. Although direct human control and judgment will continue to be required for most missions, there are others that may be entrusted entirely to automated machines. Increased automation of routine physical tasks will also serve to reduce one of the trends of recent armed forces, which has been to move "fingers off triggers," to reduce the proportion of combat or fighting personnel in the total force structure.

The authors would like to gratefully acknowledge the thoughtful comments, suggestions, and information provided by Dr. Michael Knasel, a well-known expert in robotics technology.

AFTERWORD

Two years ago, a small group of scientists, engineers, and defense experts expressed their apprehension and concern about the focus and characteristics of certain aspects of the national security programs underway in the United States and among our allies. This group of talented leaders and thinkers decided to devote some personal time and energy to introduce these concerns in the form of concept essays. The preparation of these essays was not funded or supported by government or any other commercial interests and the essays represent only the independent views of the participants. The Washington Institute of Technology (now located in Fairfax, Virginia) served as the arranger and supporter of this endeavor. However, various organizations within the federal government and industry became interested and encouraged the efforts of this group. The overarching goal of the group was to provide a foundation and forum for addressing the issues, organizations, processes, and technological developments involved in confronting and responding to the nontraditional warfare (NTW) threats.

By now, the reader has become familiar with our use of the term *nontraditional warfare* to mean activities involving opposing sides that are not organized in the conventional manner of structured echelons of forces, weapons, and support systems in use during the twentieth century. Rather, nontraditional warfare threats consist of the new types of threats from ballistic missiles, weapons of mass destruction, electronic warfare, urban and guerrilla operations, mine warfare, and terrorism. None of these new threats can be effectively countered by conventional means or forces without reshaping the tactics, organizations, and technological applications of power, communications, information, and weaponry.

We chose the term *nontraditional warfare* in recognition that "unconventional warfare" and "asymmetrical warfare" do not encompass the full range of threats to the national security cited earlier. NTW includes the introduction of several types of conflict that lead to a totally different viewpoint and methodology for developing and prosecuting campaigns and for defending our nation and our allies.

During the past 2 years, a number of these essays have been furnished to organizations within the government to serve as a catalyst for early attention to some of the critical NTW problems. It is gratifying to see many of these ideas begin to surface in the media and official government publications/ pronouncements. Just recently, the Central Intelligence Agency recognized that while the ballistic missile threats were still of grave concern, the weapons of mass destruction (nuclear, chemical, and biological) could be delivered by simpler and more likely methods. This announcement, published in the *Washington Post* on the eve of my birthday (11 January 2002), provided a needed balance toward understanding the role of ballistic missile defense (BMD) in countering the threats from rogue nations as espoused and presented by our organization in the middle of last year. Some of the essays on terrorist operations, emergency management, and advanced technologies have found their way into the Federal Emergency Management Agency, Office of Homeland Security, Defense Threat Reduction Agency, offices within OSD, and congress and are being used for planning future campaigns and responses to these new threats. Of course, our intention is that this book will be of assistance to the decision makers in the government as well as the civilian community for understanding and influencing the direction of national security programs.

As we move forward into the twenty-first century, a glimpse of the future world conditions is emerging that is quite different from the Cold War conditions. While national powers can continue to build strong conventional forces, other smaller groups that are not aligned with any particular nation are at work to achieve political, religious, and financial gains and objectives. Thus, the United States and its allies must remain diligent and be capable of responding and deterring both conventional and nontraditional threat conditions. This combination of threats places great strains on the national security budget as resources always have some limits—even when a war is underway. In short, choices in spending allocations must be based on carefully evaluated positions and rational decisions—not on cosmetic or public relations activities that often only represent short-term fixes or political influence. Moreover, the selection of options must be logical and realistic. It is not advisable to just throw money at the NTW problems, especially the perceived infrastructure needs. First, it is necessary to determine what the priorities are, how much money should be spent on particular problems, and what affect these investments will have on the national security and conditions in the world.

Part of this future world will be filled with amazing and magical electronically based technologies that will be available to many of our potential enemies as well as ourselves. Therefore, we must guard against possible vulnerabilities that could threaten our use of land, sea, and space for commercial and military applications. While information, intelligence, communications, and computers will be important enablers for our responses to NTW problems, they also could constitute vulnerabilities, and we must continue to develop electronic countermeasures to protect these resources. During the past decade, electronic systems have been an essential part of our responses and we depend on them. They have enabled the United States and its allies to respond with accurate intelligence information and new smart weapons that limit our casualties as well as collateral damage.

In response to the NTW problem areas, the size of our response ground units will be much smaller than the large echelons of forces and structures previously demanded for conventional conflicts. These new units must have flexibility to meet a wide variety of conditions and threats—so tailoring and combining elements of force will be the normal approach. More reliance will be placed on requests for critical logistics and fire support. Threats from mines, booby traps, and chemical/biological weapons may surface anywhere so the ground forces will need to avoid or survive these traps. Remote sensors and robotics will help to ease these burdens. Still, it will be a very dangerous battlefield or operating complex, encompassing a variety of weather, terrain, and visibility conditions.

In developing responses to the NTW threats, we must move away from the old idea that it is not a threat unless we obtain evidence that nations or groups are preparing to attack in a particular way. A threat is *real* when the activity or objective is feasible, can be achieved and employed with stealth, and is preferable over alternative approaches. I am reminded of a similar event that happened over a year ago when several of us discovered a critical U.S. vulnerability that was brought to the attention of several agencies, services, and intelligence organizations. Our ideas were rejected because the concept had never been considered before and there was no funding. As an example, no one seriously considered the idea of terrorists hijacking commercial airliners to use them as guided munitions until September 11, 2001. Fortunately, recent indications are now surfacing to indicate that some previously ignored and overlooked problems are beginning to be accepted as real threats and are being partially addressed. Still, there are many NTW threats that need to be considered that are not within the current mission or resources of any agency or organization. Responsibility for the evaluation of these threats and the development of appropriate responses and systems must be assigned and resources allocated.

Several essays in this book deal with aspects of the weapons of mass destruction (WMD) problem. Our primary observations that emerge from these investigations are (1) the threats from nuclear, chemical, and biological effects are very real and dangerous; (2) various means exist for delivery of these effects; (3) these types of threats are here to stay; (4) the world must continue to exist in a way that resists the human tendency to live in fear or isolation; (5) reliance on deterrence is even more important than ever; and (6) preventing worldwide access to chemical/biological technology, supplies, and delivery means must be continually and legally enforced.

Sensor technologies and HUMINT are the fundamental underpinnings of approaches to deal with the terrorist threats. In short, we must identify the terrorists and determine their location, what they are doing, and their plans and capabilities. Finally, we must apprehend these terrorists before they can carry out their plans. Of course, we must also have response remedies but prevention is still the best cure.

A serious problem caused by the lack of organizational and management infrastructures exists in dealing with the NTW threats. These essays point the way toward developing and utilizing the emergency management processes and information assets. Likewise, an initiative to apply enterprise management practices to set up integrated methods for communicating, controlling, and overseeing the organizations and missions for countering terrorist operations is imperative. Currently, the homeland security efforts are segmented under many organizations with particular strengths and weaknesses. When time permits, this approach may be effective, but usually the NTW threats demand fast, accurate responses that must be tailored to prevent the hostile actions as well as match the needs for saving lives and capturing the perpetrators.

To overcome some of the political and agency barriers to the operation of a super agency for homeland defense and security, one approach would be to have the current organizations continue to manage their normal day-to-day activities and control their assigned assets. Then, during emergency/crisis situations, the super agency would take management control of the supporting organizations' assets and resources. The President of the United States would make the decision on this transfer of authority and control. Of course, the super agency would require an experienced, nationally recognized staff with in-depth capability to deal with and coordinate the major aspects of crisis management and response.

Currently, the existing models and simulations (M&S) are inadequate to meet the NTW needs. Most of the current M&S tools were designed for conventional operations and really do not deal with any of the new problem areas in a satisfactory way. Without accurate M&S tools, the necessary planning for organization, operations, and technology development is seriously hampered. In addition, new effort is required to put in place the necessary test and evaluation (T&E) assets to develop the systems and concepts to counter the emerging threats. Aspects of the needed M&S tools and T&E assets are discussed in this book and should provide a baseline for initiating these important steps.

Urban and guerrilla operations persist in many underdeveloped areas of the world and usually threaten the stability and security of neighbors and existing governments. Many of these conflict regions also provide safe havens for both criminal and terrorist operations. The United States and our allies have become involved in many of these activities since the end of the Cold War. While the United States is not likely to participate in these conflicts with substantial ground forces, our interests must be met and protected at times by using smart sensors for intelligence and target acquisition plus accurate lethal and nonlethal weapons.

A plethora of technologies, primarily in the electromechanical areas, will continue to offer military organizations expanding opportunities for solving transportation, mobility, firepower, communications, and combat support problems for decades to come. To fully exploit these opportunities, new approaches are required that organize the military units and institutions around the technologies designed to meet the mission objectives. Besides the numerous discussions about potential technologies and operational needs presented throughout this book, Essay 21 presents some 50 current deficiencies along with about 100 R&D planning guidelines for addressing threats from weapons of mass destruction, electronic warfare, terrorists, and mines.

In light of the these concerns, issues, and responses for dealing with the NTW problems, a perspective unfolds that assists in planning for a future, more secure world. Some of those initiatives include revised, integrated military organizations and more emphasis on international agreements and participation. Of course, surprises and unforeseen problems and threats will always be around so we must be prepared to meet these unexpected challenges with strength and capability.

First, military action in the new era will involve generally smaller forces and also require a more intensive focus on high technology, especially in terms of information management and C⁴I. United States experience in the decade since the Kuwait War indicates that a great deal of military action will focus not on armed conflict per se, but rather on the employment of armed forces to perform a range of operations other than total warfare: national-building, law enforcement, disaster relief, and other activities. In many cases, regular military leadership is poorly prepared to deal with these challenges, which will likely comprise a major portion, if not the majority, of their active overseas service and duty. Certainly, military forces in the new era, regardless of whether they are Army, Navy, Marines, or Air Force, will *have* to be flexible and adaptive. This framework of consideration must also govern a gamut of national security policy issues, ranging from procurement through modeling and simulation, to research and development (R&D) and personnel policy.

Second, the gradual diminution of U.S. overseas deployment of forces, coupled with the dwindling size of U.S. conventional forces of all types, means that the United States increasingly will be less able to "go it alone." This is likely to be a serious issue in domestic politics, where a large segment of U.S. public opinion has traditionally regarded the United States as a special case, bound neither by certain aspects of international law and practice, nor by criticism of other nations to U.S. policy. This will have to change, however slowly such an evolution will progress. In the emerging multi-polar world, we may indeed be the last superpower, but we will not be able to maintain our position and our global interests without the support of other national governments, nor will we be able to maintain our geopolitical position outside the framework of international law and international agencies. The UN is scarcely perfect (and is indeed sometimes inadequate), but it is better than nothing.

Finally, internationally oriented nongovernmental organizations (NGOs) such as Doctors Without Borders and the International Red Cross are often able to provide valuable humanitarian relief services in conflict-stricken areas and nations, as shown by the recent near famine in Afghanistan. While these same NGOs are neither oriented toward, nor capable of, mounting serious policy initiatives, their aid can make the role of armed intervention easier, particularly when that intervention is aimed less toward strictly military operations and more toward activities such as aid to the civil authority, ordnance disposal, infrastructure rehabilitation, peacekeeping, and so on.

As we begin planning to write several other related books, another problem bears mention for immediate attention by the federal government. This concern deals with the experience of several talented groups of experts and organizations that have not participated in the planning and evaluation of new ideas and concepts for meeting the NTW threats. Without this front-end analysis and evaluation, much effort and resources will be wasted on poor hardware/software solutions and organizations frameworks that are limited by scope or resources. Accordingly, the government should designate points of contact and integrate contracting authority to allow this intellectual support community a means to come forward and assist in the important and necessary thinking and problem resolution involved in NTW responses.

Finally, we wish to commend the participants who contributed to this opus. We trust the readers will appreciate the scholarship and knowledge of these writers and advisors. Dr. McDonnell, Mr. Sayers, and Mr. Bongard, who participated in writing portions of this book, provided advice in the writing of these concluding remarks.

As a short personal note, I want to recognize Dr. Lawrence J. Fedewa, founder of the Washington Institute of Technology, for his assistance and encouragement in the development of this book. We are very grateful for the support of Duane, Pat, Greg, Meg, Clive, Lynne, and JoAnne, the wind beneath our wings all these many years.

Stay tuned for the next book in this series.

William R. Schilling

ACRONYMS

ABM	antiballistic missile
AD	air defense
AI	artificial intelligence
ANFO	ammonium nitrate and fuel oil, an easy-to-assemble explosive compound, used in the attack on the Alfred P. Murrah Federal Building in Oklahoma City, OK, in 1995.
APC	armored personnel carrier
AR	available resources
ARES	advanced research and experiments in sensing
AT	antitank
ATACMS	army tactical missile system
BAT	brilliant antitank submunition
BATF	Bureau of Alcohol, Tobacco, and Firearms
BMD	ballistic missile defense
BW	biological weapons or biological warfare
CBW	chemical and biological warfare
C⁴	command, control, communications, and computers (or computing)
C³I	command, control, communications, and intelligence
C⁴I	command, control, computers (or computing), communications, and intelligence
CDM	collateral damage model
CEO	chief executive officer

CEP	circular error probability (radius within which half of warheads will land)
CIA	Central Intelligence Agency
CINC	commander-in-chief
COEA	cost and operational effectiveness analysis
COIN	counterinsurgency
CONUS	Continental United States
COTS	commercial off-the-shelf
CW	continuous wave
DARPA	Defense Advanced Research Projects Agency
DEA	Drug Enforcement Agency
DEW	directed energy weapon (most likely laser or maser)
DHHS	Department of Health and Human Services
DIA	Defense Intelligence Agency
DOD	Department of Defense
DODD	Department of Defense Directive
DODI	Department of Defense Instruction
DOE	Department of Energy
DOJ	Department of Justice
DOS	Department of State
DSM	decision support model
DT&E	developmental test and evaluation
DTRA	Defense Threat Reduction Agency
DU	depleted uranium, an alloy comprised largely of partially de-radiated uranium, useful for its extremely high density in kinetic warheads and armor
ECM	electronic countermeasures
ECCM	electronic counter-countermeasures
ELF	extremely low frequency (referring to wireless communications band)
ELN	*Ejercito Liberacion Nacional* (National Liberation Army)—Colombia-based terrorist group
EM	emergency management

EMAM	emergency management and analysis model
EMI	enterprise management integration
EMOC	emergency management operations center
EMP	electromagnetic pulse
EOD	explosive ordnance disposal
ERAM	emergency response and analysis model
ERW	enhanced radiation weapon (the so-called neutron bomb)
ES	event site
ESA	European Space Agency
EW	electronic warfare
EWVA	electronic warfare vulnerability analysis
FAC	fast attack craft, naval combat vessels of under 500 tons displacement, and usually not fully ocean-going
FAE	fuel-air explosive (an explosion utilizing simultaneous detonation of a cloud of flammable vapor to produce a massive concussion effect)
FARC	*Fuerzas Armadas Revolucionarios Colombianos* (Revolutionary Armed Forces of Columbia)
FBI	Federal Bureau of Investigation, part of the Department of Justice
FBR	fast burn reactor
FD	fire department
FEBA	forward edge of battle area
FEMA	Federal Emergency Management Agency
F&F	fire and forget
FLN	*Fuerzas Liberaciones Nationales* (National Liberation Forces)
FOPEN SAR	foliage pentration synthetic aperture radar
FRU	first response unit
FSU	former Soviet Union
GHz	gigahertz (one billion cycles per second)
GL	grenade launcher
GPS	global positioning system (satellite-based navigation system)
GUI	graphic user interface

HAZMAT   hazardous materials

HE   high explosive

HEAT   high explosive antitank, a shaped-charge warhead that creates a plasma to blast through the armor of enemy vehicles

HEMP   high altitude electromagnetic pulse

HIMARS   high mobility artillery/rocket system (a reduced-weight MLRS derivative)

HMMWV   high mobility multipurpose wheeled vehicle

HPAC   (in Essay 17—Models and Simulations for Evaluating Emerging Threats)

HPM   high power microwave

HTI   high temperature incendiary

HUMINT   human intelligence, meaning that garnered from live human sources, through agents

HV/AC   heating, ventilation, and air conditioning

IAC   information and analysis center(s)

ICBM   intercontinental ballistic missile (with a range in excess of 8,000 km)

IFV   infantry fighting vehicle, such as the Soviet/Russian BMP-2 or the U.S. M-2 Bradley

IMRO   Internal Macedonian Revolutionary Organization

INS   Immigration and Naturalization Services, part of the Department of Justice

IOC   initial operational capability

IOT&E   initial operational testing and evaluation

IR   infrared

IRA   Irish Republican Army

ISR   intelligence, surveillance and reconnaissance

ISS   International Space Station

IT   information technology

IW   information warfare

JLF   joint live fire

JMEM   Joint Munitions Effectiveness Manual

KLA   Kossovo Liberation Army (pro-Albanian)

KT	kiloton, or 1,000 tons equivalent of TNT, for assessing nuclear weapons yield
LAV	light armored vehicle, specifically an 8 × 8 wheeled vehicle in use with both the USMC, and the U.S. Army's new Light Mechanized Brigades. Primarily configured as an APC, it also has antitank, air defense, logistics, command, communications, and mortar carrier versions
LEO	low earth orbit
LFT	live fire testing
LFT&E	live fire testing and evaluation
LPI	low probability intercept (used to describe electronic communications)
LRRP	long-range reconnaissance patrol(s)
MANPADS	man-portable air defense system
MBT	main battle tank
MDA	milestone decision authority
MEM	micro electromechanical
MHz	megahertz (one million cycles per second)
MILO	magnetically insulated linear oscillator (a device for projecting RFW weapons)
MIL STD	military standard
MLRS	multiple launcher rocket system
MMST	Metropolitan (Washington, D.C.) Medical Strike Team
MNS	mission needs statement
MO	method of operation (or, *modus operandi,* meaning the same thing)
MOE	measures of effectiveness
MOOTW	military operations other than war
MOUT	military operations in urban terrain
M&S	modeling and simulation
MV	muzzle velocity
NAFTA	North American Free Trade Agreement (or Association)
NASA	National Aeronautics and Space Administration
NATO	North Atlantic Treaty Organization

NBC	nuclear (radiological), biological (and) chemical
NDI	nondevelopmental item(s)
NEAR	near earth asteroid rendezvous
NGO	nongovernmental organization
NIMA	National Imagery and Mapping Agency
NMRT	National Medical Response Team
NTW	nontraditional warfare
NVA	North Vietnamese Army
NVESD	night vision and electronic sensors directorate
NVN	North Vietnam
NWE	nuclear weapons effects
OCONUS	outside the continental United States
OMS	orbital maneuvering system
OOTW	operations other than war
OSD	Office of the Secretary of Defense
OT&E	operational testing and evaluation
OTH	over the horizon
PD	police department
PF	protection factor(s)
PLO	Palestinian Liberation Organization
PM	performance measure(s)
PRP	Peoples Revolutionary Party
QFD	quality function deployment
R&D	research and development
RDT&E	research, development, test(ing), and evaluation
RF	radio frequency
RFW	radio frequency weapons
RPG	rocket-propelled grenade
RPV	remotely piloted (unmanned or uncrewed) vehicle
RTF	rapid response task force
RVN	Republic of Vietnam (South Vietnam)
SADARM	sense and destroy armor
SAM	surface-to-air missile

SBU	sensitive but unclassified
SEA	Southeast Asia
SEMP	system engineering master plan
SETI	search for extra-terrestrial intelligence
SSW	smart sensorweb(s)
SURVIAC	Survivability/Vulnerability Information Analysis Center
SWAT	Special Weapons and Tactics (police units trained and equipped for actions in terrorist and hostage situations)
T&E	test and evaluation
TEM	testing and evaluation model(s)
TEMP	test and evaluation master plan
TNDM	tactical numerical deterministic model
TOW	tube-launched optically tracked, wire-guided; U.S. heavy AT missile
TRAM	terrorist response and analysis methodology
TREE	transient radiation effects on electronics (from nuclear weapons)
UAV	unmanned aerial vehicle
UDM	unit damage models
UHT	underground hardened targets
UN	United Nations
USCG	United States Coast Guard
USN	United States Navy
UWB	ultra wideband
UXO	unexploded ordnance
VC	Viet Cong (communist guerrilla movement in South Vietnam, 1955–1975)
VTOL	vertical take-off and landing
V&V	validation and verification (generally refers to assessment of models and simulations)
WMD	weapons of mass destruction (nuclear, biological, and chemical)
WWW	Worldwide Web

INDEX

ABOUT THE EDITOR AND THE CONTRIBUTORS

WILLIAM R. SCHILLING is president and CEO of the Washington Institute of Technology and provides technical and operational leadership to the company. Mr. Schilling is heavily involved in certain aspects of nontraditional warfare, including weapons of mass destruction, electronic warfare, and terrorist operations. These activities address a host of non-traditional warfare problems, in terms of management of information systems, force structures, countermeasures to terrorist and WMD threats, models, and tools for assessing possible responsible measures, and identifying advanced technological initiatives.

Mr. Schilling received a B.S. in civil engineering from Virginia Polytechnic Institute, an M.E. in structural engineering from Pennsylvania State University, an M.S. in aeronautical engineering from the University of Southern California, and an engineer's degree in aerospace engineering from the University of Southern California. Mr. Schilling is a nationally renowned systems and operations analyst with a wide range of expertise in fields of endeavor including technological forecasting, research and development planning, mission and requirements analysis, cost and operational effectiveness analysis, system development program analysis, and field and combat system evaluation. From 1978 to 1998, Mr. Schilling was the president and founder of the McLean Research Center/Corporation. Earlier in his career, Mr. Schilling was a chief scientist and division head for Science Applications Inc. (now SAIC), head of Weapons Systems Analysis at Research Analysis Corporation, and an engineer with the Douglas Aircraft Corporation.

NORMAN R. AUGUSTINE graduated magna cum laude from Princeton University where he received bachelors and masters degrees in aeronautical engineering. In the aerospace and defense industry he served as chairman and CEO of Martin Marietta Corporation and Lockheed Martin Corporation. In government he served as undersecretary of the Army, chairman of the Defense Science Board and a member of the President's Council of Advisors on Science and Technology. He has been a member of the faculty of the Department of Mechanical and Aerospace Engineering at Princeton University, chairman of the National Academy of Engineering, and for 9 years chairman of the American Red Cross. He was awarded the National Medal of Technology by the president of the United States and has received the Department of Defense's highest civilian award, the Distinguished Service Medal, on five occasions.

ROBERT E. BENT has more than 25 years of experience as a senior military operations manager. He was project manager for the Army Theater Nuclear Force Survivability Program and the subsequent Department of Defense NSNF Survivability Program. Mr. Bent prepared survivability papers for the NATO Senior Levels Weapons Protection Group and High Level Group and transformed the approach to survivability at the Defense Nuclear Agency and the Army Nuclear Chemical Agency.

DAVID L. BONGARD has 16 years of experience as a professional military analyst and military historian, and has worked extensively in the realm of using historical analysis to support model development. He was also a long-term and close associate of Col. Trevor N. Dupuy, (USA, Ret.), the developer of the "Quantified Judgmental Model" (QJM) and its successor, the Tactical Numerical Deterministic Model (TNDM). He performed the research, and contributed to the analysis, of TNDM engagements of battalion-size and less, the results of which were published in *The International TNDM Newsletter* in 1996. Mr. Bongard is also a veteran hobby wargamer, with particular interest in guerrilla warfare and operations, and in unusual and little-known conflicts.

JOSEPH D. DOUGLASS, JR., is a national security affairs specialist with more than 25 years experience. He is director of the Redwood Institute and author of *Red Cocaine: The Drugging of America* (London and New York: Edward Harle, 1998). His areas of expertise include strategic analysis; nuclear, chemical and biological warfare issues; intelligence; national defense policy planning; international narcotics trafficking; arms control treaty verification; weapon systems evaluation; military technology development; and threat evaluation. For the past 8 years, Dr. Douglass has focused on international drug trafficking, military countermeasures, INF and START arms control verification, special earth penetrating radar technology, advanced technology chemical and biological warfare capabilities and related political problems, proliferation, and defense problems in a post-USSR world. He was formerly the deputy director, Tactical Technology Office, Advanced Research Projects Agency, and was responsible for managing research and development activities involving numerous high-leverage, low-cost technologies. Dr. Douglass has served on the editorial board of the United States Strategic Institute and the strategy advisory council of the American Security Council.

JASPER C. LUPO recently retired as director, Sensor Systems, Office of the Director, Defense Research and Engineering, Office of the Secretary of Defense. During his long career, he was instrumental in leading the developmental effort for smart sensorwebs within the Department of Defense. Earlier in his career, Dr. Lupo was responsible for the management and development of smart munitions at the Defense Advanced Research Projects Agency. He has been instrumental in the application of electronic technology for weapon system programs during the past two decades.

MICHAEL D. McDONNELL is a program manager with the Washington Institute of Technology. He received his B.S. in physics from St. Peter's College, and his M.S. and Ph.D. in nuclear physics from Fordham University. Dr. McDonnell has over 14 years experience in telecommunications and information technology in the Department of Defense and over 18 years experience in areas related to weapons of mass destruction including nuclear and chemical/biological weapons design, targeting, defense, protection, and countermeasures. He is the author or co-author of hundreds of papers and reports covering the survivability/vulnerability of a broad range of targets in an equally broad range of scenarios.

JAMES F. O'BRYON has graduate degrees from George Washington University in operations research/management science and from MIT through the electrical engineering department. He has more than 25 years of leadership experience in weapon systems technology and survivability and has testified before the United States Congress on several occasions regarding weapons acquisition and testing. Mr. O'Bryon began his work in the Pentagon as assistant deputy undersecretary of defense, a position created in response to an act of congress. Since that time, he has also served within the Office of the Secretary of Defense as deputy director, Test and Evaluation; as director, Live Fire Testing; as director, Weapon Systems Assessment; and as deputy director for Operational Test and Evaluation/Live Fire Test.

TERRY L. SAYERS is a former newspaper reporter and Vietnam combat veteran. He has more than 30 years experience as a research writer and documentation specialist. Mr. Sayers has, in many cases, independently researched a wide range of subject areas before and during the preparation of material. His exposure to scientific and technical material has permitted him to contribute to numerous technical projects. Mr. Sayers has been involved in the evaluation of information systems since 1972 and currently serves as facility security officer for the Institute.

LYNNE M. SCHNEIDER is the president of Enterprise Systems and Solutions, Inc., and a policy analyst with extensive experience within the Department of Defense. She received a B.S. in business administration with an emphasis in energy management from the University of Maryland and a M.S. in information systems from George Mason University. Ms. Schneider is currently enrolled as a Ph.D. candidate in public policy at George Mason University. She is a former member of the Task Force on Defense Reform and was responsible for developing the Strategic Level Enterprise Model, the draft DOD Strategic Plan, DOD Core Processes, and the Defense Enterprise Planning and Management Framework. Ms. Schneider worked closely with the Defense Information Systems Agency and the Office of the Assistant Secretary of Defense, Command, Control, Communications, and Intelligence to integrate changes into the Global Command and Control System, Global Combat Support System, CRISR, and other DOD-wide information system initiatives.

HOWARD J. SEGUINE is a program manager with Battelle Memorial Institute, Crystal City Operations. He is concerned with evolving threats and emerging technologies that may become threats to national security and the national infrastructure, and mitigating measures. Before joining Battelle, he was deputy for studies, U.S. Nuclear Command and Control System Support Staff.

JAMES J. VALDES holds a Ph.D. in neuroscience from Texas Christian University and has performed postdoctoral research in neurotoxicology at the Johns Hopkins Medical institutions. Dr. Valdes serves as the chief scientist, Biological Sciences, and scientific advisor for Biotechnology, ECBC, U.S. Army Soldier and Biological Chemical Command. His research interests include toxicology, biosensors, and bioprocess engineering. Dr. Valdes is adjunct professor of toxicology at the University of Maryland and adjunct professor of life sciences at the University of Texas at San Antonio. He is the author of more than 90 peer-reviewed publications.

ANDRUS VIILU is the deputy director for Land Warfare, Office of the Undersecretary of Defense (Acquisition, Technology and Logistics). Mr. Viilu has a

B.S. degree in aeronautics and astronautics from MIT. Mr. Viilu has more than 40 years of experience in land warfare related weapons technology and systems acquisition. His civilian work experience includes Research Analysis Corporation, Systems Planning Corporation, and the Institute of Defense Analysis.

CLIVE G. WHITTENBURY received a B.S. in physics from Nachester University (England) and a Ph.D. in aero engineering from the University of Illinois. He is a nationally recognized expert in sensors, avionics, missile and aircraft technology, design, and operations. This expertise has been applied in a variety of high level assignments and leadership roles in private enterprise. For example, Dr. Whittenbury was responsible for rebuilding the heavy lift Sky-crane helicopter and managed the Erickson Group's investment in new hybrid aircraft technology with Aerolift, Inc. He was manager of SAIC's Washington Operations until 1975, serving the company's largest customer, the U.S. government. Dr. Whittenbury was vice president for Science and Engineering at Research Analysis Corporation (1964–1972), following 5 years with the Douglas Aircraft Company (1959–1964), where he was a founding member of the Missile Research Group and later, chief of Systems Analysis, specializing in ballistic missile defense. Dr. Whittenbury currently serves as a consultant to the National Ignition Facility at the Lawrence Livermore National Laboratory.